Frank Johnson, a Londoner, was parliamentary sketchwriter for the *Daily Telegraph* from 1972–79, then a roving political reporter for *Now!*, leaving to go to *The Times* as a columnist.

He was Parliamentary Sketchwriter of the Year in the 1977 Granada 'What the Papers Say' awards, and was named Columnist of the Year in the 1981 British Press Awards.

D1630883

Der Verständige findet fast alles lächerlich, der Vernünftige fast nichts.

The intelligent man finds almost everything ridiculous, the responsible man hardly anything. (Goethe: *Reflections and Maxims*)

Out of Order

Frank Johnson

CORGI BOOKS

The author and publishers would like to thank the editors and proprietors of the *Daily Telegraph* and *The Times* for permission to reproduce material first published in their pages.

OUT OF ORDER

A CORGI BOOK 0 552 99053 1

Originally published in Great Britain by Robson Books Ltd.

PRINTING HISTORY
Robson edition published 1982
Corgi edition published 1984

This book is set in Baskerville 10/11 pt

Corgi Books are published by Transworld Publishers Ltd.,
Century House, 61–63 Uxbridge Road, Ealing, London W5 5SA

Printed and bound in Great Britain by
Cox & Wyman Ltd, Reading

Contents

Introduction

I have worked in the parliamentary press gallery at Westminster since 1966, having gone there as a reporter for a provincial paper. These pieces are drawn from the work of the ten years since I became a parliamentary sketchwriter on the *Daily Telegraph* in 1972. For some time before 1972 I had a silent, nagging and increasingly hopeless ambition to hold such a post. Politicians would be justified in deriving a certain satisfaction from that admission. Back-benchers are much mocked for the way in which they live in endless hope of being called by the Prime Minister and granted even the most tedious junior office. Such mockery is a staple of the Irreverent School of political journalism. But the irreverential also strive after their little satisfactions. Journalism has much in common with politics. Journalists and politicians are as one in their search for recognition, status, praise.

The clown who addresses the audience directly in the Prologue of *I Pagliacci* sums up the 'irreverent' journalist's predicament. It went particularly well in the terrible English translation I recall from the cheap seats at Sadler's Wells as a boy. 'And so, sweet people, when you look on us, clad in our motley and tinsel . . . we are but men like you, of gladness and sorrow, with the same broad heaven above us . . .' (I quote from fallible memory). On and on some hoarse baritone would bellow. I was under the impression at the time that here was profundity. How true, how true, I would reflect. It seemed so much more persuasive than poetry of the better sort. Later life did indeed reveal that the clown had described the condition of all performers—including a type of journalist. It was profound after all.

In 1972, Mr Andrew Alexander left the *Telegraph* sketchwriting job to do the same work on the *Daily Mail*, though more lucratively. I then shared his unfashionable right-wing beliefs before they became fashionably unfashionable, as they are today. He suggested I apply for the *Telegraph* job. By that time, I had moved from the provincial paper to become one of no fewer than three lobby correspondents whom Mr Rupert Murdoch's *Sun* saw fit to employ at Westminster, even though politics was not the reason for the vast circulation the paper remorselessly achieved from the moment of its launch in 1969. I was unsure whether to act on Mr Alexander's suggestion. I doubted whether the *Telegraph* would offer the job to someone from the *Sun*.

It is perhaps forgotten how appalled people were by the early Murdoch *Sun* before its excesses became a national institution. I shared a house with my parents at the time. When the paper was delivered, I used to hurry downstairs and, if there was a particularly blatant bosom on the newly-notorious page 3, would remove the page. This was in order to avoid the censure of my mother, a London matriarch who embodied traditional morality. 'Your paper's a bit short-weight today,' she would subsequently complain. 'It says here page 2 on one side, and page 5 on the opposite.'

'I know, I know,' I would reassure her. 'It's all on account of those print unions. Some nights they refuse to print whole pages.' That did not really surprise her. The unions were holding the nation to ransom, she would explain. For I had found that, with my mother, it was safe to blame most things on the unions.

There was another problem about applying for the *Telegraph* job. It was an outer branch of the higher journalism, involving metaphors, conceits, quotations, mandarin irony—that sort of thing. I had never written anything like that. Indeed, I had written scarcely anything other than 'Premier Ted Heath lashed Labour leader Harold Wilson in a new Commons storm last night', which is the other main language of the profession. How to persuade the *Telegraph* that—despite one's mode of employment—one was a man of immense culture? (Saying 'one' when you mean 'I' would do for a start, I decided.)

Mr Alexander arranged for me to see Mr Colin Welch, the deputy editor—a superb journalist and recognized polymath. At this meeting I spoke at prodigious length about the writings of Sir Herbert Butterfield—also, Hegel. We parted cheerily, but without any indication that I was likely to get the job. Alexander reported Welch's reaction. Butterfield and Hegel had gone down well. 'But he doesn't seem to have *done* anything.' Mr Welch did not disapprove of that in principle, but thought it prudent that I be asked to submit some trial sketches from the Commons.

Now, it was true that I had not *done* anything. But I had absorbed the higher journalism for years as a consumer—indeed, had read little else, certainly not Hegel. I felt I had the patter. So the trial pieces were sent. Also sent were two or three I had written in the *Sun* on the 1970 general election campaign, pieces which had been mutilated by the office—or so I had thought—but in which a few impressionist touches had survived. They were all I could offer in the way of published 'writing'.

There was next an interview with the editor of the *Telegraph*, Mr Maurice Green, formerly of *The Times*. He was a courtly, shy, unmoralizing man whom little had ever been known to amaze, nearing the end of his editorship. 'You may wonder what I'm doing working for the *Sun*,' I mumbled during one of several silences in the conversation. No, not at all, he replied. We all had to work somewhere. Why should I think it would cause him any wonder? Well, because the *Sun* was sort of . . . trivial. Also, it was pro-Labour (for at that time it was), and I was some kind of a Tory. He replied that in journalism where one worked was largely a matter of chance. He had nothing against trivia. As for politics, the *Sun*'s advice on the subject had so far done considerably less harm to the British economy (his own interest) than the *Guardian*'s, in his view. I was beginning to admire this man. Concerning the work I had submitted, he thought the trial sketches 'rather over-done, perhaps', but the *Sun* pieces were 'damn good'.

He gave me the job. It took someone of Green's social imperturbability to do so. I suspect I would have fared less well at the hands of one of those youngish, exciting, grammar-school meritocrats who had for some years been taking over the country.

The *Telegraph* had a dual nature. There was column after column of grey 'news' and seemingly endless 'sport'. It was on these pages that the paper's grip on the great British middle class was consolidated day after day. But dotted around were a few oases: the Peter Simple column; some of the more inventive editorials; Garland's cartoons; the occasional main feature when not written by a Conservative MP; some of the book reviews. Though the constitution was hazy and unwritten, the oases came under the authority of the editor: the surrounding desert under that of a managing editor called Mr Eastwood. Both were responsible to an editor-in-chief, the proprietor Lord Hartwell.

The parliamentary sketch was in a perilous position. The sketchwriter was appointed by, and answerable to, the editor. But the sketch was on one of the pages controlled by the managing editor.

9

Could he or his staff alter it, or eject it from the paper entirely some nights in favour of yet more 'news'? That was the question.

I conceived this Eastwood as an essentially expansionist power. He was out to control the sketch, I knew it. He would like to have authority over what went in it, or whether it went in at all. Ideally, he would like his own man to write it, not the editor's. The sketch was the warm-water port, control of which had been the historic aim of his foreign policy. My own strategy was to embroil the editor and deputy editor on my side, to get them to complain or ask questions when the sketch was left out. Usually this would work for a while. But always—at least during the early years of my *Telegraph* career— there would come a night when Eastwood or his men would move against the sketch once more.

The issue was never resolved in the eight years I worked on the paper. I found it gave a certain savour to life. There was the satisfaction of knowing that in Eastwood one was taking on a worthy foe. Like all aggrieved powers with an age-old territorial claim, he was prepared to renew the struggle, if the moment were opportune, after years of living in relative peace. In the early summer of 1979, when I had given notice that I intended to leave the paper, I went out to write about Mrs Thatcher campaigning in the general election. Some tactical sense warned me that Eastwood would keep a careful eye on anything I wrote about a Conservative politician during an election, much more so than the editor who had succeeded Maurice Green, the broad-minded Mr William Deedes, even though the latter had actually *been* a Tory politician. It was a day on which Eastwood was not expecting a piece from me, nor had I intended to write one. But Mrs Thatcher took herself off to a Midlands chocolate factory (*see* page 57). Here was a theme, I decided. I waited until the time at which Eastwood would have gone home to Burnham-on-Crouch or wherever, and then telephoned the piece. It went on the front page. Next day, the word was that Eastwood was displeased. He asked to see me. He was characteristically courteous—for over the years our mutual disapproval had been conducted at a distance, with never a harsh word. There appeared to have been some failure of communication, he said. He had not known I would be writing that day. Oh dear, what a pity: I thought I had told him. Too late now. Sorry. Perhaps I would let him know in future? Of course.

In my next piece, all ribald references to Tories had disappeared by the time it ended up in the paper. I withdrew from the election campaign, rendering myself silent for its three weeks. As a consolation, Deedes allowed me to write a piece on election morning on one of the pages which the editor alone controlled. So, after nearly eight years, Eastwood had won. True, I took care to put into my election morning piece all the phrases which had been taken out of the earlier piece. But Eastwood was the victor.

Let this be a lesson to all who abandon life's struggle. At Sir James Goldsmith's *Now!*, to which I went for much the same reasons that Alexander went to the *Mail*, there was no such invigorating office politics. It was an unreal existence. We were people most of whom had not previously known each other, on a voyage to we knew not where, though most suspected that it would not be a long trip. Collections of science fiction or ghost stories are full of such situations.

Because of one or two spectacular instances, popular demonology has it that Goldsmith was an 'interfering proprietor'. Most of us saw little evidence of this. His very absence added to the air of unreality. From time to time, we expected him to call us together, as someone does in those stories, and announce: 'I expect you're wondering why I asked you all here.' But he never did. When he entertained the staff, he was vastly hospitable and complimentary. Perhaps he thought that this was how all real press proprietors behaved to their employees, the sort of thing which was expected of him. We did nothing to disabuse him of this erroneous notion.

As the months passed, alliances formed among us. But the only subject of intrigue was when and how the magazine would close. One of our number claimed to be an expert on these matters, having worked on a huge number of failed publications. He was a fatalistic man who cultivated the tone of the worldly-wise. The first sign to look for was the sudden reshuffle among the executives with attendant departures, he advised. That would come just before Christmas. (The magazine was launched in September.) Christmas came and there was no such convulsion. All that had happened was that someone, whom I shall here refer to as Snooks, had fallen ill. 'It's Christmas and we haven't had your reshuffle,' I pointed out to the worldly-wise one.

He replied with the most pessimistic remark I have ever heard anyone make about any subject. 'The executives to watch for, as the victims of the coming reshuffle, are the ones who are not invited to Snooks' funeral.' Happily, our sick colleague recovered. But the pessimist was proved right. For the magazine did not.

By the time it closed, I had left for *The Times*. For a while people tended to ask me whether I had had warning of the death of *Now!* I

11

had not. I always believed that Sir James's legendary pride would prevent his admitting defeat; another of the legends about him which was proved wrong. I wish him well.

I had gone to *The Times* because I had always wanted to write for it. I have the same attitude to the paper as those elderly members of good families who, during its year's closure under Thompson, dreaded that they would have to die in the *Telegraph*. So I will always be grateful to Mr Harold Evans, the then editor. 'Would you like to work on *The Times*?' he asked, shortly after he became editor in 1981. After I replied that I would, he asked, 'What would you like to do?'

This reversal of the natural order of things was one of the unconventional aspects of his brief editorship in so far as it affected me. In between my agreeing to go to *The Times* and my arrival a development took place which was alarming from my point of view. Mr Bernard Levin announced that he was leaving. Now, my early pieces were to go on the same page as had his. The thought transfixed me: was I supposed to be some sort of a replacement for Bernard? How terrible! Politics was my trade, not the universe. I had other interests, to be sure, but they tended to be the same as Bernard's, especially opera. The punters would think they were getting an inferior remake. I thought it best not to ask. Gloom descended on me. I discovered Lord George-Brown in an eel and pie shop (*see* pages 65-7). That would make a first piece, I thought; my sort of scene.

But what of this Levin problem? It had to be confronted.

For a second piece, I wrote about Wagner. After all, nearly every second Levin piece was about Wagner. But I had a clever idea. I would come out *against* Wagner. The piece appeared (*see* pages 71-2). Evans telephoned me later that morning. 'That piece was brilliantly funny,' he said. 'But you've not come here to be the new Bernard Levin.' 'Oh,' I said. 'I'm delighted to hear it. I thought I had.' That did not solve the problem: what had I come here for? 'You're not doing yourself justice,' the editor continued. 'You're not just a funny man.' 'Oh,' I said, 'I thought I was.' But not at all apparently. Evans discerned certain profundities in me, at least that was his opinion for the duration of his telephone talk. Happily, come the end of the summer, the party conferences, and the return of parliament, the problem somehow resolved itself.

Most of the pieces in this book are parliamentary sketches, written in the two hours or so between the scenes they claim to describe and the deadline. I have taken care to remove grammatical blunders, but not bad jokes. I think that is fair. Few of the pieces are complete, any major cuts being indicated by asterisks. Care has been taken to include all bias. In defence of that attitude, I quote another Johnson on the subject of his accounts of parliamentary proceedings: 'I took care to see that the Whig dogs should not have the best of it.'

'And yet for old theatre notices there may be a kind of excuse,' wrote the *Guardian* drama critic C. E. Montague long ago, of the practice of reprinting newspaper journalism between hard covers (he was prefacing a collection of his own notices). 'You wrote them in haste, it is true, with few books about you, or moments to look a thing up; hot air and dust of the playhouse were still in your lungs; you were sure to say things that would seem sorry gush or rant if you saw them again in the morning. How bad it all was for measure, containment and balance! But that heat of the playhouse is not wholly harmful. Like sherry sack in the system of Falstaff, it hath a two-fold operation: "it ascends me into the brain—makes it apprehensive, quick, forgetive, full of nimble, fiery and delectable shapes!" '

This book will prove whether all that is also true of old political notices.

In the 1970s

Herewith my first published parliamentary sketch: from a Daily Telegraph *of October 1972. I include it because it might be of some archaeological interest. The author was aged 29. Here, in primitive form, can be discerned, beneath several layers of irony, some of his later contributions to civilization, such as a sceptical attitude towards Mr Roy Jenkins. Nowadays (1982) affectionate raillery at the expense of Mr Jenkins is a commonplace of political journalism.*

Elsewhere, the piece contains evidence of a lost world. Mr Edward Heath was Prime Minister. Mr Harold Wilson was Leader of the Opposition. Sir Alec Douglas-Home was Foreign Secretary. Mr Michael Foot was the sort of figure who could never become Leader of the Labour Party. Mrs Margaret Thatcher had not been invented.

Mr Wilson gave the lads of the Parliamentary Labour Party's shop floor—the back benches—a special treat yesterday.

As Common Market issues, such matters as butter, CAP, VAT had been all right as far as they went. But they had somehow lacked 'soul'—offering little scope for talk of war and peace, our children, our children's children, indeed children yet unborn. But yesterday Mr Wilson came up with The Bomb.***

What, demanded Mr Wilson, was all this about our bomb being wired up with their bomb (the French one, that is) to make a Euro-bomb? Don't deny it, he, in effect, warned the Government front bench. Lord Carrington, the Secretary for Defence, blurted it out last week to the Tory Party conference. (The Opposition Leader seemed under the impression that this was a forum notorious for being entrusted with the gravest military and diplomatic secrets of state.)

To Mr Wilson, it was a venture fraught with the direst con-sequences, among much else, for 'NATO and the Atlantic Alliance'. Labour back-benchers gargled sagely, fidgeting in their seats to emphasize their concern. Among them were several of the Left—where love of NATO and the Atlantic Alliance has always been endemic. *** Mr Wilson tossed in that hobgoblin in excelsis: the danger of a German finger on the nuclear trigger.

'Aaaaaargh,' rumbled his back-benchers. Mr Robert Mellish's homely crab-apple of a face was creased in smiles. The Chief Whip's trade is unity and keeping everybody happy and there's nothing that spreads happiness in the party more than talk of the nuclear. It goes down a bomb, as it were.

Mr Heath was vastly amused by all this, and may even have permitted himself a heave of the shoulder. So Mr Wilson was forced to tell him: 'This is nothing to laugh at.' 'Behave yourself,' shrieked Mr Heffer, the Labour MP for Walton whose impeccable record in matters of parliamentary decorum entitled him to administer the rebuke. Eventually, the Prime Minister rose to reassure Mr Wilson that there was little prospect of British and French mariners—still less, German—going buccaneering together aboard Polaris in the near future.

A kind of Holmes-Watson exchange ensued.

Mr Heath: The Treaty of Rome does not deal with defence.

Mr Wilson: Exactly! (Do not be deceived, my dear Heath, the Opposition Leader was clearly thinking. Your Continental is much too wily a cove to put anything of real significance on paper.)

Broad strategic matters having been dealt with, Mr Wilson moved on to scarify the Foreign Secretary—the debate's chief Government speaker—by demanding answers from him to no fewer than twenty-five questions on economic matters. They included a call for Sir Alec's views on 'the snake in the tunnel'—not a reference to some treacherous Shadow Cabinet colleague, but to an arcane device of European exchange rate policy. Not really Sir Alec's scene.

The Foreign Secretary wisely confined himself to a bout of that Euro-mysticism that always descends on Common Market debates sooner or later. After the by-now routine reference to Charlemagne, Sir Alec's contribution petered out after only fifteen minutes or so, with cries from the Foreign Secretary of 'partnership . . . the future . . . unity.'

Appropriately, this led on to Mr Roy Jenkins, the Labour Member for Stechford. He offered the sort of wrist-flapping, torso-swivelling, adjective-emphasizing performance that has been good enough to establish him, for many tastes, as a parliamentarian of the golden age. But his famed courage was, it seems, to be deployed sparingly from now on. He would be in the same lobby as Mr Wilson come the division. It was a speech studded with the sort of reflections on which have been based Mr Jenkins' repute as a thinker. 'You can never go back,' he observed. 'You always have to start from where you are.'

True, how very true.

Over the next pages are to be found unconnected episodes from the politics of 1972–79. They are unconnected in order to avoid concentration on major events. For major events a decade later have a tendency to look minor, whereas an event of the period such as, say, the left-wing Labour Member Mr Dennis Skinner has proved more lasting.

Nonetheless, in the years covered, Mr Heath called a general election in February 1974 on the issue of a miners' strike, and lost. Mr Wilson, who had been Prime Minister from 1964 until 1970, returned at the head of a Labour Government which did not have an overall majority. Mr James Callaghan became Foreign Secretary, Mr Denis Healey Chancellor of the Exchequer and Mr Roy Jenkins Home Secretary. Mr Heath retained the leadership of the Opposition. Mr Wilson called an election in October 1974, in order to secure an overall majority, which he did, though it was small. Early in 1975, Mrs Thatcher defeated Mr Heath for the leadership of the Conservative Party. Mr Heath retreated to the back benches, where he has remained. In the spring of 1976, Mr Wilson unexpectedly retired and shortly afterwards became a Knight of the Garter. Mr Callaghan defeated Mr Michael Foot, Mr Healey, Mr Jenkins, Mr Tony Benn and the late Anthony Crosland for the leadership of the Labour Party and became Prime Minister. Crosland was appointed Foreign Secretary and Mr Merlyn Rees Home Secretary. Mr Healey remained Chancellor. Mr Jenkins resigned his seat and became President of the European Commission. The Government's majority was steadily eroded as a result of by-election defeats and parliamentary votes occasioned by opposition to its policy of 'devolution' of government to Scotland and Wales. Its continuation in office began to depend on the support of the Liberals and various Scottish Nationalists, Welsh Nationalists and Ulster Northern Irish members. In the winter of 1978–79 there was much industrial unrest, as a result of opposition to the Government's incomes policy. In the spring of 1979, as a result of defections caused primarily by devolution, the Government lost a parliamentary vote of confidence. The Conservatives won the resultant general election and Mrs Thatcher became Prime Minister.

Mrs Thatcher had first seemed worthy of attention in a debate about the economy in December 1974, though she had no chance of becoming leader of her party. The Conservatives had gone into Opposition. Mr Heath was still their leader, though not for long.

On sitting down after her speech yesterday, Mrs Thatcher became the first Tory front-bencher in this parliament to win from Tory back-benchers a cheer prompted by enthusiasm rather than hope of distant knighthoods or peerages. In her first appearance as her party's finance and public expenditure spokesman Mrs Thatcher proved, as was once said of a deceptively easy-going operatic prima donna, that she has dimples of iron.

Her principal target was the Chancellor. But before she launched into Mr Healey a glancing blow was sustained by Mr Lever, the Dr Schacht of the present Wilson régime. Mr Lever's answer to any problem was to borrow, she claimed. 'There are four ways of acquiring money—make it, earn it, marry it and borrow it. The right hon. gentleman [Mr Lever] seems to know about all four.' Moving from Mr Lever's personal finances to those of the nation, she said: 'Yesterday it was suggested that there should be a penalty on companies which went beyond the Social Contract. It seems very odd that employers who were not party to the Social Contract pay a penalty if the Contract fails, but those who were parties to the Contract seem to take no part in the penalty.'

She also drew attention to the economy of detail shown by Mr Healey in his Budget speech over the precise magnitude of the price rises, and other privations, inherent in the Budget strategy. 'The first was petrol, followed by nationalized industry, price increases, then deductions arising from public expenditure cuts, and then, in April, increases in taxation and rates,' she said. 'It is going to be sacrifice by instalments.'

Finally, she made admirable play with the corny patter in Mr Healey's Budget speech about accumulation of material goods not bringing happiness. She produced a newspaper cutting in which Mr Healey was quoted as saying that he never saved, and that whenever he got any money, he would 'go out and buy something for the house'.

Mr Healey jumped up to demand the source of the quotation. 'The *Sunday Telegraph*,' said Mrs Thatcher. The Chancellor and his supporters seemed unwilling to regard that publication as a scholarly guide to the personal habits of the major politicians in the Workers' Party.

For Mr Healey denied having ever said it. Alas, his evidence for not making the remark rested solely on the ground that it was 'preposterous'. He did not behave in that way towards money, we gathered.

Mrs Thatcher said how pleased she was to receive this assurance that, far from being a spendthrift, Mr Healey apparently took the excellent investment advice of his colleague, Mr Lever. 'Certainly, I know he's spent money on buying houses in good Tory areas,' she added.

The male chauvinist thought crossed the mind that she might be about to scratch his eyes out. But soon she was learnedly discussing the Treasury's net borrowing requirement. Reluctant though I am to risk the lady's wrath by questioning her undoubted femininity, let it be said that the Tories need more men like her.

Mr Wilson's announcement in early March 1976 that he intended to retire took almost everyone by surprise, and caused considerable speculation.

Mr Wilson had so timed things that his first Commons appearance since the sudden announcement that he was relinquishing all earthly power was for his twice-weekly answering of questions to the Prime Minister. And he timed his entry into a heaving crowded Chamber to within a minute of 3.15 pm, the hour at which he was due to take the boards.

Question Time, rather than the British economy under his stewardship, or high diplomacy under his guidance, is what had always provided him with his greatest triumphs. It had been for Mr Wilson what La Scala was for Callas or (if you find that one a little too ethereal) what downtown Chicago was for Capone.

The House was nearly full a quarter of an hour before he was expected. Even the Peers' Gallery was crowded. That normally means war, or sexual scandal. No one had yet recovered from the shock of the Downing Street announcement of three and a half hours earlier. True to form, Mr Wilson the Great News Editor had made known his departure by means of a Shock Bombshell Sensation. Mrs Thatcher waited on the Tory front bench, flanked by Mr Whitelaw, deputy Opposition Leader, and Mr Prior, shadow Employment Secretary. Mr Heath, who nowadays keeps his distance from that class of person, brooded below the gangway—with Mr Wilson perhaps not his ideal choice of party leader who should stand down.

Each of the real or imagined contenders for the Wilsonian succession was greeted with Tory ho-hos, and nudge-nudges. Mr Roy Jenkins, Home Secretary, strolled in at 3.10. In the leadership election, he is expected to sweep Belgravia and the offices of *The Times*. Securing comparable support from the Labour Party may be more difficult for him. Anyway, he sat next to Mr Mellish, the Chief Whip, and they chatted. All the potential contestants were opting frantically for casualness. Mr Crosland, hands in pockets, walked in past the benches where the Tribunites lurk. He smiled in their direction. They will form a cohesive voting bloc. He may have had it in mind to explain there and then that when in the past, he had often privately described the average left-winger as mad, he meant mad in the inspired manner of, say, Beethoven.

Mr Crosland got his share of Tory irony. So did the next arrival— grey, sepulchral Mr Edward Short. A candidate? Surely not! It's impossible! One's worst enemy's stable should contain such a dark horse! Finally, an enormous round of ho-hos for Mr James Callaghan—who sees himself, at nigh on 64, as the candidate of the New Generation. Mr Callaghan squeezed himself on to the crowded bench—almost squashing Mr Crosland (Aha! Symbolic!). Mr Healey, the Chancellor, did not sit in a prominent position. Perhaps he was pondering that had he known (when he said such rude things about all those Tribune voters last week) what he knew now about Mr Wilson's future . . .

The conspiratorial chatter and all that Tory irony were drowning the Junior Employment Ministers, who were supposed to be answering routine questions. 'Order! Order!' shouted the Speaker. 'I don't know what's wrong with the House today.'

Alas, the poignant moment of Mr Wilson's arrival coincided with a Dispatch Box answer from an earnest, highly unemotional Minister of State, Mr Booth—an artist capable of removing the pathos from the closing moments of *La Bohème*. But Mr Wilson got his cheer— though only Mr Mellish, and a few of the most slavish of Government narks, waved their order papers.

First Mr Wilson answered a routine inquiry about when an interim Royal Commission report was due. But because of the special circumstances of this Question Time the Speaker allowed questioners to stray from the point. Thus Mrs Thatcher conveyed to the Prime Minister some conventional good wishes. But you had to be fleet of ear to catch them. For, to her credit, she did not submerge us in the brand of House of Commons humbug usual on these occasions. Instead, she rasped something about hoping Mr Wilson would enjoy a happy retirement, and went on to demand that his successor call a general election.

Mr Wilson thanked her for her good wishes. But lest he lead anyone to think that she was prone to that sort of thing by nature, he quickly pointed out that 'on occasions such as this, nice kind words such as hers have been used'. But he added: 'I totally reject what she said in the second part of her remarks. I am not sure she is all that keen on it [an election] either,' at which there was a bellow of Labour laughter.

The acid, in place of celebratory champagne, continued to flow between the two leaders. Mr Wilson warned Mrs Thatcher against 'a certain degree of hubris about recent by-elections'. It seemed that he had taken the trouble to look up by-election swings against previous governments at this stage during previous parliaments—thus showing that, at a time when the pound was sinking fast and his public expenditure policy was in doubt, our boy had made sure he had got his research priorities right. The swings were much smaller now, he explained.

Mrs Thatcher rose again and sweetly asked: 'Would he try three weeks on Thursday? We would be ready.'

'No,' he replied, and, glancing along the Government front bench but allowing his eye to fix on one in particular, added: 'My right hon. friend who succeeds me . . .' The rest was engulfed by Tory inquiries as to who that would be. Mr Wilson shouted back: 'We have long had a practice of democratic election, not the scatty system you introduced, but for which the right hon. gentleman the Member for Penrith [Mr Whitelaw] would have been leader.'

Many Tories would take the view that the truly scatty system would have been the one that produced just that result. In any case, Mr Whitelaw thought it his duty to nod in disagreement with Mr Wilson.

Mr Heath paid Mr Wilson a long and elaborate compliment about all the elections the Prime Minister had won, and how courteous he had always been towards him—thus showing that there is no telling who you will end up regarding as a good egg if you have been toppled by Mrs Thatcher. Mr Wilson thanked him equally glutinously.

The main advance interest in the contribution, on behalf of the Ulster Unionists, of Mr Enoch Powell, was how he would use the occasion to attack Mr Heath. Impossible? Not so. Mr Powell could use the Second Coming for that purpose. Following the 'disastrous' Ulster policy of the Tory Government, said Mr Powell, Northern Ireland 'will look forward to greater stability and peace under the policies the right hon. gentleman [Mr Wilson] has enacted.' Mr Whitelaw, the last Tory Ulster Secretary, nearly had apoplexy at that, and spoke agitatedly to Mrs Thatcher. Mr Wilson thanked Mr Powell 'for what I think he meant as a compliment,' but added that the then Opposition had supported the Tory Ulster policy. Mr Whitelaw recovered his physical health.

Finally, Mr Molloy, the Labour Member for Ealing North, who can be relied upon to be the representative of the ridiculous no matter how sublime the occasion, proudly said that Mr Wilson was going 'without any knives in his back whatsoever'.

'Of course, that is true,' replied Mr Wilson, as other shoulder-blades along the front bench did all the twitching necessary for the time being. In fact, he had intimated 'to you, Mr Speaker, many months ago' that he would be resigning about now.

Hmmm, thought Mr Healey. Pity he didn't indicate it to me before last week.

*

Drawing on his lifelong lack of interest in foreign affairs, Mr Crosland made a successful début as Foreign Secretary at Question Time. The fact that it was successful is no argument for extending the principle of the gifted amateur to, for instance, brain surgery. But Mr Crosland's appointment is a reminder to Britain's expensive and frequently patronizing Diplomatic Service of their true place in the scheme of things. For he is reportedly only at the F.O. for a few months in order to fill in time before succeeding to the Treasury. The Foreign Office, then, is nowadays just a superior sort of dentist's waiting room—whose inmate leafs through briefs about, say, Ethiopian Cabinet reshuffles instead of copies of *Punch*.

But no disrespect is here intended to Mr Crosland, who is one of the cleverest men in the Commons, as he would himself concede. And yesterday he donned world statesman's drag and comported himself in the manner associated with the Great Department of State that harboured Canning. Sir Edward Grey, Burgess and Maclean.

Moreover, when it comes to being patronizing, most people on the F.O. payroll will find Mr Crosland a hard man to beat. He was asked yesterday about his meeting with Dr Kissinger. Now almost certainly he believes Dr Kissinger to be a chubby, rather boring little fellow, perfectly amiable in a superficial sort of way, but not up to much intellectually. Furthermore, he should grapple—as Mr Crosland himself had done for years—with something really difficult, such as the British rating system, instead of going in for all that easy, 'broad sweep' stuff about Metternich—who was no doubt an equally tedious character—and The Decline of the West.

The evidence suggests that Mr Crosland would not be far wrong. But he thought it prudent to tell the House that the doctor's speech this week on Africa was 'a major contribution to African policy'.

He was also asked about Mr Ian Smith. Now he, of course, in the Crosland lexicon, would be a very vulgar and tiresome figure indeed—worse even than all those hysterical and tiresome black men from all those outlandish countries about which people like Mrs Judith Hart become sentimental in a perfectly ludicrous fashion. If he had his way, he would have no part of any of it.

However, he explained that: 'The essential thing is for Mr Smith and the White community to grasp the full significance of the Kissinger speech and realize that they are dealing with an opinion now held by the whole world community.' Furthermore, 'in terms of national interest and the global balance of power, I would suggest that if the UK Government and Dr Kissinger had not taken the line they have taken, we would have undermined every moderate Black leader in the entire continent of Africa.'

Note such 'broad sweep' touches as 'world community' and 'global balance of power'. Mr Crosland had mastered the patter without any trouble at all, proving that being Foreign Secretary was nowadays a form of up-market, unskilled labour. He did spoil it at one stage by showing a certain amount of knowledge of the cod war, but that could be explained by the fact that he is MP for Grimsby.

Mr Tugendhat, an Opposition foreign affairs spokesman, asked him what he thought about Mr Jimmy Carter's reported sporting of an 'England-get-out-of-Ireland' button. To Mr Crosland, Mr Carter would be a really rather absurd person whose advance towards the Presidency only went to show what preposterous and boring people the Americans could be when they set their minds to it. But the Foreign Secretary stuck to deploring the illegal American arms shipments to Ulster.

As for Rhodesia, we must not lose sight of the conditions for a settlement recently laid down by the British Prime Minister—'Otherwise we should simply set off again on that long, stony road we have tried to inch up in the last twelve years.'

A telling phrase, if I may say so, Foreign Secretary. God bless you, in these troubled times, sir.

*

Without once having to read from notes, Mr Tom Swain—a Derbyshire miners' MP whose syntax is normally more muddled—exclaimed to a Tory: 'If you say that outside, I'll punch your bloody head in.' It was the best, and most articulate, speech Mr Swain had made in his seventeen years in the House.

A moment later he illustrated his observation with a diagram. He seized the Conservative by the tie, but by that time other Members had understood the broad sweep of Mr Swain's argument and interposed themselves—at some personal risk—between the two men.

This example of punk politics took place during Question Time—a peak viewing hour—while many impressionable politicians and sensitive journalists were watching. I myself subsequently jammed numerous switchboards in protest. It happened as questions to the Education Department were drawing to an end and Prime Minister's questions were about to begin, which immediately raises the interesting issue: what is the hitherto concealed link between Mr Swain and education? But no matter, Mr Swain was in his place. Opposite him sat Mr Tebbit, the Conservative Member for Chingford—tall, thin, dark-jowled, ideally equipped for his role as Labour's current Tory back-bench stage villain, but who would also be excellent as the wicked Sir Jasper in one of those Victorian melodramas now being fashionably revived.

Mr Tebbit was recently described by Mr Michael Foot as 'the most studiously offensive man in the House'. A signal honour. Let us hope Mr Tebbit proves worthy of that sacred trust. Certainly he did his duty yesterday. Mr Swain was complaining to the Speaker about not being called by the Chair to put questions to the Education Ministers. Mr Tebbit muttered something studiously offensive. It was then that Mr Swain spoke eloquently about the likely fate of Mr Tebbit's head. Mr Swain turned to the Chair, complained to the referee that 'the hon. Member accused me of being drunk,' and sat down.

Out of earshot of the rest of us, Mr Swain and Mr Tebbit continued to exchange ideas across the floor of the House. Then, suddenly they rose and walked to the Bar—the Bar of the Chamber, that is. Mr Tebbit was smiling. Mr Swain seemed to grab Mr Tebbit's tie, and pulled back a huge miner's fist of the kind idealized by D. H. Lawrence.

A Tory back-bencher continued to drone through a question to the Government front bench. But Mr Tebbit had stopped smiling. After all, Mr Swain—a large, beetle-browed person shaped like a bulky wardrobe—is no joke. Well, he is a joke. But you know what I mean. Rescue action was very clearly required. Only MPs could supply it. That was only proper. They are always urging sacrifice.

The Press, one must report, displayed exemplary cowardice. Throughout it was left to several Members standing by the Bar to usher Mr Swain away. The two returned to their seats—Mr Tebbit with his head still mercifully intact. Mr Swain with *his* as intact as it is ever likely to be.

Anthony Crosland's death in February 1977 deprived the Labour Party of one of its ablest members, and the House of Commons of an outstanding politician.

Mr Crosland, who at least in youth could have played the Sweet Prince, was sung to his rest, not alas by flights of angels, it being the House of Commons, but by his fellow politicians. The Prime Minister, the deputy leader of the Conservative party, the leader of the Liberals, and the leader of the Scottish Nationalists (who spoke also on behalf of the Ulster Unionists and the Welsh Nationalists) paid tribute to the late Foreign Secretary.

The venue was a reminder of an aspect of Mr Crosland too little mentioned in the otherwise apt obsequies paid him over the weekend; his qualities as a performer at the Dispatch Box. For a man who was said rather to have despised the dark but (to many of us) irresistible arts of the parliamentarian, Mr Crosland was extraordinarily good at them. Indeed, in the set-piece debate, this reporter never saw him worsted. This was the case—and here is the mark of the born debater—irrespective of whether, at any given moment, he was in the right or in the wrong.

He proved this only some ten days before sustaining the stroke which was to kill him. For in the emergency debate on the Black Rhodesian school-children who had crossed into Botswana, he secured at least a drawn verdict. He thus confounded those who had implied in advance that, in a full debate on the matter, he would be unable to give a good account of himself—the implications having come from Conservative opponents, and from certain observers (including this one).

Indeed—with his panache, amiable devilry and taste for Mandarin invective—one would rather listen to Mr Crosland wrong than to a lot of other politicians right.

Yesterday, the mourning was superbly led by one who is also a master parliamentarian, though in a different, more avuncular style. Mr Callaghan, in a speech marvellously free from sentimentality or false rhetoric, told the House: 'He was a major political figure of the present generation, gifted beyond the reach of many of us.'

Rare among speeches on such occasions, Mr Callaghan's conveyed some of the flavour of the man being commemorated. He had first met Crosland when addressing a meeting at Oxford thirty years ago. They had talked in Mr Crosland's room. Mr Crosland confided his desire to become a politician.

'I could not help but note the rather distinctive manner he had.' Mr Callaghan had asked this apparently donnish figure whether he would feel at home in politics. 'I then had the first taste of what we all got to know very quickly afterwards. He took me aside very civilly and left me in no doubt about what he intended to do.'

Later, and after Mr Crosland had been elected to the Commons, they were both delegates to the Council of Europe at Strasbourg. 'He and I shared many of the delights of Alsace, we drank the wine in great quantities and we walked in the mountains around Strasbourg together.'

Mr Crosland 'always carried the aura of a university don, even into his local Labour club at Grimsby, but he was accepted there because people knew he was not a humbug . . . and when he watched "Match of the Day" each week, it was not a pretence but a real interest in football.'

And so, in a few deft strokes, Mr Callaghan—instead of writing an epitaph—had conveyed, as far as was possible at such a time, the impression of a flesh and blood figure. There followed references by the Prime Minister to the offices Mr Crosland had held, to the great influence of his writings, and to Mrs Susan Crosland. 'All of his friends felt it was fortunate he met and married her, forging a true partnership of loyalty and affection.'

Mr Whitelaw, deputizing for Mrs Thatcher, Mr David Steel, and Mr Donald Stewart paid more formal, less intimate tributes. And the House moved on to the business of the day, bereft of one of its diminishing number of outstanding figures—and with our having lost, too, a splendidly sketchable politician.

As Labour's majority was whittled away, an accommodation with the Liberal Party was sought. By the spring of 1977 this had been formalized to give Liberal spokesmen access to Government Ministers.

Many Members who had been absent for the thinly-attended first two speeches of the resumed debate on the Budget yesterday trickled back into the Chamber the moment Mr John Pardoe, the Liberal economics spokesman, rose. This was not because Mr Pardoe is normally regarded as a Compulsive Listen; it was because MPs hoped that he might show more signs of the amusing megalomania which has gripped him since, under the terms of the Lib-Lab Alliance, he was designated as The Liberal Who Walks With Chancellors.

The House was not disappointed. Mr Pardoe was suitably self-important. Indeed, we now face a considerable Pardoe Problem.

The lad has been given just one glimpse of, as the saying goes, the black underwear of power, and he has not been able to keep a grip on himself. He needs to take a few cold baths. None of us is safe from molestation by this new Whitehall lurker.

There he was yesterday, asking the Press to take note of such and such a clarification of Liberal policy, making his attitude clear on this or that totally unimportant position once adopted by his party. He was concerned about what he thought was Mrs Thatcher's simplistic attitude towards high policy and to the sort of gigantic problems with which he had perforce to grapple throughout his public career. 'She makes governing Britain sound a darned sight too easy, and it frankly is not,' he said, drawing on his years as the close colleague of Gladstone, Asquith and Mr Clement Freud. What she lacked was 'the responsibility of office,' he added in a sombre tone, implying that, unlike him and his party, she had never had to fight the First World War or the Orpington by-election.

He began by explaining that, contrary to some press speculation, 'I did not write the Budget. And it shows!' But that was the kind of disclaimer designed to show off the sort of circles in which one moved—the sort of thing indulged in by those models, formerly married to property speculators, who are always denying that they are about to marry Prince Charles. We had got the message. Mr Pardoe was now important.***

*** Mrs Kellett-Bowman, the Conservative member for Lancaster, demanded of the Speaker that an emergency debate be held about public money being given to an Indian institution called 'the Anand Marg'. This turned out to be not one of those Tandoori resturants with a potentially lethal cuisine but merely (as she told the House) 'an Indian terrorist group which practises homosexuality and ritual murder'. Mrs Kellett Bowman was indignant. Understandably. Ritual murder is one thing, but homosexuality is always to be deplored.

Mrs Kellett-Bowman, who represents a marginal constituency and could therefore lose her seat if she offended any significant minority taste, courageously came out against both. But it was a sign of these permissive times that the ritual murder seemed to be causing her most concern. For, when certain Labour back-benchers laughed as she described the twin activities of the Anand Marg, she sharply told them: 'I am surprised that Members of the Government side should find ritual murder amusing.'

She swept on. It emerged that these brown-skinned gay

27

necrophiliacs, or whatever is their precise hobby, had a branch on Merseyside. They had received a £60,000 grant from the Government's Manpower Services Commission. But, as Mrs Kellett-Bowman explained, Professor Ridley, the chairman of the Merseyside Job-Creation Committee, had said it was all right because the ritually murderous gays from the subcontinent had been given the cash so that they could rejuvenate a Victorian theatre in Liverpool. (Are you able to follow all this? I confess that I cannot. For instance, why did Professor Ridley think that the most obviously suitable people to rejuvenate a Victorian theatre in Liverpool were these dusky deviants of a homosexual, and indeed homicidal, tendency? Perhaps it is all part of the timeless, unfathomable mystery that is teeming, changeless Merseyside.) We never did get to the bottom of it all.

Soon it was time for the Speaker, Mr George Thomas, to read out the application for an emergency debate. He said that, under Standing Order Number Nine, Mrs Kellet-Bowman was asking for precedence over other business to be given to a debate about a grant to a group 'which practises ritual murder'. He left out the homosexuality, the squeamish man!

'And homosexuality!' Mr Norman Tebbit, the Conservative MP for Chingford, smilingly obliged.

Mr Speaker is a Welshman and a Methodist. Presumably, although ritual murder is well-known in the valleys, folk know nothing of that other matter. He ignored Mr Tebbit and refused an emergency debate.

In a debate later, the speech by Mr Merlyn Rees, the Home Secretary, was clearly designed to demonstrate that the Tories were not more anti-crime than Labour. Nonetheless, he lapsed into a sort of Open University sociological chatter—'Crime is shaped by the growing complexity of modern society and the unpredictability of human behaviour.'

The strong 'law and order' speech in reply by Mr William Whitelaw, Shadow Secretary, was rather upstaged by the later contribution of an unusual Labour Member, Mr Peter Doig of Dundee West.

Mr Doig wanted criminals treated in the same way that they treated their victims—e.g., 'Those who threw acid in people's faces should have acid thrown in theirs.' When his Labour colleagues protested he explained that he was not saying that such sentences should be compulsory, but just an option available to the judges (the old softie!). While agreeing in principle with this admirable speech, one saw certain practical difficulties. For example, how would Mr Doig's policy apply in the case of rapists? Also, a call for volunteers to punish, in kind, Indian homosexual ritual murderers might attract undesirable elements.

*

In the House, Mr Callaghan as Prime Minister is proving to be many of the things which his predecessor, Sir Harold, was widely said to be—but really was not. Mr Callaghan is genuinely cunning. Such is his deviousness that he always knows the right moment at which to be straightforward. He also gives the impression that he is seriously engaged in the activity of politics, something which Sir Harold could never bring off.

Stravinsky (I think) said, in a most elaborate jibe, that 'Richard Strauss is the Puccini of music.' Well, James Callaghan is the Harold Wilson of politics.

Sir Harold was constantly trying to be the National leader. But he always looked like a cornered ferret. Mr Callaghan looks the part. Yesterday he was shamelessly playing it to the full. For instance, he was superb in the firm-but-fair soliloquies which the role entails.

He was equally serene when dealing with his own enemies within as with his Tory enemies. For mention of fire provoked an intervention from Mrs Barbara Castle, now merely the Labour Member for Blackburn, who, ever since Mr Callaghan relieved her of Cabinet office on his becoming Prime Minister, has been smouldering on a back bench. Mrs Castle told him that the Government should underwrite a long-term firemen's pay claim to the same extent that it was underwriting the findings of the independent inquiry into the police.

He replied: 'When there are negotiations to be conducted, I prefer not to be pressed on that matter across the floor of the House.'

Shortly afterwards, on a non-Euro-matter, Mr Cryer's colleague at Industry, Mr Kaufman, showed how to deal with troublesome questions of this kind. Mr Tebbit wanted to know if the British Aerospace Corporation had yet made any proposal to proceed with a new civil aircraft project.

Mr Kaufman: 'British Aerospace is actively examining all the possible civil aircraft options.'

Mr Tebbit: 'What does that mean?'

Mr Kaufman: 'What it says.'

*

Mr Michael Foot made a dramatic 'We are innocent' plea in the face of mounting evidence that the Government had master-minded a massive fraud involving millions of pounds worth of taxpayers' cash being spent on bribing thousands of Tyneside and Clydeside shipyard workers to vote Labour at the next general election. The plan was for the money to be passed to the shipyard men not (as is usual in swindles on this scale) via Switzerland, but via Poland.

Almost certainly, the Government had intended to follow international criminal precedent and use Switzerland for the job. But a key part of the plot involved using ships as a cover. And someone in the Cabinet who was a swot during geography lessons at school—that goody-goody, Dr David Owen, perhaps—must have remembered that Switzerland was only a minor maritime power.

Part of the gigantic deception which has now been uncovered involved the men on Tyneside and Clydeside making out that the money they were getting was in exchange not for their votes but for building ships. This is where the sinister 'Cracow connection' comes in.

One of the most vicious gangs in Europe—the so-called 'Polish Government'—agreed to pretend that they were *buying* the ships. But in fact—and here is the racket's master stroke—the British Ministers were more or less *giving* them the money with which to do the buying, after having first snatched it from millions of British taxpayers (the money was to be disguised by such descriptions as 'credit' for the Poles).

That, then, was the deal. The Poles were to get some big ships for virtually nothing: the British politicians were to get a lot of votes which were admittedly very expensive but which would be paid for by somebody else. As a scandal, it is on a par with the South Sea Bubble, Marconi, Lloyd George's sale of titles, Sir Harold's Resignation Honours List and British Leyland. It makes the Crown Agents look like a tea party in a Warsaw vicarage.

Yesterday, Mr Foot, the Leader of the House, was at the Dispatch Box during Prime Minister's Question Time, deputizing during the absence in Brussels of Mr James Callaghan—who is said to be the 'Mr Big' behind the whole affair. Also present was Mr Eric Varley. He is thought to be the 'Mr Little'. But none of the men involved had bargained for the investigative abilities of Mr William Whitelaw, the Deputy Leader of the Conservative Party. It soon became clear that he had uncovered the whole plot by unrelentingly reading about it in the newspapers.

Yesterday Mr Whitelaw protested about the deal, on behalf of the official Opposition, a mere couple of months or so after various Conservative journals had done so. He told Mr Foot: 'There is a growing suspicion that there is something to hide over the Polish ships deal and that there is an urgent need for a Government statement.' This was a reference to the actual size of the sum which the Government was advancing to the Poles in exchange for their buying the ships and which so far has been kept secret.

Mr Foot explained that without arrangements of this kind, many Labour MPs in Scotland and the North East might be thrown out of their jobs. The way in which he phrased this was to say that 'Many British workers would be thrown out of their jobs,' but his meaning was understood.

*

From the Government Dispatch Box, the always dependably outrageous Mr Gerald Kaufman last night wound up a debate forced by the Tories on the Polish ships deal with a brilliant speech which won him a deserved cheer from his party.

He was particularly impressive on this occasion because, like all the most heroic actions, his speech was a defence of an impossible position. The Poles have shown no inclination to buy British ships under normal circumstances, but this difficulty is to be overcome by our more or less giving Poland the money with which to do the buying.

As the debate wore on, Labour Members from shipbuilding areas twitched with irritation. It was now reported that the Indians were going to get a similar deal, one Tory complained. 'So what?' a Labour voice inquired. 'It's the unemployment that's important,' another Labour man cried. A collective mania for such ruinous commercial arrangements seemed to be sweeping the Labour benches. One could quite believe that these MPs were angry at the lack of similar shipping deals with Czechoslovakia, Switzerland and Tibet—regarding such a lack as sheer water-ism: discrimination against landlocked countries.***

Mr Kaufman accused Mr Nott of wanting unemployment in the shipbuilding areas. Mr Nott rose and noted that unemployment in his constituency of St Ives was worse than in the shipbuilding areas, and what was the Government going to do about that?

Mr Kaufman replied that if Mr Nott was calling for more Government expenditure he had better sort it out with his Tory front-bench colleagues who were against more public expenditure. Next Mr Kaufman mocked the Tories for apparently being against these sorts of deal with Communist countries. He noted (to a large Labour cheer) that on her recent visit to Yugoslavia Mrs Thatcher had praised a certain project which involved British credits) as an admirable example of 'Anglo-Yugoslav cooperation'. Then he took up an earlier complaint from Mr Nicholas Ridley (the Conservative Member for Cirencester) that the Government had not released enough details of the Polish shipping order's financing.

He said that Mr Ridley, when a Minister for Industry in the Tory Government, had been asked to supply similar details, but had refused in a parliamentary reply which had noted that 'this is a purely commercial matter'. Finally Mr Kaufman pointed out that work was being carried out at Warsaw Airport by a British firm called Cementation. It involved British Government credits.

'Like the *Daily Express* [an opponent of the Polish ships deal], this company is a subsidiary of Trafalgar Investments,' Mr Kaufman said. And he triumphantly added: 'I am sorry I cannot give further details of this deal because in the immortal words of the hon. Member for Cirencester, this is a purely commercial matter.'

On April 3, 1978, sound broadcasting of parliamentary proceedings began.

As the BBC has for days seemingly been reminding us every five and a half minutes, yesterday was the historic first day of the historic permanent broadcasting of the historic House of Commons.*** Transistor pressed to an ear, and with the day's business about to begin, one heard the BBC commentator, the historic Mr David Holmes, explain that: 'Mr Speaker will take the chair. He will start things off with the cry of "Order, order".'

Into the Chamber.

Sure enough, the Speaker, Mr George Thomas, was taking the chair. He is a Welsh Methodist, unmarried teetotaller who, so far as is known, is not on drugs either. He is not typical of previous transistor stars.

'Order! Order!' he cried, historically. And, indeed, hysterically; for one could be forgiven for suspecting that someone in the Beeb had told dear George to speak up for the benefit of the microphones and to put on something of a show for the occasion.

Such advice would not have come from the admirable and stupendously Reithian Mr Holmes. But one feels sure that the Corporation is full of trainee-producers named Cindy and Mandy (probably even those who are male are also called Cindy and

Mandy) and one of them perhaps asked the occupant of the chair to 'camp it up a bit, Speakie darling'. Anyway, Mr Thomas yesterday gave his all for the listening millions or hundreds. For example, when Mr Ridsdale, Conservative MP for Harwich, rose on a point of order to complain about slow progress of Question Time that day, the Speaker observed: 'It may be my imagination, but I have been under the impression that the supplementary questions have been longer than usual today and I cannot think why.'

The subject chosen for the first broadcast was Welsh Questions. This was of course sheer sensationalism on the part of the broadcasting authorities. One has to warn those members of the public who listened that parliament is not always as exciting as Welsh Questions. Mr Gwynfor Evans, the Welsh Nationalist MP for Carmarthen, asked a question about Dyfed. Mr Kinnock, the Labour Member for Bedwellty, was worried about Bronglais, which was either a place or an illness. An Under Secretary at the Welsh Office named Mr Jones had an announcement to make about something which had happened at a place which sounded like 'Mouldy Fluid'. Another Under Secretary at the Welsh Office—who was also named Mr Jones—was for a while annoyed with a Welsh Nationalist named, for the sake of variety, Mr Thomas. In an interview just before the historic day, Mr Michael Foot, the Leader of the House, had said that these broadcasts would mean that newspapers would have to 'report better' the proceedings of the House because the public would now be able to 'hear how it really happens'.*** Also, one hopes that the broadcast will put an end to the distortion and trivialization of politics indulged in by MPs. (Why don't the politicians report the good things which happen in our society?)

How, then, did yesterday's broadcast compare with the unreal thing inside the Chamber? Well, Mr Holmes did wonders at explaining the inexplicable, and the sound was excellent, down to the last rhubarb-rhubarb. But disinterest compels one to admit that, whatever miracles this latest phenomenon called the wireless performs in years to come, it will never take the place of the old fashioned, steam parliamentary sketchwriter. With our funny old misprints, and unfunny old jokes, we will still be around long after many contemporary politicians have come alive. Only we could tell you, for instance, that throughout yesterday's historic proceedings Mr Russell Kerr, the Labour MP for Feltham, was wearing fluorescent green socks. Perhaps he thought the socks would enable him to be seen better on the radio.

SOCKNOTE: This column yesterday reported Mr Russell Kerr as wearing fluorescent green socks. But they were described as yellow by another newspaper.

In its morning review of the newspapers, the BBC drew attention to this discrepancy. Yesterday Mr Kerr was wearing socks of the same colour (which raises a point of hygiene: was he wearing the same socks two days running? This being a charitable column, we will assume that he has two pairs of the same colour).

The issue should be resolved in the proper manner, as is usual with controversial utterances by Members. I move, Mr Speaker, that a copy of Mr Kerr's socks be placed for inspection in the Commons library.

*

A scholarly controversy developed in the House as to how many Tory back-benchers were asleep during the speech, opening the resumed debate on the Budget, by the Shadow Chancellor, Sir Geoffrey Howe. The Liberal leader, Mr Steel, who spoke later, told the House that 'a distinguished political commentator recently described the Shadow Chancellor as Mogadon Man, but I counted only three back-benchers asleep during his speech.'

Mr Rooker (Labour MP for Perry Barr): 'Four.'

Mr Steel: 'Well all right then, four.'

The precise figure must be left for future historians to decide. The present writer would like to be able to produce the answer, but he was asleep at the time.

*

Yesterday brought signs of industrial unrest among Church of England clergy. These emerged when Mr Nelson (the Conservative Member for Chichester) asked Mr Terry Walker (the Labour MP for Kingswood), who is the representative in the House of the Church Commissioners, for a statement on the condition of the Church's investments. This joint consortium between God and Mammon was doing rather well, we learned. Mr Walker reported that the Church's investments were providing a better yield than the average for the country's investment as a whole. Mr Nelson seemed to interpret this to mean that the bosses could therefore afford to relinquish more of their profits in favour of the men on the spiritual shop-floor. 'Many clergy feel that the work is not adequately rewarded,' he said—apparently believing that he was acting on the authority of Him who is the final Advisory, Arbitration and Conciliatory Service.

Was Mr Nelson threatening that his lads would hold the nation to ransom? Faced with this example of the Church Militant, Mr Walker remained calm. Troops had lately fought fires: they could deliver sermons. Mr Walker was not taken in by this propaganda that no Government could beat the vicars. The Conservative Member for Halesowen, Mr Stokes, intervened with a suggestion that the Government supplement the clergy's pay out of public funds. He was thus courageously defying the simplistic, hard-faced right-wing Tory policy which says that, if the Church of England cannot hold its own against Japanese competition, it must go to the wall. Mr Walker was noncommittal. Understandably. If the Government bails out the C. of E., all Heaven will break loose.

*

In the furtherance of its policy of more 'open government', the Callaghan régime yesterday released the details of the efficiently incomprehensible formula it apparently employed for determining 'the relationship between prices and wage costs'. Mr Joel Barnett, the Chief Secretary to the Treasury, was asked to supply this information during Treasury Question Time by Mr Tom Arnold, the Conservative MP for Hazel Grove. Presumably it was news which they had long been awaiting in the pubs and launderettes of Hazel Grove. Mr Barnett began by saying, with some relish, that 'the formula is rather complex'. It went, he explained, as follows: 'ERPR over ERPR to the power of minus one equals, Z Square bracket 0.5 sigma alpha 1, where 1 equals 0 to 2, bracket PR over PR to the power of 4 minus one.'

In view of the fact that he was addressing an audience of MPs, Mr Barnett had of course to simplify it a great deal. For it was clearly not as simple as it sounded. The more mathematically-inclined back-benchers would have noted, for example, that after the first bracket, one would have to change at Crewe: double the sigma you first thought of, return to go, and be sure not to buy the Savoy Hotel.

Anyway, Mr Arnold was no doubt suitably bludgeoned. 'I think it better,' Mr Barnett gleefully told him, 'if I refer the hon. Member to the publication *HM Treasury Macro-economic Model Technical Manual 1977*, a copy of which is available in the library. The formula he wants is set out on pages 8A, 4, 5 and 6.' Or put another way, if Emma passes Rupert on a London Underground escalator twice during alternate leap years, the driver of the next eastbound train must be the same Mr S. J. Patel.

As Mr Barnett read triumphantly on the wretched MPs looked suitably cowed. For us trained mathematicians, it was very much a case of Liebniz, bowled Einstein, caught Gottlob Frege for sigma alpha. Once Mr Barnett sat down, however, there developed much unseemly giggling on the back benches. Eventually Mr Enoch Powell (who is now an Ulster Unionist, representing Down, South) rose. 'If that is how they do it,' he said, 'is it surprising that the macro-economic advice of the Treasury has been persistently wrong?' Mr Barnett was suitably disappointed with Mr Powell. 'I should have thought that he at least would have understood it.'***

*

Such is the strength of our British tradition of parliamentary give-and-take, it is possible for two statesmen of diametrically opposing philosophies—one right-wing, the other left-wing—who have from time to time to say harsh things of one another, nonetheless to get on tolerably well together.

One refers of course to the Shadow Secretary for Education, Mr Norman St John-Stevas, and Dr Rhodes Boyson, his deputy. There the two of them were yesterday—sitting together on the Opposition front bench during education questions, as if they were colleagues.

Mr St John-Stevas is long and thin. So, from time to time, are his speeches. But that is only when he is forced to conceal Tory educational policy from the main opposition—Dr Boyson.

Dr Boyson is short and rotund. So too, by all accounts, are some of his private observations about Mr St John-Stevas's policy.

But there are similarities between them. They both dress elegantly. Yesterday Dr Boyson wore a purple shirt and Mr St John-Stevas a purple tie. When thinking of each other, they each wore a purple face. Their social backgrounds, however, are very different. It was to end the rule exercised by Mr St John-Stevas's class that Dr Boyson joined the Conservative Party.

One of the arenas in which this decisive, historical struggle is waged is Education Question Time. The weapon they use is not, as in less happy countries, civil war—but silence. Traditionally, neither hardly ever says a word throughout the hour or so in which the Education Ministers are being questioned.

Mrs Shirley Williams, the Secretary for Education, and her departmental Ministers scarcely miss a chance to draw attention to the divisions in the Conservative Party on the subject of education. And, through it all, Mr St John-Stevas and Dr Boyson titanically vie with one another in noiselessness.

But one suspects that, after these epic jousts, Mr St John-Stevas and Dr Boyson are in the habit of sinking a pint together in the smoking room—the transient antagonisms of public life having passed. That would be true to the Westminster tradition for such virulent opponents. It was true of Churchill and Bevan. 'Get some ale down yer gullet, lad,' Dr Boyson no doubt cries, fetching his old enemy a tremendous slap on the back and, indeed, a kick in the teeth. 'Thank you, Boyson,' the Shadow Secretary for Education replies. 'But you may give me a sweet Martini with a cherry on top.'

There was probably some such sequel to yesterday's Question Time. For it had been a notably tumultuous episode in their long duel. Both kept up a steady stream of silence. Mrs Williams was asked a question about 'the educational voucher scheme'. This is an untried method of financing education which is favoured by the Right.

Support for it is therefore regarded by Mr St John-Stevas as evidence of insanity. Dr Boyson is in favour of it. That reinforces Mr St John-Stevas's medical judgment.

Mrs Williams said the scheme was 'absurd'. Then, in an apparent reference to the difference of opinion between Mr St John-Stevas and Dr Boyson as to the efficacy of vouchers, she said there was 'a most enjoyable cacophony' among Tory spokesmen on the subject.

This was nothing less than a challenge to Mr St John-Stevas to agree with something supported by Dr Boyson. Unflinchingly, Mr St John-Stevas rose and talked about something else.

He pressed upon the Secretary of State his own scheme for widening parental choice of schooling, a scheme designed to mollify some of the supporters of the voucher scheme. Mrs Williams replied in effect, that the Government was already doing the sort of thing which Mr St John-Stevas wanted—a reply which was no doubt not lost upon Dr Boyson. Mr St John-Stevas resumed his seat. Dr Boyson said nothing. Their at turns knockabout, impassioned, but at the same time strangely sentimental, silence resumed.

The following account of manure being thrown in the Commons is, for once, not a metaphor. The substance was indeed thrown from the public gallery. The throwers were a man and woman who were under the impression that the act would further the Irish Nationalist cause. The woman was, for some reason never fully explained, the daughter of Mr Mintoff, the Maltese statesman.

Manure was propelled in the direction of MPs yesterday. Your correspondent was in the Press Gallery bar at the time, engaged upon in-depth research. He therefore cannot, for once, be held responsible. By the time he arrived in the Chamber, MPs were filing out with impressive calm—women and children first. Various attendants were busy with brushes and brooms.

Relatively few MPs or journalists were present for the incident. This was because the House was debating the Scottish Devolution Bill.

The news that excreta was raining down upon the Scotland Bill sent one hurrying into the Chamber for an eye-witness account from, among others, the parliamentary sketchwriter of Another Conservative Newspaper, who has a perverse and expert interest in the subject (the Scotland Bill, that is). This informant was shaken—although possibly with glee. From his, and other, accounts it seems that a man and woman in the public gallery yielded to a temptation which a lot of people must feel from time to time, and launched the rude substance in what appeared to be several half-open plastic bags.

Mr Tam Dalyell, the Labour Member for West Lothian, was in mid-point of order. This of course rapidly became a point of odour.

The Speaker shouted 'order!' but, according to some reports, it might have been 'ordure!'. (The reader will be burdened with no further puns.)

The fall-out covered a wide area and was non-ideological in its choice of victims—it ranged from the Tribune benches to the right-winger Mr Ian Gow (the Conservative Member for Eastbourne). Our condolences to relatives, particularly wives.

But it was the Tribune benches, just under the public gallery, which got the worst of it—thus causing a lot of people in all parties to reflect that life may not always be unfair. And the worst affected area was Mr Dennis Skinner, the Labour Member for Bolsover, but he has always claimed that politics under capitalism were a dirty business. There was a direct hit on the new sports jacket which Mr Skinner has worn for the first time in the Chamber this week. Understandably, he jumped up and rushed to the door. MPs looked on aghast, almost as much as they would have had the stuff missed Mr Skinner.

Visitors in the public gallery gazed down impassively—the Americans, Japanese and Arabs among them being presumably under the impression that it was all a regular part of the unchanging ritual of the oldest Parliament.

Mr Dalyell, a remorseless critic of Scottish devolution, was forced to stop speaking—something which only dung from heaven could have achieved.

The couple in the gallery shouted slogans at least as odorous as their missile. They were removed.

Small deposits of the substance settled throughout the Chamber. Even the very Dispatch Boxes were defiled. Mr John Smith, the Minister of State in charge of devolution, looked down to find that his briefs were soiled, so to speak. The first instinct of the Speaker, Mr George Thomas, must have been to consult Erskine May, the parliamentary rulebook, to discover the precedents. But under what heading to look? Pollution? Agriculture? No, George was on his own. So he established the historic precedent that when proceedings begin to leave a nasty smell, the House has to be suspended for twenty minutes.

*

Mr Merlyn Rees, the Home Secretary, made a statement to the House yesterday explaining the Government's plans for the future of broadcasting, particularly of television.

A certain type of person takes the subject of television with great seriousness and tends to talk about this absurd and highly enjoyable medium by deploying such phrases as 'the need for an educated democracy'.

Speculation as to the content of yesterday's announcement had lately covered a substantial Scandinavian forest of newsprint. At least, this was the case with those progressive newspapers which are obsessed with television's power struggles and the obscure personalities involved. They contain such headlines as 'Cowgill Moves to Deputy Controller (Expenses)'.

Mr Rees' statement, then, was eagerly awaited by ordinary, average, decent television executives up and down the country. Likewise, the politicians. They too take television seriously. That leaves only the viewers to adopt the correct attitude of complete ribaldry. Anyway, the Home Secretary rose.

He proceeded to read a huge and complicated encyclical the essence of which was that, in creating a Fourth Channel run by a new television authority independent of the BBC and the existing commercial companies, at least three new quangos would also mysteriously come into being—no doubt staffed by the usual statutory women and deceased trade unionists. This seemed harmless enough on the face of it. But what sort of programmes would we get?

Would the Fourth Channel maintain the tradition whereby most documentaries took place in the Brixton area of London or were about lesbians or about Brixton lesbians? Also, would the present ratio be maintained of ten programmes about the denial of human rights in, say, Chile and the Isle of Wight to none about the denial of human rights in, say, Tanzania or the Isle of Cuba?

The answer to both questions appeared to be: of course.

For Mr Julian Critchley, the Opposition front-bench expert on broadcasting, revealed that the Government's policy had been largely inspired by Mr Phillip Whitehead, the Member for Derby North. He is a stupendously progressive former producer of television documentaries who has a beard and wears those suits with the bell-bottomed trousers which were the fashion of the 1960s—the deadly decade which invented such people. One suspects that—as far as his current taste in documentaries is concerned—he is very much a lesbian man, if he will not misunderstand the expression.

Mr Critchley's worst fears were confirmed when Mr Whitehead welcomed the statement. Mr Whitehead spoke about the need for an educated democracy. It will be no laugh-in, this Fourth Channel.

Reporting party conferences almost makes a change from reporting proceedings in the Chamber. This was the Conservatives' in 1978.

Tuesday
This year's Conservative Party conference opened with one of those days of uncontrollable unity which is the traditional sign that the party is divided. Even the religious service starting the proceedings was affected. It contained contributions from an Anglican, a Free Churchman and a rabbi. This was carrying unity too far. One was prepared to listen to Mr James Prior and to Sir Keith Joseph without much wanting anyone to demand of them an explanation of their obvious differences with each other. But, as rabbi rubbed shoulder with gentile cleric, one yearned for a heckle along the lines of: 'What about the Divinity of Christ?'

Someone, however, had blundered. There was no Hindu priest, nor Sikh or Rastafarian. They did not even wheel on a small portable mosque. This, one is happy to report, completely ruined the later efforts of the party managers to so rig the debate on immigration that the party appeared moderate on the subject.

The Free Churchman delivered a message from St Paul, via the Ephesians, which was the best English we would hear all week. St Paul appeared to be something of a monetarist. 'Put on the whole armour of God,' the Saint told the conference. This was a clear warning against the flimsiest of man-made armours: incomes policy. 'Stand against the wiles of the devil,' St Paul added, in an obvious reference to Mr Heath.

The opening debate was about employment and industrial relations. The motion called on the Government to find solutions to the problem 'both short-term and long'. But neither the motion, nor the speech from Mr Prior ending the debate, said what those solutions should be—short, long or oblong-term. Instead Mr Prior offered a speech designed to be election campaign-term. 'This [Mr Callaghan's ability to get on with the unions] was Labour's secret weapon,' Mr Prior said. 'And it exploded in their faces. We should ram it down their throats.' With an exploded secret weapon rammed down his throat, the Prime Minister was now powerless against further Prior blows. 'The economic boomlet is running out of steam,' Mr Prior mocked, to show that he is not a man to be taken in by any old steam-driven economic boomlet.

Everything had been arranged in this debate to convince voters that the Tory Party was made up of ordinary people. Among the speakers brandished were: a West Indian gentleman; Mr Reg Prentice; and a mover of the motion who was a trade unionist named Fred. As a joint definition of ordinariness, this left something to be desired. Among other things, trade unionists called Fred are surely among the most unpopular groups in the country.

Wednesday

Mr Heath arrived in the hall and advanced menacingly on the platform shortly after the economic debate started—neatly dressed as ever, facially impassive, arms thrust straight down his sides. It was as if he had stepped out of the window of a nearby branch of Burton's. He was warmly applauded and seated himself one place away from Mrs Thatcher. They gave each other a welcoming stare. Lord Carrington was a kind of peace-keeping zone between the two. Mrs Thatcher leaned forward towards the rostrum and pretended to be engrossed in a lugubriously-delivered speech from Mr Iain Mills, the candidate for Meriden. In the middle of his monotone about the need for incentives, he somewhat superfluously exclaimed: 'Forgive my passion!' But he felt strongly about these matters 'because they are facts in the lives of many middle-managers'.

Mrs Thatcher continued to be enthralled by the passionate Meriden middle-manager. But, alas, this wonderful, fleeting moment, which she was snatching with him amid life's turbulence, could not go on forever. Any minute now he would have to go back to middle-managing and old Heath would barge in. So it happened.

Mr Heath was stupendously statesmanlike—indeed, rather more so than he ever was when actually employed as a statesman. He reminded the conference that when he last addressed it two years ago he had said that the country was at the end of the road. But in the next breath today he said that the country had been saved then by the IMF and North Sea oil. He did not seem to draw the conclusion that he must therefore be a lousy prophet. Instead, he said we were reaching the end of the road again. It seemed to be a sort of mobile road-ending. This inconsistency apart, his bark for national unity was mightily impressive. He warned against 'dogma'. The speech had a vaguely 'coalition' tone about it. But it is difficult to say in what way. The speech could mean something or nothing. One would not want to be dogmatic.

It was well received. So too was Sir Geoffrey Howe's reply to the debate. He praised Mr Heath's contribution and went on to advocate more or less the opposite.

The conference either did not notice this nuance or was not bothered about it. They gave Sir Geoffrey a considerable ovation. Mr Heath need not have worried about the conference being dogmatic. Sir Geoffrey's oratory, often so earthbound in the Commons, took flight. He threw his arms about and was larky. He said that Mr Clive Jenkins, Mr Richard Burton and he had all come from the same Welsh town. Then the normally plummy-toned Sir Geoffrey showed that he could do voices. He instructed Mr Jenkins to 'look behind you, boyo' at the number of members of Mr Jenkins's union who are opting out of paying the Labour political levy. It was an authentic Pakistani accent. Sir Geoffrey, who once administered the Heath incomes policy, is now a born-again monetarist. It was good to see this most agreeable of politicians having a triumph at the conference.

Ever since scoring his own first triumph with a big speech to the conference a few years ago, Mr Heseltine, the Shadow Secretary for the Environment, has lived for his annual moment. He does not much force himself on the attentions of the Commons in the intervening twelve months. He seems content to be the Yearly Man. Probably he did not study British Constitution to 'A' Level and therefore does not know that it is the Tory MPs who choose the leader, not the conference.

Each year the jealous party hierarchy seems to try to put him on at a time awkward for many conference attenders and television viewers. Last year they staged a brilliant coup by getting him faded out in favour of 'Play School'. This time I watched him on television from an informal position in my bed at the Old Ship Hotel, having had rather a detailed lunch. Sure enough, ten minutes into his speech they faded him out in favour of the much less entertaining Open University—a sort of pretentious 'Play School' and a disseminator of even more unconvincing information than Mr Heseltine's annual speech. One leapt out of bed, threw off one's pyjamas and hurried along the promenade to the conference hall, pausing only—this being the conference of the anti-permissive party—to put on one's trousers. One arrived to find Mr Heseltine engulfed in his own peroration. A huge audience was enthralled. He bellowed at them from beneath that blond mane which causes him so often to be mistaken from behind for Mrs Sally Oppenheim. He was thundering along the lines of: one nation, one Reich, one Heseltine. Then he sat down. Ovation! Whereupon the Yearly Man subsided for another twelve months. Next year those envious party managers will probably resort to holding the conference at Blackpool and telling him that it is at Brighton.

Thursday
Various idealistic and decent Young Conservatives were more or less kicked to death by the rest of the conference for advocating a fairer electoral system. But it was not all good news today. Between the adjournment of the conference the previous evening and the resumption this morning, disloyalty had come like a Heath in the night. The former leader had taken to the television screens in support of the Prime Minister on pay. Thus, although he was no longer in the hall, Mr Heath's monstrous presence dominated the morning's economic debate. He was the spectre at the Ancient Mariner's wedding, though not having one's library to hand in Brighton one is unable to check the accuracy of the Coleridgean allusion. So perhaps it would be more correct to say that he was the albatross on the wall. Anyway, he was the spanner down the trousers of party unity, all right, that's for sure. But this time he had clearly gone too far. The conference draws the line at going on the box and saying that the Labour Government is all right. They demonstrated their disapproval by giving a standing ovation to a speech by

Sir Keith Joseph, a man scarcely a word of whose speeches they have ever understood. Sir Keith is, however, no Heseltine. They tend to listen to him with awe rather than affection. How could he have got all those books into the average-sized head, they wonder.

With Mr Heseltine the problem is the opposite: how could that handsome, large head contain so little evidence of books? But, although they may not have been able to grasp the details of Sir Keith's message about capitalism, the conference knew it was not: vote Labour. The motion which he supported on 'free enterprise and industry' was carried with acclamation. Indeed at this unity-crazed conference it was difficult for a Shadow Minister to make a motion towards the Gents without it being carried with acclamation.

Friday

After her big speech ending the conference, the leader received a long standing ovation and could be said finally to have 'arrived' as leader of the party. The long standing ovation and final 'arrival' as leader of the party constitute an annual event. After one such occasion, during the years of the Heath Occupation, it was observed that that man had had more arrivals than Dame Nellie Melba had farewells. The 'media's' repetitive coverage of the occasion is on a par with the inevitable report of that small motor-boat which takes turkey and pudding across a treacherous sea on Christmas Day to the remotest Scottish lighthouse; or of the West Indian young ladies who kiss policemen at the Notting Hill carnival each year shortly before the equally traditional mass arrests of West Indian young men.

But, as an elaborate *hors d'oeuvre* before she spoke, we had Mr Norman St John-Stevas replying to a debate on education in the best and most intentionally funny speech of the week. The mood of the debate had been right-wing. After a noisy conference debut by Professor Max Beloff of a Black Paper-ish hue, Dr Rhodes Boyson jumped up and led a standing ovation. Mr St John-Stevas joined in with a crouching ovation. Finally, he rose, made his jokes, and carefully jumbled the motion and the amendment into a left-right mix which was carried unanimously. He achieved this by using such rightie code-phrases as 'the need for discipline in our schools'—even though, as a mother in a Noel Coward play says on hearing that her son had taken up boxing, Norman is so terribly *un* that sort of thing.

Mrs Thatcher arrived to scenes of near-dementia. Young Conservatives had pinned to the balconies banners bearing such devices as 'Love Maggie', though it would have been even more fun had the Old Conservatives pinned to the balconies various Young

Conservatives. Her speech pointed up the left-right conflict which dominates our time: that between her left-wing speechwriters and her right-wing speech-writers. The righties seemed to have done reasonably well. The speech was more or less against incomes policy.

At the end, a suitably deranged audience gave her a Blue Teddy Bear. Being mute and easily locked up in a dark attic, she will prefer him to the other Blue Teddy. There was a happy ending, then, to what, for the professional observer, had been a good week in the still-marvellous town of Brighton. Balmy weather! Barmy speakers! Mrs Thatcher fighting off an attempt to murder her by controversial Ted Vicious! What more could a reporter ask?

And so to the Callaghan Government's 'winter of discontent', about which a Labour back-bencher, sometimes said to have been Mr Arthur Lewis of Newham, is accredited with saying: 'Whoever thought up that phrase in Tory Central Office is a propaganda genius.'

Sooner or later a Minister was going to have to make a statement to the House about the most macabre of our industrial disputes. This is the strike in the north-west of England by workers responsible for grave-digging and crematorium-operating: the dying industries. Messy work of this kind, among Ministers, is normally palmed off on Mr Denis Howell, the Minister of State for the Environment. In his time he has looked after Sport, Drought and Snow. But this time he seems to have dug in against being landed with Death.

So the statement was made by the Secretary of State who is the head of Mr Howell's department, Mr Peter Shore. It was a tricky one both for him and for any Member who might want to put a question to him. It is agreed on all sides that this particular dispute is fabulously horrible. But supposing some Tory suddenly told Mr Shore that it was a grave situation? Supposing some left-winger accused the Tories of inflaming the crematorium problem? It did not bear thinking about. In particular, we in this column, conscious of the way in which we tend to set the tone in these matters, would have to proceed warily.

In the event, we all acquitted ourselves rather well. Not a single MP doubled his entendre. Everyone was appropriately mortified by this strike.

Actually, Mr Michael Heseltine, the Shadow Secretary for the Environment, rather overdid it. His tone became more and more theatrically sombre as he pressed Mr Shore to make another statement within a day. One harboured the suspicion that if he was *that* upset he would surely be on the train to Lime Street, with the intention of wielding a shovel himself.

Mr Shore, on the other hand, seemed genuinely aghast. 'The matter goes much wider than one of just public health,' he said. 'It affects the feelings of those confronted by death in the family and in the community.'

Mr Heseltine rose again and, tuning in his sepulchral tones, he once again played undertakers—although, since he was standing beneath that elaborately sculptured blond hair-do, and was encased in several yards of expensive suiting, he would have been one of those prosperous American members of the funeral profession to be found in Evelyn Waugh's *The Loved One*. He vaguely demanded action. Mr Shore asked him 'to wait until a little later' to see what the response was to various talks among the local authorities and unions concerned.

The left-wing Liverpool Member, Mr Eric Heffer, who had long seen himself as the First Gravedigger of many a Labour Government incomes policy, said he was 'deeply concerned at the distress being caused to bereaved families. But the men must have a decent living wage,' he added, with the nearest we came to an unfortunate phrase.

All the piety proved rather too much for Mr Dennis Skinner. He told Mr Shore that both sides of the House were 'with only a few exceptions indulging in a bout of utter hypocrisy'. Mr Skinner probably regards death as a bourgeois custom. It holds no terrors for him. The House and the Government could 'get rid of these dead bodies', he said, by paying 'a decent wage'. And he added: 'There is no one, but no one, in this House who would do the job these people are doing for a take-home pay of £40.'

This was an honest and impressive outburst. It was very different from the false emotion—surely the definition of sentimentality—which was deployed by other Members. But honest and impressive, too, was Mr Shore's reply. He rounded on Mr Skinner with real feeling, something one does not often see displayed in the House. He said he hoped that Mr Skinner 'will at a later stage today consider what his sense of priorities and values are. Death is not hypocrisy, nor is human grief, nor is a common sense of humanity. There ought to be some sense of common fellowship and decency between members of the same community.' (Huge Tory cheers: Labour silence.)

Mr Skinner sat back in his seat with a look of considerable disapproval. Two of his left-wing cronies appeared to commiserate with him. He stared at Mr Shore. These middle-class Labour Ministers, he seemed to say, would be the death of him.

*

Searching amid our economic troubles for some of the glamour and escapism associated with people still capable of really outrageous spending, one chanced upon Mrs Judith Hart, the Minister for Overseas Development.

Mrs Hart, who was at the Dispatch Box at Question Time, is in charge of Britain's aid to Afro-Asian countries. With the possible exception of Mrs Jacqueline Onassis, this must make her the world's most expensive woman. And like all expensive women, she is irresistible. Indeed, if you are resident in Britain, it is illegal to resist her, since she gets her money from the taxpayers. Certainly, she nearly always has her way in the House. This is because all of those Members, on both sides of the Chamber, who are widely regarded as intelligent, never question the case for overseas aid. Only the acknowledged oafs suspect that there may be something not quite right about our going around the world thrusting sums of money on other countries' politicians and civil servants.

The policy of the OAF party on the matter—and of those of us who vote OAF—is strongly non-racialist. We take the view that, just because those Third World politicians and civil servants are black or brown or yellow, it does not mean that they do not waste most money entrusted to them, just like white politicians and civil servants.

But we have no chance in a society dominated by pro-intelligent propaganda. For example, Mr Ivor Clemitson, the Labour Member for Luton East, rose at one stage yesterday. He has a beard. This is a notorious sign of intelligence. Sure enough, he produced much nonsense. In so far as one could understand him, he seemed to be complaining that the Indian Government had failed to spend £35 million of the money which we had given them. He appeared to be demanding that we do something about it.

Like all women who get control of huge amounts of other people's money, Mrs Hart is ruthless. The essence of her reply was that she intended to turn really nasty with the Indians. Unless they spent that money she would throw a lot more at them. She reminded the House that she had looked into the matter last year when she made an official visit to India, which itself must have set us back a bob or two.

Mr Malcolm Rifkind, Conservative MP for Edinburgh Pentlands, intervened. He is thin, rather intense, highly articulate and wears horn-rimmed spectacles: one feared the worst. But instead he entered a timely complaint about a poor country like India spending so much money on building so many large merchant ships.

One suspects that India needs such ships rather as it needs fertility drugs. But Labour members scoffed at Mr Rifkind's question. But, then, they would be in favour of our Government subsidizing shipbuilding in Malawi, which is landlocked. Mrs Hart dealt with the inquiry effortlessly. 'If India, as part of its development programme, feels satisfied about that, there's nothing inconsistent,' she replied. She said that India needed the ships to help it get foreign exchange. That explained everything. The ships were needed to enable Indians to sail here and collect their foreign aid.

Mr Donald Stewart, a Scottish Nationalist from the Western Isles, asked Mrs Hart to deduct, from our aid to Zambia, a large sum in accident compensation owed by that country to one of his constituents and which there was no sign of the Zambians paying. She replied that she hoped the Zambians would pay the debt out of the money they are receiving from us in aid. 'The more assistance Britain provides, the more likely it is that Zambia will pay the compensation due to UK nationals,' she said, in a literally priceless remark.

The Britons owed money would be paid it in the end then. But the cash would first have to be sent to them via Zambia—a further demonstration of the widespread lack of confidence in the internal British postal service.

*

Prince Charles paid a visit to the House to see how parliament works—or, as the case may be, doesn't. There had been much advance interest in how the Labour left-wingers would react to his presence. The last time a royal personage with his first name became particularly interested in parliament, their predecessors on the extremist wing of British politics cut off his head. This was going to be a hard act for the Tribune Group to follow. But one had the fullest confidence in Mr Dennis Skinner.

The Prince strolled into the Peers' Gallery accompanied by the amiable, smiling figure of Lord Peart of Workington, Lord Privy Seal and Leader of the House of Lords, who in real life is dear old Mr Fred Peart. Mr Peart's duty was to sit next to Prince Charles and explain what was going on. This would have made the Prince notably confused. Every now and then, he would lean forward and whisper in the Windsor ear. 'See that fellow sitting in the big chair in the middle, Your Royal Highness, the one with the full-bottomed wig and the black tights,' Fred was no doubt saying, pointing towards the Speaker. 'That's the Prime Minister.'

At the time of the Prince's arrival, the Minister answering questions at the Dispatch Box was that other Fred-figure: Mr Mulley, the Secretary for Defence. This was appropriate. Mr Mulley and the Prince have something in common. They have both fallen asleep on or near the Prince's mother's lap.

The sight of a member of the Royal House seemed to revive, in the Secretary for Defence, memories of that single heroic action for which he is famous, and for which his name will live for ever in the annals of the British Armed Forces—so long as men still tell of these things. He began to sound distinctly drowsy.

*** And the Labour Left's reaction to the Royal visit? They turned out to be a cowardly lot. For they treated both us and his Royal Highness to a disgraceful show of good conduct. One cannot see the point of having a Left if they are going to behave like this.

And Mr Skinner? The visit of such a person as Prince Charles would no doubt have been particularly provocative to him. But Mr Skinner, with centuries of tradition and breeding behind him in these matters, knew exactly how to behave. He left earlier than usual.

*

On the Opposition front bench, an expensive-looking blonde was denouncing the Government. Heseltine? No, Oppenheim. (She is the clever one of the two.)

Mrs Sally Oppenheim, the Conservative spokesman on prices, was dutifully doing her job of attacking Mr Roy Hattersley, the Secretary for Prices. This is not difficult. During the period in which we have had Secretaries of State for Prices—the office was started under the Tories—prices have continued to rise, generally by as much, if not more than, before the invention of this great office. This makes whoever is the occupant into the softest target for the Opposition 'shadow' since whoever was Minister of Health during the Black Death.

Labour members scoffed at her. But then she has always aroused a prejudice on the grounds of her being a millionaire's wife. Indeed, when she once mentioned 'the shop floor' in a debate about wages, a Labour member said that the only shop floor she knew about was Fortnum and Masons's. But one fails to see why this makes her any less of an authority on prices, especially high ones.

Other points of interest:

Mr Russell Kerr (the Labour Member for Feltham), who occasionally wears bilious canary-yellow socks, has taken to wearing a bilious canary-yellow pullover. Either that, or he spilled his lunchtime Commons Catering Department omelette down his shirt.

Later, one looked into the Chamber to see if anything was becoming known about the Government's survival. A near-deserted House was harmlessly debating housing. On the Opposition front bench, an expensive-looking blond was denouncing the Government. Oppenheim? No, Heseltine.

In the late 1960s, largely as a result of by-elections won by Scottish and Welsh Nationalists, 'devolution' joined the ranks of words denoting things which most politicians thought they should favour, or be seen to favour. By the late 1970s, partly to conciliate Scottish and Welsh Nationalist Members on whose parliamentary votes it depended for a majority, the Labour Government introduced a Bill devolving governmental power to Scotland and Wales, by which time many MPs of all parties had decided that it was safe to be against devolution after all, or at least to be apathetic one way or the other.

A Bill relaxing the laws against prostitution won a majority yesterday from members of the world's oldest, but most frowned upon, profession (politics).

But first the latest on the subject in which you are all really interested: devolution. Yesterday's was the first Prime Minister's Question Time since the blows sustained by the Government in the referendums last Thursday. It rapidly emerged that the Prime Minister had as yet no idea what he was going to do about devolution. Back to prostitution.

The Bill was, appropriately enough, a Private Member's measure. (From now on, this column will do its best to keep all its entendres undoubled.) The authoress was Mrs Maureen Colquhoun, the Labour MP for Northampton North. She is either the most stupendously courageous MP or the most exhibitionist: perhaps a little of both. Some time ago she announced to the world that she was a lesbian. Short of announcing that she was also a practising monetarist, it was difficult to think of what else she could do to outrage her apparently rather bigoted constituency Labour Party, many of whose members have been trying to prevent her from being their candidate at the general election. But there she was yesterday, getting up to put the case for women who go out to work. And the case she put was highly convincing.

Her Protection of Prostitutes Bill would abolish prison sentences for soliciting and would ensure that, before a prostitute could be convicted of a street offence, there would have to be evidence that she had actually annoyed someone by approaching him. It would also abolish both the law whereby a building in which more than two prostitutes lived could be classified as a brothel, and the offence of being 'a common prostitute'.

Mrs Colquhoun persuasively demonstrated that these laws 'actually prevent a woman, once convicted, from getting away from prostitution, forcing her to carry the stigma of common prostitute for the rest of her life, and forcing her back on to the street in order to pay ever-increasing fines'. She added that the present laws ensured that it was the incompetent, ageing, immature or emotionally disturbed prostitute who got into trouble—'Successful and competent prostitutes operate very well within the law in a different way.' Present arrangements 'force prostitutes directly into the hands of organized crime, making them totally dependent on ponces and pimps and part of a terrifying Mafia'. Although she was a common MP, Mrs Colquhoun, then, turned out to have a heart of gold.

'Eminent psychiatrists have told me that it is accepted in their profession that prostitutes have great therapeutic value in society and are practitioners of professional therapy,' she said. 'Many psychiatrists accept that prostitutes are the oldest therapists in the world.' The calling in aid of eminent psychiatrists forced one momentarily to part company with her, especally since one of those whose opinion she quoted was Dr Wilhelm Reich, a cult figure of the liberated, boring 1960s. On these delicate matters, one should no more be guided by Wilhelm Reich than by the Third Reich. Moreover, Mrs Colquhoun's insistence that the prostitutes were more or less hospital ancillary workers perhaps meant that under her Bill they would have to join NUPE. They would then go on strike. There would be demands that their work be done by troops. (WRACs? Guardsmen?) It does not bear thinking about.

In the public galleries, Mrs Colquhoun's speech was listened to raptly by several women in fluffy coats or sweaters who, one was given to understand, were eminent therapists. These visitors were something of a disappointment. Just as some of the miners, when they lobby MPs, bring their lamps and helmets, so one had hoped that the therapists would bring what, according to the more entertaining and disgraceful newspapers, are the apparatus of their profession: chains, divers' suits, Father Christmas boots. Not so yesterday. The women looked like respectable typists, although

51

these days respectable typists sometimes look like, so to speak, therapists.

A couple of the visitors squealed with approval when, after Mrs Colquhoun's speech, the Speaker asked if she be given leave to bring in the Bill and a majority of MPs shouted in favour. The girls were clearly under the erroneous impression that the Bill had been passed. Apparently they were not students of parliamentary procedure. No reason why they should be. Therapy's their game. They were hustled out by the attendants.

Before the vote, the Rev. Ian Paisley (U U U Antrim, N.) bawled a speech which must have persuaded many a Tory who was against the Bill either to abstain or vote in favour.

He quoted Christ's attitude to the woman taken in adultery, correctly interpreting the parable as meaning that 'no MP has the right to point the finger of judgment or pass condemnation'. 'Sit down, then,' cried Mrs Renee Short, the Labour Member for Wolverhampton North East, drawing a perfectly reasonable inference, but Mr Paisley crashed on. He failed to address himself to the crucial point that the existing laws actually made it more difficult for women to give up prostitution. Instead, he concentrated on such assurances as 'I believe in the sanctity of women,' thus proving to his opponents on both sides of the House only that he believed in the sanctity of Mr Paisley.

*

Sir Bernard Braine, the Conservative Member for Essex South East, is a very agreeable and industrious back-bencher who specializes in imperial matters. Of late he has been somewhat restricted by the fact that we no longer have an empire. This has rather cramped his style. Nonetheless he is seemingly able to keep on discovering various outlandish parts of the world over which we apparently still hold some sway. Whereupon, he asks questions in the House about them.

Yesterday, for example, he was on his feet to put an emergency question to a Foreign Office Minister about 'security on Ocean Island following the breakdown of talks on the Banaban question'. To their credit, most MPs registered instant interest and concern. 'What,' they seemed to ask one another to a man, 'is the Banaban question?' Most Members clearly had not the faintest idea. Some undoubtedly knew the Banaban answer which, if memory serves aright, is: 'Yes, we have no Banabans!' but the Banaban *question*! That must be something else entirely.

Mr Evan Luard, the Parliamentary Under-Secretary at the

Foreign Office, rose to enlighten us. 'According to the latest reports available,' he said, 'the situation on Banaba is at present quiet.' He had met representatives of the Banabans in Tarawa. Negotiations were continuing.

Sir Bernard thanked Mr Luard for that reply, but accused the British Government of 'a tragic blunder'. This blunder, he added, was to tell the Banabans that they had to be part of the Gilbert Islands which were to become independent shortly. Brows furrowed throughout the Chamber. What part of the world were we dealing with here, exactly?

One could almost see Members struggling to draw on their reading of Arthur Mee's *Children's Encyclopaedia*, or on memories of stamp collections long ago. Ah, that's it, the large hole on the right hand side of Australia, or perhaps the left. That was always covered with these wretched islands.

But who were the Banabans? Why were they upset anyway? How do you spell Tarawa? Was it the same as in 'Tarawa, for now?' Why do the Banabans have to be part of the Gilbert Islands? Who was Gilbert? Are there also the Sullivan Islands? Above all, what is it to do with us?

Meanwhile, Sir Bernard banged on with his enormous supplementary question deploying vast knowledge. 'The Fijians cannot be insensitive to the Banabans' position,' he assured us, at one stage. *The Fijians*! How did they come into it? They were apparently the sort of superpower in this strategic powder-keg of a region. Furthermore they were, it seems, the traditional allies of the Banabans. They would not stand for the Banabans being forced into, so to speak, a Gilbertian situation. If that happened, then Fiji might march or, more probably, swim.

One derived all this knowledge from subsequent questioners of Mr Luard. For, as is invariably the case with any subject brought before the House, there are always some Members who know a bit about it—or claim to.

For some unaccountable reason, Mr Donald Stewart, who is the leader of the Scottish Nationalists and sits for the Western Isles, intervened. He complained of 'the appalling injustice done to the Banaban people'. Perhaps he thinks the island is one of the Western Isles.

Mr Christopher Price, the Labour Member for Lewisham West, made matters still more impossible for Members to follow. The whole affair might make it 'difficult to get the Kiribati Independence Bill through the House', he said. Presumably in what was a bid for the Kiribati vote in Lewisham West.

Mr John Roper, Farnworth's Labour MP, spoke of 'external interference and aid' in relation to the Banaban cause. Sir Bernard disagreed. 'They're Methodists,' he exclaimed, in a final, surrealist touch to a notably implausible afternoon.

On 28 March, 1979, the Callaghan Government, having been defeated on the Devolution Bill, faced a confidence motion. The outcome essentially depended on how the Liberals, the Scottish and Welsh Nationalists and the Northern Ireland Members would vote. The motion was lost. Mr Callaghan called a general election.

All evening we waited for the answer to the question: Would we get a drink? For the Commons catering staff had chosen this of all nights to go on strike.

Even those of us whose history is rather hazy had no doubt that this was the most dramatic debate since Simon de Montfort did for Ramsay Macdonald over Norway. Yet it was taking place in an eerie void without tea, without coffee, without the famous House of Commons rock-cakes made from genuine rocks, and without booze.

Mr John Stokes (Conservative Member for Halesowen and Stourbridge) rose on a point of order immediately after the Prime Minister's speech and demanded a Government statement on what it was doing 'about this disgraceful situation'. The Government front bench ignored him.

There were hopes that, on humanitarian grounds, the unions would allow essential supplies of alcohol to reach the Press Gallery. Otherwise there would be no alternative, as the evening wore on, but to listen to the speeches. But no relief came. The political columnist of the *Guardian*, who has a sense of history, informed one that, as well as being the first time for over fifty years that a Government had lost a confidence vote, it could also be the first time ever that a Government had lost a confidence vote with everyone sober.

He spoke too soon. As the night wore on, passersby were confronted with that most frightening spectacle: a sober mob of journalists. It roamed the streets of Westminster in search of a pub that had not been taken over by the equally-desperate mob of MPs. Police with dogs were on hand to keep the two groups apart.

Back in the Chamber, the debate had opened amid the traditional packed House and constant hubbub. The galleries heaved with onlookers—diplomats, MPs' wives, MPs' mistresses.

As ever on these occasions, one's eye was constantly drawn to the

Peers' Gallery and its picturesque collection of defunct politicians resembling the Twentieth-century History section of Madame Tussaud's. Some of the likenesses were rather unconvincing. There was a shrivelled owl purporting to be Lord George-Brown. It did not look a bit like him. There was also a large, round character—resembling one of those jolly porcelain figures surrounded by children which one sees in the windows of Chinese restaurants—purporting to be Lord Thorneycroft.

A sighting was reported, on a distant Labour bench, of Mr Frank Maguire, the Independent Irish Republican who has hardly set foot in the place since being elected in 1974, but none of us really knew what he looked like. It could have been someone in from the street. Next, word went round that it was impossible to get into any of the loos because Liberals were locking themselves in as their explanation of why they did not vote. So anything could happen. The excitement was tremendous.

For about half an hour, however, it was dispelled. Mrs Thatcher spoke. Within minutes of rising to open the debate and move the motion of no confidence, it was clear that she was in pedestrian form. Labour Members sensed it and fell silent. The bounders decided to give her a fair hearing. Apparently she sounded responsible and statesmanlike on the radio. But that sort of thing never goes down well in the House. Remorselessly, she heaved statistics at us to demonstrate Governmental failure in every field of human endeavour. Her back-benchers began to fidget and even to talk among themselves. The much-loved Mr Freddie Burden, the Conservative Member for Gillingham, appeared to nod off.

Suddenly Mrs Thatcher brought a heavily statistical passage to an end by raising her voice. Her back-benchers took this as their cue to stop muttering to one another and to cheer. Unfortunately the unaccustomed noise caused dear Freddie to wake up with a jolt. Labour Members gave him a huge cheer.

Mrs Thatcher sat down after only half an hour amid Labour cries of 'That all?' and 'More! More!' But, although she had not done herself much good, she had not done herself much harm either. No one was much interested in the speeches, only in the vote.

The Prime Minister's was nonetheless a great success, its close bringing Labour back-benchers to their feet cheering and waving their order papers. This was because the speech was a roguish mixture of denunciations of Mrs Thatcher's heartless capitalism, of clever playing upon the divisions in the Shadow Cabinet, and of talk about micro-processors. (He was either for them or against them.) It ended with an impressively shameless announcement of higher pensions soon for the old folk. Many Tories helped by heckling him. They included Mr Burden at one stage. 'I'm glad the hon. gentleman has woken up,' Mr Callaghan told him.

Later the House thinned. But it kept filling up every time some normally-obscure Celt rose, because such speeches might disclose voting intentions. Mr Gwynfor Evans (the Welsh Nationalist MP for Carmarthen) talked at length about the bad things the Government had done to Wales. His denunciation covered housing, education, 'equalization of water charges', Welsh language policy, and the large numbers of people who, he claimed, could only walk a few steps without pausing for breath, because they suffered from mining and quarrying diseases.

This portrait of a land of breathless, immobile people who could not speak to one another because they were being denied their language, and who had trouble equalizing their water, added up to a poor advertisement for the Welsh Tourist Authority. But Mr Evans ended by saying that he would vote for the Government.

With a fine sense of drama, the usually-stolid Mr James Molyneaux, the Ulster Unionist leader, confined himself to implying that he would vote for the party which would restore Ulster's local government. He sat down amid Labour cries of 'What does that mean?' This was exactly what he intended.

A look of utter relief crossed the face of a tired and pale Mrs Thatcher at 10.18 p.m. A tall Conservative Whip was standing over her and whispering something. She drew in her breath. Mr William Whitelaw, seated next to her, put his arm around her shoulder. She had won.

A few seconds later the Conservative and Government Whips lined up in front of the Speaker's chair and a Tory among them barked—as is the prerogative of the winners of a division—the news that the Conservative motion of no confidence in the Government had been carried by one vote. A huge cheer went up from the Tory benches, which became a forest of waving order papers.*** The final scenes of the debate and vote were the most exciting anyone could remember. Mr Michael Foot, the Leader of the House, whooped and bawled his way through a magnificent, outlandish winding up. He was in full Footage. If Mrs Thatcher is half as much a threat to socialism as he made out, the country is saved.

After denouncing her every policy, he found himself still with ten minutes to go. So, in a marvellously gaga passage, he started raving about how it was always Labour who had to save the country—for example, in 1940. When this went down a treat with his back-benchers, he developed the theme. 'Yes, we saved the country in 1940,' he bellowed. 'It was a Labour motion in this House which brought Churchill to power.'

The Tories became rather angry at this failure to mention that Churchill was a member of their party at the time. But Mr Foot stormed on. 'Yes, we saved the country then, and we'll save it again.' The fact that Labour was already in charge of the country seemed lost on the Labour benches, which were receiving Mr Foot's speech with delirium. He sat down to a vast ovation.

After the result, Mr Callaghan rose and the House fell silent. Smilingly, he announced a general election. Both leaders were cheered out of the Chamber by their followers. Amid Tory jeers, some Labour Members, including Mr Heffer of Walton, Mr Cryer of Keighley and Mr Price of Lewisham West, stayed behind and sang 'The Red Flag', which must have been worth a few votes to the Tories in the marginals.

*

Mrs Thatcher continued to travel around the country telling everyone she met that a Conservative Government would be all right. On a more serious note, she also ran amok in a Birmingham chocolate factory. For those of us who have been on the trail with her this was indisputably the big event so far.

Finding herself by chance in the extremely marginal constituency of Selly Oak—Labour majority 326—she decided to call in on the voters on the Cadbury assembly line who bring you your walnut fudge in soft caramel, hazel crispy cluster, and bitter lemon crunch and who are therefore responsible probably for more coronaries than anyone in Britain apart from the pro-jogging lobby. It was a discreet visit—just the Leader of the Opposition and about a hundred television and Press photographers and reporters.

Before we were disgorged into the factory we all had to put on white coats and hats to make us hygienic. We then advanced on the unsuspecting folk on the conveyor belts. The famous factory is as superbly organized as legend has it, but is rather noisy. Apparently the manufacture of chocolates is a process which makes a noise like Niagara Falls. Into this existing uproar erupted Mrs Thatcher pursued by a hundred white coats. The whole effect resembled perhaps a lunatic asylum in which the doctors had themselves gone berserk; or possibly a convention of mad surgeons.

The entire surrealist canvas was the most picturesque which your correspondent has witnessed in a decade or so of observing politicians trying to become Prime Minister. Mrs Thatcher would descend on a chocolate woman (that is to say a woman making chocolate). They would have a conversation. Because of the din, neither could hear the other. This is the ideal arrangement for conversations between party leaders and voters at election time since it cuts out a lot of unnecessary detail.

Meanwhile, Mr Denis Thatcher the husband would lurk on the fringe of the affray conversing with employees who did not quite get to talk to his wife. He has developed an impressive line in Duke of Edinburgh factory visit chat. It goes something like: 'This is the assortments section, I gather . . . Interesting . . . Do you export much? . . . Really? Africa as well . . . but surely it would melt?'

Back at base, the Leader of the Opposition would inevitably be urged to try chocolate packing herself. The problem, of course, would have been to stop her. Maniacally, she would raid the hazel crispy clusters and shove them in passing boxes. At this, those of the deranged doctors who had cameras would ecstatically close in with their tripods, lights and in the case of the TV men those strange objects which look like small bazookas and are to do with the sound. Some of them would clamber on chairs and machines to get a better angle. Thus clustered together at many different levels, they became not just mad surgeons but mad Martian surgeons as a result of their extra, deformed electronic eyes and cables coming out of their heads. In the midst of the tiers of lenses and faces the visage of the occasional Japanese photographer or correspondent would peer out framed perhaps by huge piles of Bournville selection. This was an extra loony touch.

What a scene! The genius at Conservative Central Office who thought it up must get a knighthood.

In the middle of it all the little chocolate woman who was the object of Mrs Thatcher's rapt attention would rather tend to get forgotten. Eventually we would all move further on down the conveyor belt or up to the next floor, the entire progress taking place before the disbelieving gaze of the Cadbury's employees on the conveyor belts. The squeals were understandable. It was exciting for me. It must have been mindblowing for folk who have to sit all day transferring the plain-coated nougat into the boxes of 'Contrast'. From department to department there was no abating of the noise. Squeals! roaring machinery! and Denis still doing his stuff: 'Fascinating . . . but how do you get the walnut exactly in the middle of the fudge?'

It was occasionally hazardous for those of us caught up in the heavy, swaying throng. Machines bubbled and clattered within inches. The Leader of the Conservative Party, borne irresistibly on by the deranged mob, was herself at times fortunate not to be converted into a large mass of delicious hazel crispy cluster.

Next week, with luck, a cement factory!

The publication of Barbara Castle's diaries in 1979 gave an interesting insight into the workings of the Labour Government which had presided over so much of the 1970s. (The following piece is from Now!*)*

Mr Enoch Powell protests at the spectacle of a Cabinet Minister (Mrs Barbara Castle) keeping a diary obviously intended for lucrative publication.

It was bad enough when Crossman did it, Mr Powell implies, but at least Crossman was clever and was trying to explain how government really worked; Mrs Castle cannot enter that defence; she is none too bright and her writings are trivial. Also—and Mr Powell is the sort of man who regards such an argument as clinching—they are in breach of the Privy Councillor's oath and of collective Cabinet responsibility.

Now, though he would deny it, Mr Powell's complaints are entirely concerned with what is in the best interests of the governors, not with what is in the best interests of us, the governed. Mr Powell is being true to himself by taking such an attitude. Mr Roy Jenkins, in his life of Asquith, divided politicians into two kinds: men of the state and tribunes of the people. Mr Powell is the former. So too is Mr Jenkins, although it is the only thing the two have in-common. Long ago, Mr Powell may have appeared to be the tribune of the people on the subject of immigration. And he may once have harboured hopes that opposition to membership of the Common Market might afford him a similar role. But his writings, temperament and manner all mark him as essentially a man of the state. The Queen's Government must be carried on. There must be a general air of decorum. No Minister's trousers should be seen suddenly to collapse, mysteriously, around the ankles. It is a bleak vision of what politics is about.

Most politicians take the same attitude, including most of those who pretend to be wags or scourges of the Establishment. Mr Michael Foot certainly does. But he, too, is at heart a state man. Mr Dennis Skinner is not. And although a lot of his former colleagues would deny it, neither, one suspects, is Mr Benn nowadays. But the left-wing tribunes of the people have a difficulty: on the whole, the people are terrified of them. That does, however, not make them any the less tribunes by temperament.

The state men have a vested interest in the state maintaining its pomp and dignity. This is all very well. But, in the public mind, the state is not embodied solely in some person of universally acknowledged dignity such as the Queen or Lord Goodman. It is also a matter of politicians. And politicians traditionally have presented a much less dignified appearance to the rest of us. We know that they spend most of their time scheming either for our votes or against the teams of politicians fielded by other countries.

This is not the result of a moral failing on their part. It is in the nature of their trade. Why should the rest of us agree to the conferring of dignity on such a knockabout activity? Yet this is what Mr Powell asks of us.

Ah, Mr Powell would reply, it is not a matter of dignity. The Castle diaries deny 'to the sovereign and to the nation that confidentiality and collective responsibility of the Cabinet which is basic to modern British parliamentary democracy'. This would be all very well were modern government the limited activity which it was in the nineteenth and early twentieth centuries. But many aspects of modern government are little better than a conspiracy against the governed, although a relatively un-sinister, slapstick kind of conspiracy (so far). Their members flourish manifestos in front of voters which, were they prospectuses flourished at the shareholders of private companies, would involve the authors in subsequent prosecution for contractual failure. Whereas, in the past, governments taxed and inflated to buy the votes of a small electorate, they today tax and inflate on a correspondingly vaster scale to provide the subsidies which buy the votes of whole regions and classes—council house dwellers, the North East, Wales, the suburban commuters.

As in the eighteenth century, they are everlastingly handing out prizes, at the public expense, to their friends and to themselves, prizes once known as sinecures and known now as quangos. We voters therefore justify our desire to see the politicians' confidentiality breached by correctly arguing that we must keep an eye on folk who are carrying out so many depredations. In this we have one great ally: the politicians' rivalry with one another for our high opinion. This leads them to want to give their version of what went on.

But there is another, less lofty, reason why we should welcome the new candid political diaries—idle curiosity. Those of us who keep up with all classes of gazette know that these political serializations are simply the up-market version of the kiss-and-tell memoirs to be had in the lower sheets. Mrs Castle's diaries were contemporaneous with 'I've Been A Bad, Bad Girl' (the memoirs of Miss Dana Gillespie, a popular artiste of the halls) and 'My Amazing Story' by Nina Carter (the un-amazing reminiscences of a distinguished model), both in the *News of the World*. The basic principles are exactly the same, but the readerships expect different details.

The Misses Gillespie and Carter offer drugs and pop. Mrs Castle offers less fragrant tales of various Budgets, although her second episode in the Sunday paper did have a yarn about Barbara and the private doctors' beds.

All three women are obsessed with their clothes—Miss Gillespie and Miss Carter with getting them off, Mrs Castle with getting them on. 'Hurriedly, I dress in my decolleté for James Callaghan's annual diplomatic banquet,' writes Dana, no, Nina, no, Barbara. 'I had decided to wear the sixty-year-old Edwardian blouse I had discovered among mother's things,' writes one or the other of them before describing how she debated the Common Market with Mr Heath at the Oxford Union. 'My trouser suit caused a lot of favourable comment,' says naughty Barbara. 'One of the civil servants whispered, "Every time you come to Chequers, Secretary of State, you wear an even more distracting ensemble. It isn't fair to the secretaries."' Here one pauses in disgust. What sort of a dribbling, grovelling, whey-faced, specimen must that penpusher be to utter thus?

Barbara Castle's diaries are rich in malice and human vanity. Her loathing of Mr Callaghan is brought to a shattering climax because he sacks her, an event she depicts as akin in its tragic grandeur to the execution of Mary, Queen of Scots. Mr Ted Short first gets shown as a bore and a toady. Then he sympathizes with the sacked Mrs Castle and is immediately a good bloke. She is surprisingly complimentary to Mrs Thatcher. At one stage she notes how pretty the new Leader of the Opposition looks. 'She is in love: in love with power, success and with herself. She looks as I did when Harold made me Minister of Transport.' One knew there was a catch.

After a few acres of Barbara's hiss-and-tell confidences you warm to her. She is confirmation that those who make up the state are as vain and trivial as the rest of us, though Mr Powell would have us not know it. In the end, however, a certain irritation grips the reader. It is the day of the funeral of her junior minister, who died cruelly young: 'I wondered distractedly what to wear.' At which point native chivalry deserted this reader: '*Black*, you self-centred moo!'

Politicians Today

Lord George-Brown

Professor Robert McKenzie—he of the large, round face and large, round swingometer—once said that he regarded elections the way other people regarded cup finals; my own sentiments entirely.

Some of us will go anywhere to watch an election. Indeed, these days we have no alternative. For the old game is not what it was. They no longer seem to put on by-elections. Dietary change, jogging, and improvements in their personal hygiene have brought about a tragic situation in which the mortality rate of modern MPs is appallingly low.

So, for us fans, it had to be the Greater London Council election. As it happens, it was no second best. For the years seemed to fall away, and it was possible to go and watch Lord George-Brown campaigning again. He was appearing in Chapel Market, Islington, in support of a certain Mr Douglas Eden, of the Social Democratic Alliance, who was seeking to represent Islington South and Finsbury on the GLC.

Time was when the intrusion into an election campaign of the then Mr George Brown, the Deputy Leader of the Labour Party, was enough to scarify even the most gnarled of his enemies. And that was only in his own party. But he always had his defenders, since on the large issues he tended more often than not to be correct. 'Better George Brown drunk than Harold Wilson sober,' someone wrote at the height of the Brown Terror of the 1960s. Personally, one thought that a somewhat down-market observation at the time. Like the Prime Minister of the day, one tended to be terrified of what the Foreign Secretary might do next. One only felt the loss to our national life once he had retired from politics and the occasional drink.

Happily, he was at it again in Chapel Market—politics, that is. What was he doing there? You may remember that a few years ago, appalled at the new power of the Labour Left, he announced his resignation from the Labour Party and shortly afterwards fell over.

The Labour Left argued that there was a causal relationship between the two phenomena. Not so the Labour Right. They regarded his resignation as evidence of extreme sobriety.

After the passage of a mere half decade or so, some of them summoned the courage to do the same (resign, that is, not, alas, fall over). None the less, the nobs of the new Social Democratic Movement—Mr Jenkins, Mrs Williams, Dr Owen, Mr Rodgers— seem so far to have been wary of Lord George's impact on the rather genteel punters whose support in the country they seem to be seeking. These nobs have behaved as if they fear he might keep on falling over. They have offered him no position of pomp.

So Lord George accepted the presidency of the Social Democratic Alliance. The SDA is the new movement's rough trade: the extreme wing of the moderate grouping.

Thus it was that Lord George was soliciting votes for Mr Eden in one of the last of the romantically proletarian London street markets. As he made his progress along the narrow thoroughfare, we could observe the phenomenon of the formerly famous face. That is, a face which was once one of the most famous in the land—but a few years ago. People know such faces, but they cannot always put a name to them. The face is not recent enough to have been on the news the night before, like that of the Chancellor of the Exchequer, but not long enough ago to have been in one of the costume series later on in the evening, like that of Queen Elizabeth I.

'Look over there . . . It's that fella . . . That bloke . . . y'know . . . Who is it?' But sometimes the name simply would not come. Shoppers sought each other's historical judgment. Disinformation no doubt spread wonderfully. 'I know . . . I know . . . R. A. Butler. That's him. The one who hanged Christie.' 'R. A. Butler, be buggered. He was the tall, thin one with the bushy, black moustache. He didn't have anything to do with Christie.'

When Lord George did encounter a student of recent history, the results were heartwarming. 'George Brown, in'it? Well done, George. Keep it up. Where's the ermine?'

Admittedly, George was subdued compared with the by-election monster of his great days. But there was still The Voice. This, contrary to some popular belief today, was never a proletarian roar, more a honeyed, pleasantly strangulated tenor similar to that of Sir Peter Pears. Moreover, the vowels are pronounced with that beguiling imitation, indulged in by many Londoners, of what is assumed to be toff speech. It is the sound favoured by regimental sergeant majors and commissionaires at the Royal Opera House,

Covent Garden. Thus, George replied to a stallholder who suggested that his visit to the market from the House of Lords was a bit of slumming: 'New, new. Note at all.'

Television cameras were present, and a few of us pencil men. So everybody started acting in the way in which they had read, or viewed, that they should act. So chirpy Cockneys behaved like chirpy Cockneys. Stallholders with crab-apple faces started to look even more so. The decades slipped away and one was suddenly among the fantasized working class of Noel Coward's *Calvacade* or *This Happy Breed*. People found themselves saying things like: 'Tell 'em straight from me, George, old son,' although it was not clear who the 'them' were. The mêlée, the antiquity of the market, the general difficulty some people had in ascertaining exactly who the visitor was, created an atmosphere of amiable confusion in which some passing Pearly King could well have enjoined George to 'Give old Hitler one for me, Mr Bevin.'

Eventually we reached Manzi's pie and eel shop. A strategic stop, this. For the GLC Social Democratic candidates are out to prove that they are more working-class than the Labour Left: prolier than thou. Mr Eden follows the traditional Cockney trade of polytechnic lecturer in history and politics and makes a special study of Abraham Lincoln. The hated left-winger of Lambeth, Mr Ted Knight, lives in a council house and has never made a special study of anything. So you can see the SDA has a problem here. That was why they aimed George at the eel and pies. The cameramen, and the rest of us, crashed in behind him.

Matters were not initially helped by the fact that George was wearing a royal blue cashmere overcoat with an elegant velvet collar. He might at least have added a Stanley Holloway-type flat cap. No matter. He seized a plate of pie and mash. In the media age, a celebrity, a number of cameras, some lights and a bazooka-shaped sound device, all intruding themselves into a confined space, seem not to arouse the slightest interest or disturbance in the citizenry originally occupying that space. They regard it as one of the hazards of shopping, like the presence of West Indian lads on roller skates. So the folks carried on munching the pies or torturing the eels.

George and Mr Eden started to do roughly the same. We professional observers gathered around. After a while, a woman came up to me: 'Is that . . . who is that?' she asked. 'R. A. Butler,' I replied, for I do not believe in encouraging politicians in their self-importance, even ones as benign as Lord George-Brown. She seemed to be only partially persuaded. Soon, Mrs Lydia Manzi, the proprietress, advanced on George. He told her: 'I first got my taste for this at Woods in The Cut' (a street in his native south London). Mrs Manzi suddenly started talking about whether it was true that George once worked for the John Lewis partnership and was such a good fur salesman that he could sell furs even at the height of summer. George mumbled partial agreement, but was obviously not sure that the subject chosen by Mrs Manzi struck the right proletarian note. Wisely, he continued with his culinary autobiography.

'Better than the stuff in the House of Lords, this meal . . . Not that I eat there much . . . tuppence each, they were in my day . . . tuppence ha'penny for the large ones.' (And you could still have a night out on the change, one was tempted to interject, so as to ensure the script was word-perfect.)

Mrs Manzi pressed on about the furs. George simply talked through her in his demotic routine. Although they were not jointly discussing the same subjects, each seemed perfectly happy with the other. Eventually they wished each other well and exchanged warm thanks. The surrealism was complete when another woman, noticing the name on Mr Eden's rosette, politely inquired: 'Are you any relation to Mr Anthony Eden?' There seemed to be rich possibilities in this exchange. All Mr Eden had to do was say 'Yes' and people would have hurried over to assure him that it wasn't his dad's fault that the Anglo-Italian invasion of Morocco in 1956 was mucked up; it was all on account of that Roosevelt. Infuriatingly, Mr Eden told the woman: 'No, I'm not.'

Myself: 'You should have said Yes. Abe Lincoln, in his early campaigns, would have said Yes.'

Mr Eden: 'Well, according to your well-known, cynical view of politicians, if I lose this election it will be because I'm an honest man'. (I was beginning to warm to this Eden.)

Soon George's day was over. He disappeared in the direction of central London where there are fewer pie shops, but more velvet collars. What a superb campaigner! But his present role in the new movement is not consistent with his dignity and talents. Why should a George Brown play second to a David Owen? The situation in which George finds himself is similar to that adumbrated in a song of his cockney youth—a song almost Schubertian in its suggestion of disappointment stoically borne:—

> *Please don't tell my mother,*
> *I'm half of a horse in a Panto,*

Never let her know that I'm a sham,
But if she learns in due course,
That I'm only half a horse,
Please don't let her know which half I am.

Mrs Margaret Thatcher

Mrs Margaret Thatcher, her husband Denis and Mr William Whitelaw, the Home Secretary, sat through a charity performance of a West End play in which they were the main characters—being depicted as, respectively, a henpecker of her husband; a suburban sot; and a generalized buffoon. When all three were asked whether they enjoyed the show, there was only one sort of thing they could say under the circumstances: Yes, certainly, most amusing, excellent, etc.

The play was of course *Anyone for Denis?* by Mr John Wells at the Whitehall Theatre. Mr Wells played the title role.

Mr Denis Thatcher was therefore at the centre of attention both on stage and in the audience. It was perhaps the most difficult engagement of his career since he assumed the part of consort to Britain's first female prime minister. Furthermore, he was appearing in the theatre which virtually invented the whole concept of the falling trouser. The play and the feature in *Private Eye* on which it is based has transformed Mr Thatcher in late middle age from a humble oil company executive into one of the great comic figures of English literature. The Denis character's euphemisms for the booze—lotion, tincture, snorter—have entered the language. So we descended on him at the interval for his reaction to having seen himself portrayed for an hour as a gin-crazed Home Counties golfer.

'Are you enjoying it, sir?' one inquired, for what else could one ask. 'Er, yes,' he replied. Did he recognize himself? 'Er, no.' What sort of tincture or lotion had he drunk in the interval? Perhaps a G and T? 'Lotion! Tincture! G and T! Well, yes, indeed,' he responded. Whereupon he started up a conversation with Lord Sieff, who was jostling past, 'Hello, Marcus, how good to see you.' What of his wife's opinion? 'Amusing, most amusing,' she said. There was a pause then, to avoid any misunderstanding, she added: 'But it's not DT.' So she calls him 'DT', does she? It sounds the sort of thing Mr Wells has people call one another. Mr Whitelaw did not think the actor playing him looked at all like him. 'He's thinner than me. But, then, I've lost weight.' Was that through worry? 'Not at all. It has been deliberate. But he's still thinner than me. And he's not as funny as you people make me.'

This was the one consolation in an otherwise rough night for the Government. All our heads would swerve to the Prime Minister and her husband every time anyone on stage said something funny, or filthy. The audience was therefore rather like the crowd at Wimbledon. The Prime Minister seemed to take the view that she had got off more lightly than others over the full evening. Of the actress Miss Angela Thorne who plays her, she said: 'She was wonderful, absolutely terrific. I am lucky. She's a good deal younger than me and a lot prettier.'

Mr Whitelaw seemed amused by a character with a distinguished accent called Roy Jenkins who for a reason not fully explained, was the butler at Chequers.

The play itself started well, flagged somewhat, but ended splendidly—which is rather what the Prime Minister is hoping of the Government.

*

A few months ago the Prime Minister was in conversation with the Master of Peterhouse. (He is still better known by the rather arid-sounding name of Professor Hugh Trevor-Roper, which somehow befitted a figure of such scarifying scholarship although he has lately assumed the romantically evocative title of Lord Dacre of Glanton, which makes him sound like one of Miss Cartland's heroes. There has been no such transformation since blunt, bleak Mr Ted Short became lilting, seductive Lord Glenamara of Genridding.)

The subject of the conversation was Christianity and freedom or some related topic. Lord Dacre did not agree that Christianity was dependent on freedom. If the Russians overran western Europe, it did not necessarily follow that things would be bad for Christianity. Look at Poland. Christianity was pretty strong there. Remember the Roman empire. That was overrun. Christianity did not do too badly subsequently in those parts.

Now, you have to be especially careful when attributing practically any opinion to a mighty academic, as the letters column of *The Times Literary Supplement* proves. I am perhaps vulgarizing what may have been a more elegantly subtle piece of reasoning by Lord Dacre, although his argument sounds wholly persuasive to me. But Mrs Thatcher was not persuaded: 'You are being deliberately provocative,' she told him.

Mr Enoch Powell was present. He did not agree with the Prime Minister that we could defend Christian values: 'Values cannot be defended,' he said. Mrs Thatcher: 'What do you mean?' Mr Powell slipped into overdrive. Militarily, values could be neither defended nor destroyed. They existed in a transcendent platonic realm beyond space and time. Territory was what could be defended. For territory was not in space or time but here on earth. All this remorseless logic was issuing forth in that haunting voice with its Black Country accent so that Mr Powell sounded like a mixture of St Thomas Aquinas and an Aston Villa trainer. As he pressed on, Mrs Thatcher shot him a look of 'wise guy, eh?' Then, index finger to cheek, she began to study his work like a grammar-school teacher confronting a brilliant but perverse essay by a boy who had a great future ahead of him but little commonsense and who needed to be taken down a peg or two for his own good. 'Create, Enoch dear, don't destroy,' she said.

In this, the week of the second anniversary of her election victory, it should be emphasized that Mrs Thatcher is if anything even more interested in what may seem to many to be idle speculations but which can loosely be described as right-wing ideas and ideology. She still loves to chatter about them to clever people whom she regards as being broadly on her side, just as she did in opposition. But temperamentally she is something of a Stalinist. Freedom, Christianity, Western values, the theological justification for nuclear weapons . . . They all swirl around together under that coiffure. And she would prefer that those who support her on one should accept the right-wing line on all the others.

Possibly this is because she seems to have come rather late in life to all these profound matters. For the first decade or so of her parliamentary career she was influenced by such figures as Mr Macmillan, Rab Butler and the late Reginald Maudling—clever men, but men distrustful of all that abstract theorizing. It was the Tory loss of office in 1974, coinciding as it did with the emergence, for good or ill, of some sort of Conservative intelligentsia, which seems to have galvanized her. Consequently all the ideas seem to have got hastily and happily jumbled up together.

At the gathering to which I have referred she seemed content to stay on into the night—going on fascinatedly about the nature of authority or whatever. As people started to debate the perhaps still more pressing issue of which trattoria or tandoori to make for it would have surprised no one had the Prime Minister suddenly chirruped, like Miss Brown at that party in *Vile Bodies*: 'Why don't you come to *my* house?' (Miss Brown was living at home with her father who, if you remember, was Prime Minister at the time.) Fortunately Mrs Thatcher did not do so. The spectacle of various professors, Conservative thinkers and sundry poseurs piling out of taxis would have caused some concern to the Downing Street police.

None of this is to suggest that she actually *does* much about all this ideology. Possibly it is a form of escapism or relaxation. She knows that, come the morning, she will encounter some starchy Permanent Secretary or wet Minister telling her that such and such an ideological course of action would be counter-productive or upset the Arabs. She has not been a particularly 'ideological' Prime Minister.* She constantly changes her policies in a wettish direction. The ideology is literally 'all in the mind'.

This makes her a more, rather than less, serious person. She ponders the inert moderate mass that is 'government', 'Whitehall' and 'expert opinion' in the only manner consistent with seriousness—with disappointment and irritation at how little can be changed. This week, after two years, she still sounds like a Leader of the Opposition. Her first response to any outrage is to say that the Government should do something about it, only to realize 'I *am* the Government.'

Well, perhaps she is not really. It could be that she is a right-wing counter-revolutionary trapped in an essentially social-democratic state. As did Chairman Mao, on the opposite wing of politics, she presides over a government apparatus against which she is spiritually in revolt.

But at work during the day reality supervenes. When she rose to answer routine questions in this anniversary week, supporters of the Brandt report on help for the Third World were lobbying the House. The place was besieged by progressive vicars and like-minded souls. Harassed Tory back-benchers, summoned by aid-crazed constituents, could be heard explaining in the Central Lobby that they agreed with the lobbyists' aims. For economic reasons, the Government had been forced to slow down aid a bit, but it would pick up after the recession.

But, according to the New Right, that is not the correct line at all on foreign aid. The correct line is that the poverty of all those countries is not caused by insufficient Western aid and that, in any case, the money cannot be other than wasted and only makes the

---

*That was written in the summer of 1981. By the summer of 1982 her premiership had become very 'ideological' indeed.

whole situation worse. Mrs Thatcher was briefed on the argument many times in gatherings during the years of the Long March in opposition. It is probably still her view. But, maddeningly, the world on such matters seems to go on much as it did before, with nearly everybody automatically assuming overseas aid to be a good thing.

Still, whatever happens to the Government in the end, the Prime Minister will have the consolation of being, on most of these awesome subjects, correct—if consolation that be.

Richard Wagner* and Mr Roy Hattersley

Unsuccessfully, as it will now emerge, I had resolved from the outset that there were two subjects which had received sufficient airing on this page and would not be mentioned further: Wagner and Mr Roy Hattersley.

Concerning the one: nobody in his right mind would deny his capacity for the sublime, his surges of lyricism, his sheer weight and scale, but there is also his torrential prolixity, his essentially outdated nineteenth-century ideological attitude towards his art, his foggy symbolism and an epic tedium which modern audiences should surely not be expected to endure. These are some of the drawbacks of Mr Hattersley.

Wagner, for all the intimidating left-luggage that comes in his train, is a less fascinating figure. But, entombed as one was in a performance of *Lohengrin* at the Royal Opera House, one was forced into some embittered reflections about him. After an incandescently wonderful prelude has put us into an ethereal mood (for I do not deny that, when Richard really wanted to, the boy could write), we are suddenly washed up on the banks of some dank river somewhere in the Low Countries or Rhineland. For getting on for forty minutes or so, various disagreeable Teutons stump about bawling '*Heil Koenig Heinrich*', and similar observations, to a dullard of a bass who seems to be in charge. My relatives fought in the war to put a stop to that kind of thing.

Eventually there is a mysterious visitor carried in by a swan. He is the tenor (the mysterious visitor, that is, not the swan: the swan does

---

*The reader may object that, despite his strong views on such issues as race, Richard Wagner was not a full-time politician and should not be included in a chapter headed 'Politicians Today'. This carping reader is referred to page 13 of the Introduction. Mr Hattersley comes in because Mr Levin disliked him.

not sing, being one of the few characters in any of Dick's operas who is mercifully silent all evening). In this production, the tenor was an East German. He was driving this swan without a crash helmet, itself an offence under English law, and without a rear-view mirror. He explains himself by saying that he has come from a far-off land to champion the beautiful Elsa in combat with the wicked Friedrich, not to be confused with the boring Heinrich, provided Elsa does not ask him his name. Any British copper, routinely hauling an East German tenor off an illegally-ridden swan and faced with such a tale, would robustly respond along the lines of: 'Oh, yeah, and I'm the Ayatollah.' Not so these German rozzers, who astoundingly allow the lad into their country for his big fight with Friedrich. Whereupon, the tenor addresses the beast as *'mein lieber Schwan'*, which potentially suggests tastes which, though unfortunately common in rural areas, would also be illegal in this country, but which do not seem to put off the beautiful Elsa over in the Low Countries.

To be fair to Dickie, all scenes involving the swan are radiantly beautiful. But the rest of the work consists of music endlessly stopping and starting. The Wagnerians defend *Lohengrin* by saying that it was an early show and that their boy only hit peak form later in his career when setting up a really big gig like *Götterdämmerung*. This is undoubtedly true. But the biggies also contain many an hour of *Lohengrin*-type windbaggery. *Parsifal* contains a character, the wounded Amfortas, who does nothing else but moan all evening on a stretcher. 'Amfortas is the wisest man in the theatre this evening,' the *Manchester Guardian* critic Samuel Langford once whispered to Neville Cardus during a notably slow performance of the work, 'he's brought his bed with him.'

Debussy, a composer disgracefully maligned by Mr Levin, was one of the earliest to see through the massively-hyped German. 'The two Sunday concerts were in competition,' he wrote when he was the superb critic of *La Revue Blanche* in 1901. 'Each played us Wagner. The result? No score on either side.'

None the less, it will be some years yet before the dilettanti, cowed by the mighty reputation, stop allowing themselves to be herded into the opera house for all those hours of monologues and papier-mâché dragons, mention of which brings us to Mr Hattersley. Those racists who beat and kicked him at a public meeting which he addressed recently were 'the product of society in the same way that the people in Brixton were: in the same way, we have alienated them and made them feel rejected'. In effect he is arguing that they were disturbed, not responsible for their own actions, and not simply evil. Here, encased in Mr Hattersley's sickly and obviously bogus compassion towards his assailants, was the behaviourist fallacy: the claim that someone's behaviour is primarily caused by 'society'.

But to want to sock Mr Hattersley is not evidence of mental disorder. No one would be incarcerated in a special hospital on such a rap. For the desire is widespread in his party and in the country as a whole. It is just that most of us, on the whole, do not give in to it.

Such is the dominance of the sociological explanation of riots and criminality, we seem to be losing sight of the fine old British concept of the yobbo: the low type who simply wants to throw Molotov cocktails, pillage telephone boxes, or assault Mr Hattersley because it is fun. Such conduct should be condemned, not verbosely explained.

Still, as a rule, we will no longer be anti-Hattersley in this space. As this latest, shameless playing to the radical gallery shows, he is a divertingly professional politician who knows precisely when to go left and when to go right in the practice of his profession, which is to become leader of the Labour Party. Society is not to blame for that, either.

*

Mr Roy Hattersley, the Shadow Home Secretary, made an eloquent, concerned and compassionate speech advocating a reduced rate television licence fee for old age pensioners. What a shameless rascal he is. But he is lovable with it. We know that, when he is visibly moved (as happens often) about the plight of elderly people or of the disabled or of racially disadvantaged groups in our so-called equal society, he does not really mean it. That somehow makes it less offensive.

There is a certain type of person the admiration for whom is almost entirely confined to others practising the same profession. There are lawyers' lawyers; journalists' journalists; conductors' conductors. Generally, they are not the same as the ones who are admired by outsiders. Mr André Previn, for example, is admired by us outsiders, but not by his fellow conductors. Perhaps it has something to do with the fact that he is a little ridiculous. That is always popular. Well, Mr Hattersley is a politicians' politician; one for the connoisseur; not the sort of figure popular with the masses. It would not be safe to use him in wallpaper advertisements or party political broadcasts. No Previn, he. Instead, a performer to whom his fellow professionals flock whenever he consents to give a virtuoso display. Actually, they took some time to do the flocking. For a long period, the Labour benches were rather deserted. This is always the way after an Opposition demands an urgent debate on some Government announcement.

A few days ago, Mr Whitelaw, the Home Secretary, announced the increase in the television licence fee. Seemingly hundreds of Labour Members rose, lamented the effect on old people's incomes, and insisted that nothing less than a full debate would suffice. Came the debate and the Chamber was practically deserted. The art, you see, is to saddle the Government with the tiresome debate. The assumption is that the old pensioners, or whichever allegedly stricken group is the subject, should have noted the original uproar, and perhaps the debate itself—but not the empty Chamber.

Mr Hattersley rose with about a dozen Labour Members strewn across the large expanse of the benches behind him, including several older folk for whom the Chamber is a place to stay in the warm and not be moved on by authority. Not that this deterred Mr Hattersley. Effortlessly, he moved into his act—speaking now sombrely, now passionately, as if a full House hung on his words. In a masterly opening passage, he lamented the necessity for exempting old age pensioners from any payments for anything. 'In an ideal world, pensioners would have what we've all got,' he said. This was of course shamelessness on an heroic scale. Mr Hattersley has not the slightest intention of allowing pensioners to have what he's got. But by now he was well into his stride. Of the wretched pensioners, he claimed: 'Television is their single, sustained pleasure.' What impertinence! Does he assume they are capable of no other pleasure? He will be old himself one day. Then he will change his tune.

Mr Hattersley swirled compassionately on. Eventually, Mr Michael McNair-Wilson, a Tory back-bencher, intervened to ask why Mr Hattersley, when in the Labour Government, had not supported his much cheaper bill to provide free television for a still more deserving group: the deaf. Mr Hattersley was stopped in his tracks. He admitted he did not support that scheme. No doubt he toyed with the idea of reminding us about his compassionate policy of free radios for the deaf. In the end he settled for saying that his present reduced rate proposals would have a 'wider application'.

But we professionals can forgive Mr Hattersley. He is a master politician. Incidentally, he writes (in *Punch*) one of the few good columns anyone has ever written about the press, though, on the principle that they should have what he's got, he will presumably be giving that work eventually to some deserving pensioner.

A nice day out

A deputation of women, including Miss Jill Craigie, the wife of Mr Michael Foot, had handed in a letter at No 10 summoning the Prime Minister to a day-long 'women's rights' festival in London to stand trial for 'putting her class above her sex' and other crimes. Came the day, and I hurried to the secondary school north of King's Cross where the festival was being held: too late, unfortunately, for the morning seminar, advertised in the programme as: 'Why the Tories want us to be heterosexual.' So one is unable to bring you the answer to that age-old question. Perhaps it is something to do with the public schools. Those institutions keep on trying to instill a vigorous, healthy homosexuality into the young, but a furtive, tragic minority of Tories are still roaring heteros. Indeed, every now and then, the practice results in one of them having to resign from a government.

But I was in time to snap up from a stall the last copy of *Sisters in Song: a collection of new songs from the women's liberation movement*. A certain amount of heterosexuality kept creeping into some of the lyrics, it must be admitted. There was, for example, a rather bourgeois love song called 'Ben' (p 70), although its language was appropriately sociological. *'Ben and I were young together, said our lifestyles would be of our choosing'*, it began. And there was a tragic ending when their lifestyles went all wrong. On p 30 you could sing along to 'Class Struggle Widow' and on p 34, to the tune of 'There's a Hole in the Bucket' you could be moved by the hauntingly entitled 'There's a Hole in the Condom'.

There was no sign of Mrs Thatcher. Perhaps she had skipped bail. But there was plenty to do while we waited. Here were seminars and workshops and pamphlets about sexism in schools; El Salvador; nuclear weapons; rape; abortion; National Health Service cuts; rent strikes; South Africa; every conceivable form of racism and exploitation; more rape; a spot more abortion; women's health hazards at work; nursery closures; the need for women not to be browbeaten by capitalism into using deodorants—while, warned the programme, from 3.0 to 3.30 in Room Al, Miss Pat Arrowsmith was threatening to read her poems. On the dozens of bookstalls, what the organizers regarded as all respectable political points of view were represented: Trotskyism, anarchism, Maoism, Sinn Fein, plus ordinary Communism for any passing moderates.

A booklet reporting the proceedings of a dayschool on *Children and Socialism*, organized by a ladies' socialist organization demurely named 'Big Flame', contained an invaluable report of the findings of the school's Possessiveness and Jealousy Workshop. 'To start the ball rolling, A. from Leeds discussed the problem of living with kids with whom he had no biological connexion. In his case he wanted Ben [presumably not the same Ben who was having trouble with his lifestyle in the song] to have an ongoing relationship with him specifically. . . . However, he felt possessive about Jesse, his kid, 15 months . . . a lot of this he felt had to do with feeling indispensable with your own kid. He wondered whether it was part of our bourgeois conditioning . . .' The realization dawned that the radical Left are no less soppy and sentimental than the rest of us. Whereas the worried among the non-radicalized masses write to Miss Proops and pose such questions as: 'Will my boyfriend respect me?' the radicals turn up in Big Flame's Possessiveness and Jealousy Workshops and ask: 'Is it bourgeois to want an ongoing relationship with my biological child?' Reassuringly, then, soppiness and sentimentality are part of the human condition. The Left just like to change the outward subject matter.

Swarming all over the building were thousands of pairs of jeans containing women of all shapes and of none. But there were *some* men and women wandering around hand in hand. One fell idly to speculating about courtship rituals among the radical classes. 'I think you're wonderful,' he presumably says to her. 'There's not a sniff of deodorant on you. In fact, you stink like a polecat. Will you share my lifestyle?'

Come late afternoon, and there was still no sign of Mrs Thatcher. She was still on the run. She'll never get away with it. Loudspeakers called us to the final rally in the playground. Orators talked of such matters as rape and abortion.

The radicals always seem to have an extraordinary relish for the latter. It would never be surprising to hear them suddenly argue that, not only should there be abortion on demand, but non-pregnancy should be no bar to abortion either. They just can't get enough of abortion.

A ferocious Irish woman called on us to support the IRA prisoners in the H-block. An astounding and somewhat confused resolution was passed about the Ripper who, because of his assaults on women, was a figure only slightly less hated this afternoon than Mrs Thatcher.

Coverage of the Ripper case, said the resolution, ignored 'women, who experience danger and fear from men, not merely this one, every day of our lives'—the suggestion being, presumably, that we chaps as a general rule wander around with a pinhead hammer and a screwdriver just on the off chance.

Next, a minute's silence for the late Robert Sands. More speeches, doubtless about abortion. Suddenly a cry from the crowd: 'What about the prostitutes?' To which a voice from the microphone promisingly replies: 'They will be later.'

What was all this about prostitutes? Where did they fit into the general ideology? I went in search of a prostitute, so to speak. Soon I found a woman who offered me a leaflet from the English Collective of Prostitutes. What to say to her? 'How much?' did not seem quite proper. One wanted to inquire: 'Are you yourself a Fallen Woman?' but that did not seem right either. The pamphlet was much the best written of the afternoon and put forward an overwhelming case for changes in the law.

Here was the central problem. The feminist cause is a great one. As Paul Foot's fine book on Shelley shows, it has been championed by some of the greatest souls. How to stop it being swamped by idiocy and worse? Easily the day's best speech came from Mrs Ditta from Rochdale, who successfully fought the Home Office Minister, Mr Raison, to allow her three children admission to this country from the sub-continent. In her Gracie Fields accent, she was very good at his expense: 'Why doesn't he have a blood test? After all, his children might be Mrs Thatcher's.'

But there seems to be some iron law of radicalism which ensures that good causes like this one—and the prostitutes'—get subsumed in darker struggles such as that of the IRA.

Another day out

To divine the present state of the Labour Party, some people study specific manifesto pledges on industrial planning agreements as amended by annual conference, acting pursuant to the recommendation of the National Executive. Others of us take ourselves off to the Labour Party Musicians Union May Day concert at the Dominion, Tottenham Court Road.

By rights, a concert by any country's radical party should not be at all like this one was. It should consist of *Time Out* progressive rock with perhaps a dash of Stockhausen for the old folk. Instead, Labour offered a first half from Mr Johnny Patrick and his big band in a programme hovering around some indeterminate point in the late Forties and early Fifties. Then came a speech from Mr Michael Foot for those listeners with a taste for the Thirties. In the second half we got a concert from the Royal Philharmonic owing much to the inspiration of *Your Hundred Best Tunes*. This was under the direction of Mr Harry Rabinowitz, a giant of the old BBC Light Programme—indeed, if memory serves correct, the conductor of the musical bits in the *Take It From Here* of the high 1950s.

The Dominion, with its sweeping balconies and chocolate cake decor, is itself a monument to a lost civilization. With such collossi as the Granada, Tooting, it is a relic of the heroic age of cinemas. This middlebrow reverie was enjoyed by an audience of defiantly unglamorous trade unionists. In the dreary 1940s so much of that big band music must have seemed touched by stardust. At a Labour Party gathering of today it is spangled with dandruff.

Today's Labour Party is said to be the party of Mr Benn and the Polytechnic-cum-Social Worker Left. But in reality it is touch and go in the struggle between them and the Harry Rabinowitz wing of the movement. Certainly, there were few of the new Left in evidence at the Dominion. But one is not sure what their line is on music. As at present organized, orchestras are not particularly Bennite institutions. As he would presumably point out, why should a group of people who are, after all, simply workers who happen to find themselves, through no fault of their own, in a concert environment, submit to the purely arbitrary authority of a conductor who has never been voted in by anyone?

Mercifully, Mr Benn seemed to be far away as, with Mr Foot and Mr Healey aloft in the royal circle, the Johnny Patrick Orchestra unleashed Tommy Dorsey's 'I'm Getting Sentimental Over You', Harry James's 'Carnival' and Duke Ellington's 'Do Nothing Till You Hear From Me'—which latter piece could have been written in honour of Mr Healey's apparent advice to the Labour moderates.

At various points the conductor introduced, one by one, his orchestra. They were portly, comfortable men, with such names as Alf and Reg and 'Duggie Robinson on baritone saxophone, who used to play in the very famous Geraldo Orchestra'. They looked Tories, almost to a man. Johnny Patrick told us to give a very big hand to Mr Morton, the general secretary of the Musicians Union, and dedicated to that no doubt sinister functionary a 1940s piece called 'I Got It Bad, and That Ain't Good'—a choice presumably connected with some dingy infighting within the union.

A trombonist called Andy was introduced as the central figure of a somewhat confused incident in trade unionism's struggle for human dignity. As far as one could follow, he had played so loudly on the picket line outside a television studio during the musicians' strike you could hear it on the *Pebble Mill* show. He was greeted as an authentic hero of organized labour. Eventually Mr Ron Hayward, the general secretary of the party, appeared and lapsed impeccably into the big band patter: 'Thank you, Johnny. That's my kind of music. And now: my kind of leader of the Labour Party—Michael Foot.'

Michael took to the stage and moved smoothly into that great old standard about unemployment and the destruction of the welfare state with backing from a group of female Irish demonstrators—one of whom grabbed the microphone in an effort to turn his solo into a duet.

Michael added a sort of 'I'm getting sentimental over practically everything in sight' number in which he crooned about the mission of the British Labour Party to save the entire world from the horrors of war. The folks loved it. In the second half, maestro Rabinowitz hurled Rossini's *Semiramide Overture* at us, plus some Gershwin and Chabrier. But, noticing that the programme was due to end with an ominous-sounding overture called *Peterloo*, by Malcolm Arnold, commissioned by the TUC, and fearing as a possible encore, say, some 'passacaglia for the Shrewsbury Two', I left.

Mr Michael Foot

Simply to look at, he was like any other old age pensioner from the traditional public service class enjoying Bournemouth: white-haired, courtly, still with his wits about him though occasionally a little forgetful, and perhaps rather out of place while the resort was taken over for the annual delegate conference of the Iron and Steel Trades Confederation. Yet this was no ordinary leader of the Labour Party. This was Mr Michael Foot.

In these days of rapid change, he tends to be forgotten. But he still takes a lively interest in what is going on. For example, they tell him that the country now has a woman Prime Minister. Bless my soul! And from what he has heard, he didn't like the sound of her. 'I repeat, the economic policy of this Government is a CATASTROPHE,' he bawled at the steelmen.

Mr Healey and Mr Benn have got all the publicity this early summer as they have toured the union conferences at the seaside resorts, fighting each other to the death, or to the Deputy Leadership of the Labour Party, whichever is the sooner. But Mr Foot goes too. While Mr Healey and Mr Benn are saying terrible things about each other at the fringe meetings, Mr Foot travels quietly down on the train, makes a speech to the conference itself, and receives a presentation consisting of some product connected with the workers concerned (at Bournemouth, it was some fine steel goblets; at the General and Municipal Workers' it is presumably a huge rate demand; at the hospital workers' it is probably something contagious).

Then he ambles around the town a little with his walking stick, and catches the train back to the London terminus from which he is taken by the Leader of the Opposition's official Rover back to Hampstead.

What thoughts are passing through that noble old head as all this is going on? What does he make of this modern world of ours? Let it be emphasized at the outset that no adverse criticism is intended of Mr Foot by drawing attention to his age.

Since the 1960s—the truly low, dishonest decade—we have had enough of brilliant young politicians. It was always astonishing that youth should ever have been associated with ability, idealism or even vigour. Still more astonishing was the fact that Kennedy's age on assuming the presidency, forty-three, was widely considered to be of itself a point in his favour, it being much overlooked that Hitler also assumed power at the same age.

It is difficult to know what the Leader of the Opposition makes of it all. But one suspects that he is rather melancholy. After a lifetime of romantic left-wingery—in journalism, in biography, on a thousand television panels and editions of 'Any Questions?', in set-piece orations in the Commons—he suddenly, against all augury, became Labour Party Leader.

Sometime in the late 1950s a popular newspaper did a jokey piece about the things least likely to happen. One of them was Mr Michael Foot becoming Leader of the Labour Party. I happen to know the man who wrote it. For, until propelled by fortune into his present position, Mr Foot had attained a quite different, though equally formal and traditional position, in our national life. He was Her Majesty's Leader of the Left.

He succeeded to his great office after the death of Aneurin Bevan. Mr Foot was the functionary who on great national occasions—such as sterling crises and speeches by Labour prime ministers in support of American policy in Vietnam—had to get up and picturesquely rave so that we all knew what the Left was thinking about it.

It was a position just as dignified as Black Rod or the Lord Warden of the Cinque Ports. But, as a result of an unforeseen concatenation of circumstances, Her Majesty's Leader of the Left finds himself Her Majesty's Leader of the Opposition. Moreover, on achieving this further dignity, Mr Foot has made a mortifying discovery: there are lots of people to the Left of him.

Indeed, we now have a completely different kind of Left. He is now in the Centre of his party, perhaps on the Right. For, while Mr Foot was ranting happily away all those years under the impression that he was the Left, a different, less respectable less comfortable Left was coming into being wherever two or three were gathered together in a polytechnic.

The signs have been gathering over the last five years or so. Consider, for example, the *New Statesman*. Like Mr Foot, the old Staggers was part of the warp and woof of England. Elitist, snooty, grammatical.

All that has been laid waste. A similar sort of thing happened to Cambodia. A workable, though superstitious and backward, traditional society has been swept away at Great Turnstile.

Whereas the old Staggers writers used to compose elegant gossip about politicians and review the whole range of bourgeois literature, they have now been forced into the fields to dig up facts for vast articles illustrated with pictures of nuclear reactors. The *New Statesman* is a microcosm of the Left as a whole.

To a traditionalist such as Mr Foot, accustomed all his life to a Left which shared his bourgeois taste for parliamentary oratory and for *belles-lettres*, it must be a baffling, faintly menacing, universe. Watching him at Bournemouth this week, it seemed that he resolved the difficulty by ignoring it.

He was helped by the fact that the steelworkers were an old-fashioned lot who were on his side—solidly-built characters loyal to Old Labour who seemed to embody a vanished industrial Britain, folk tough enough to chew steel as well as make it.

Mr Foot must have been further helped by the fact that, from its outward appearance, the resort remains an idyllic place which might have stayed still at some happy point in the mid-Fifties or even earlier. It is very much the town of a certain Mr Heath (no relation) whose very name should inspire waves of nostalgia. Neville George Clevely Heath! A classic mid-Forties story; a handsome fellow who, in the town's genteel hotels, would charm impressionable women until such time as he would dismember them. He was hanged. Since then there has been no further unpleasantness in Bournemouth and Mr Foot did not disturb that situation this week.

He gave the delegates some familiar, much-loved Footage. He scorns a text or notes or even any particular theme. He spins it out as he goes along, repeating the last idea, or a related idea, in various forms while he thinks of the next one.

'The Common Market, the EEC, the European Community, or call it what you will.' That sort of thing. It is the Roget's Thesaurus school of oratory. For some minutes, Mr Foot—or Mr Boot or Mr Sock or call him what you will—simply kept the steelmen happy by running down the list of members of the Government. The mere phrase 'Sir Keith Joseph' was enough to get them amiably falling about.

'Then there's Denis Howell, the Minister of Energy,' he added. 'The only reason he's got an energy policy is because he's been told one by Joe Gormley.' He was thinking of Mr *David* Howell. Denis Howell is a member of Mr Foot's front bench—having been, in the last Labour Government, Minister for Sport and for Natural Disasters in so far as, in the case of soccer, the two are separate. But Mr Foot is a man for the broad sweep rather than petty detail. His speech was a great success.

Mr Foot got his goblets and set out for London, leaving the conference to abstruse speculation about the precise nature of their industry's ownership and similar matters. One left just as Mr Mick Skelton, of Corby, was alarmingly demanding the further nationalization 'including the private parts'.

Where was the *Daily Mail*? ('State Grab Threatens Private Parts'.)

Back at Waterloo, one hovered in the background, as Mr Foot made his way past a group of his fellow senior citizens. They noted him warmly. He adopted a genially seigneurial manner: 'Where you off to? . . . splendid . . . hope it keeps fine . . . jolly good . . . carry on.'

But the Bournemouth Idyll was already gone. He was back in London and reality.

Mr Denis Healey

One of the many pleasures of the seaside conference round is that the visitor sometimes chances of an evening, on pier or in winter garden, on entertainers from another age, another world. Liberal Party assemblies and the smaller union conferences, because held in a wide range of resorts, have provided the present observer with the happiest of such discoveries over the years. Elsie and Doris Waters! Semprini! Max Jaffa! Jeremy Thorpe! Only a native caution prevents one from claiming to have caught up with Pavlova in Paignton, Caruso in Cleethorpes.

Contemporaneous with the steelmen's conference at Bournemouth the light tenor of Mr John Hanson was still chirruping on and on about being only a strolling vagabond and similar predicaments. And in Bournemouth, Brighton and Bridlington, the visitor could enjoy Mr Denis Healey. He was seeking union support to retain the Labour Deputy Leadership against Mr Benn.

Mr Healey is that rarity among politicians: a clever man who, in front of an audience, pretends to be an average man. Most politicians are very strange men who, in front of audiences, pretend to be very clever.

He is one of the very last of our important politicians to be the beneficiary of a pre-1930 élitist education: classics as degree subject, knowledge of German and Italian as well as French; ignorance of economics; a general command of mandarin culture. Though of a different social background, the late Richard Crossman was similar.

This does not mean that we should accept the tale, which Mr Healey himself sometimes puts about, that he is really a sensitive soul who would like to have been an art historian. He is power-crazed all right; otherwise he would *be* an art historian. It is simply to suggest that he is a more civilized man than his contemporaries. For, by the time Mr Healey was at Oxford in the 1930s, Greats was already beginning to be overtaken by the swottish, charlatan-prone Modern Greats (Philosophy, Politics and Economics) as the favoured degree of aspirant politicians, the fallacy being that these were the subjects which helped towards an understanding of the modern world. Sir Harold Wilson was the first PPE swot to become Prime Minister.

When he became Shadow Chancellor of the Exchequer in the early 1970s, after a political lifetime in foreign affairs and defence, Mr Healey clearly knew next to nothing about economics. He would arrive at the Dispatch Box festooned with cuttings from the *Financial Times*. But within a few weeks he had mastered the patter. Nowadays you could not tell the difference between him and a PPE type. Yet, unlike them, he can also do the Renaissance Man turn.

On the train to Bridlington, I had been reading for the first time *Conversations with Goethe*, by Eckermann, who seems to have been a sort of superior, Teutonic Kenneth Harris.

Asked by Mr Healey to explain what I was doing following him all the way to Bridlington, I explained 'I'm your Eckermann,' hoping he would inquire, of the latter, 'who?' But he caught the allusion. How irritating! All one could do was comfort oneself with the hope that, like most politicians, he would have assumed that by 'Eckermann' one must have meant Haldeman or Erlichman.

But no, Healey the aesthete or man of parts is probably no fraud. That makes even more remarkable the extraordinarily banal and demotic oratorical style which he affects—heightened by the fact that all these knockabout commonplaces issue from someone who looks like an old stereotyped *Punch* cartoon of an Irish navvy.

His punch-lines and rhetorical flourishes date from the saloon bar or playground of a couple of decades ago. 'Put that in your pipe and smoke it,' he will demand of some heckler at whom he has just hurled a few statistics about growth rates under the last Labour Government. 'Not a sausage,' he will exclaim after asking how many council houses the Tories were building. *Healey: Renaissance Man as Buffoon.* That is the theme on which his future biographers will build.

He arrived cheerily in the Bridlington pub where he was to address a fringe meeting during the conference of health service workers (COHSE). As he passed through, a middle-aged couple asked each other who was that man who looked vaguely familiar. Believing it necessary at all times to save our politicians from the sin of pride, and remembering all those veteran performers who turn up at the seaside, I assured them with great confidence: 'It's Joseph Locke' (the burly, noisy Irishman who, in flapping bib and tucker, was always having to say Goodbye because he was off to join the Foreign Legion). The couple seemed perfectly satisfied with this piece of information. They remembered Mr Locke warmly. Perhaps they would not have felt the same about Mr Healey.

One followed Healey/Locke into the meeting room. There was no one there. 'They forgot to give out the leaflets,' he explained. We waited. Three members of COHSE arrived. 'I'll just nip out and see if I can see anybody,' Mr Healey said. Mr Edward Heath, in a similar situation, might by now have sacked someone, if only some barman whose sacking was not in his power. But Mr Healey, as they say in the North, has 'no side'. Eventually rather a large audience drifted in.

Mr Healey's speech was un-cerebral in tone even by his standards of delivery. Presumably he saves any nuances for all that art history at weekends. But there was another reason. He likes a rough-house. A group of young delegates in jeans, badges and T-shirts, Benn-voters to a person, started to heckle him. He relished it. Suddenly the entire split in the Labour movement was before us in microcosm, in a low-ceilinged bar.

He talked of the Labour Government and housing. They changed the subject to unemployment. He switched to housing. He said the economy did well under Labour in 1978. One of them said that all economies had done well in 1978. They detested him. He, being the product of a culture which does not place supreme importance on mere politics, was just genially argumentative towards them. A middle-aged loyalist asked why the press concentrated on Labour's split. Mr Healey said the press did not print Labour's actual policies. 'Not a sausage.'

A heckler shouted something about fascism in Ireland. Mr Healey said, 'I am an Irishman.' Someone volunteered 'rubbish'. Labour is even split on whether Mr Healey is Irish.

Mr Michael Heseltine*

For over seven days and nights now, Mr Michael Heseltine has been running amok all over Merseyside. At his temporary office in the Royal Liver Building, they said he was to be found at the community centre at Skelmersdale. At Skelmersdale, they said he had been there but had just left for Runcorn. At Runcorn I asked a policeman where Mr Heseltine was. 'Who was he?' this constable gratifyingly replied. Some years on the political trail have taught me that one of the great strengths of British democracy is that there are always pockets of ignorance about even the most self-publicizing of our rulers.

One explained to the policeman that Mr Heseltine was the new Minister for places like Merseyside and that sort of thing. You could not miss him. He was about seven foot tall, with what looked like a blond wig but was, so far as we knew, real hair. This man was believed to be in the area. 'The public have been warned not to approach him, but to call the police instead,' I said, adding a tentative 'Ha, ha, ha.'

The constable looked bleak. Never try to be funny with policemen, one's auntie used to say. The policeman radioed headquarters: 'I've got a fella 'ere who says he's a reporter and he's looking for Mr Heseltine, who's the Minister of Merseyside. He's about seven foot

* In July 1981 rioting on Merseyside—particularly in Toxteth—led to Mr Michael Heseltine, Secretary of State for the Environment, paying a visit to the area.

tall and he's got blond hair that looks like a wig . . . no, not the reporter, the Minister.'

Someone at headquarters told the policeman to turn down his radio, presumably so that I could not hear what was being said. After a conversation, the constable explained: 'No, we don't know where he is.' It seemed clear that the forces of law and order knew of his whereabouts, but assumed, as authority always does, that Ministers do not want to be bothered by their subjects.

Parting from the constable, I explained that Mr Heseltine had been sent up after the riots. 'I blame the parents', said the policeman. 'Oh, I don't think old Heseltine's parents are to blame for the way he's turned out,' I replied. The policeman stared. It was time to be off.

'Perhaps Mr Heseltine doesn't want any publicity,' said another constable later. Mr Heseltine not wanting any publicity! As soon argue that Dracula did not want any blood. None the less, it was time to retire to the hotel and bed. But there, the following morning, in the lobby, encased in 7ft of Savile Row suiting and 4ft of Jermyn Street shirting, awash in half a gallon of after-shave, was Mr Heseltine. He was roaring off to a couple of job-training centres. It was not, of course, entirely true that he was avoiding publicity, but there was some truth in it.

Becoming an 'emergency' or 'crisis' or 'special' minister is a perilous adventure for a politician. Everybody says it is a gimmick and, in any case, too little too late. Afterwards, when nothing much happens which would not have happened in any case, he gets blamed. Also, people are apt to laugh at him and ask questions like: 'Who needs a riot when you've got Michael Heseltine?' Look at Lord Hailsham on the North-East, Mr Denis Howell on the drought.

The assignment does have its good side. He gets in the papers and on television a lot. But the publicity is difficult to control. He gets pictured going importantly in and out of meetings, staring at slums with a look of concern, and he gives interviews in which he can say statesmanlike things, such as that there are no easy solutions, and that he is at present here to listen.

But it is difficult to control what is said at all these meetings if there are difficult people there.

Terence Moore, of Caryl Gardens—which are no gardens but an unrelenting block of flats—was waiting for him with a few inmates, being rather cynical. 'Tarzan, they call him,' Mr Moore explained. 'So they should tell him to plant some trees around this place.' Terence's brother, Albert, said his wife had read out from that morning's *Mirror* where it said Mr Heseltine had spent £10,000 over the weekend on his daughter's birthday party—£10,000 quid, Albert emphasized. It would have been better spent getting the fungus off these walls.

The suit containing the crisis minister turned up. Terence waylaid him. 'Why wasn't Mr Heseltine meeting the people here in the houses they had to live in?' Mr Heseltine replied that he had gone into some houses yesterday. 'He's got three houses himself,' I whispered to Terence's brother, Albert, hoping to make the full and frank exchanges still more constructive. 'You've got three houses yourself,' said Albert, 'I saw it in the papers.' But Mr Heseltine was still engaged with Terence.

'My job is to see as many things as possible. I think I've got a picture of the housing problem . . .'

Terence interrupted: 'It's a corrugated jungle.' Mr Heseltine had not seen these particular houses. 'I looked up carefully as I drove in,' Mr Heseltine replied, adding reassuringly: 'I've seen dreadful housing conditions.' But today he was dealing with jobs. He couldn't deal with houses when he was dealing with jobs. Only in this way could he 'try to get a better impact for you'. Mr Heseltine made for his car: 'I'm awfully sorry,' he said.

The minister was being perfectly reasonable. And observing him on his rounds there is no doubt that he is moved and appalled by much of what he sees. We hurried off to an employment exchange, or a 'job centre', in the Old Swan district.

Lured by the television cameras, a small crowd had gathered. A Mrs Durant, of Alston Street, approached me to ask whether this Mr Heseltine was worried about employment. If so, her husband had a scrapyard, but they were making him close it down because they wanted the land for trees. 'They don't need trees around there,' she said, 'they just break them down to hit each other with.' (Terence's complaint, if you remember, was the precise opposite. He wanted *more* trees. The public, you see, can not agree on these matters.) I urged her to raise the problem with Mr Heseltine, who would be here in a moment.

'Do you think I should?' she said. Certainly. He would be very interested. The suit entered, suffused in television lighting, and was escorted forward by the manager. Fortunately, Mrs Durant managed to nip in. 'Mr Heseltine,' she said. 'You're here about jobs. Well, my husband's got a scrapyard but they want it for trees and . . .'

Mr Heseltine thanked her and said he couldn't deal with that now and turned her in the direction of 'one of my officials'. A luckless official was right behind. Mrs Durant got going again. He produced a pen and a notebook. 'I'll follow it up with the city,' he could be heard saying, 'I can't promise anything. Scrapyards *are* unpopular . . .'

Mr Roy Jenkins

By road to Warrington. We knew we had reached the militant North, for a feminist slogan on a roadside wall explained: 'Sutcliffe, not mad, male.' Militant North London, that is; Archway Road, Highgate, on the way to the M1.

One had read in *Time Out* about the hard life of folk up there in the Hampstead-Swiss Cottage conurbation—the lack of adequate crèche facilities for mothers studying psychology with the Open University, and so on. It was not surprising that Marx and even Mr Benn appeared to have support in these parts. Yet the lecturers and documentary film-makers who have historically provided the area with its industrial base are clearly attracted to the Social Democrats. Mr William Rodgers lured a crowd of 600 the other evening. Past row upon row of humble, yet proudly kept homes, furnished in the region's traditional 'Habitat' materials, we pressed on towards Warrington.

On the journey the radio messages from London were indistinct. The Liberals would stand down for a Social Democrat, but only if the Social Democrat were famous. Fame undoubtedly sits on Mrs Shirley Williams and Mr Roy Jenkins, one mused. They would probably know of them in Warrington.

But did the definition include Professor David Marquand? No one doubts his ability. He once wrote the definitive life of Ramsay MacDonald. It was weighty. Indeed, it weighed about half a ton. But is he famous? Well, he looks a little like Mr Alan Bennett. Perhaps that will do.

Later crackling messages received from the capital when we were past the Newport Pagnell service area intimated that Mrs Williams was wavering. She might be too busy. This raised the possibility of Mr Jenkins. That in turn raised the possibility of an epic confrontation between those famous, drawling, W-sounding Rs, and the equally picturesque speech of the people of Warrington.

Mr Jenkins would stroll grandly around the town expressing the view that such and such a problem was a 'sewers martyr'. The locals would be baffled. Who was this unknown hero of the local public health department? Eventually it would dawn on them that what he meant was that it was a 'serious matter'. When nominations close today we shall know whether Mr Anthony Keane, a Manchester barrister with a grievance concerning the Social Democratic Party's alleged breach of the copyright of the title, makes good his reported threat to change his name by deed poll to 'Roy Jenkins' and stand as a Social Democrat in this by-election.

If he does so, interesting aesthetic and philosophical issues will intrude into the campaign. How will it affect the real Roy Jenkins? Furthermore, can the real Roy Jenkins—the grand, stupendously distinguished and largely incomprehensible magnifico from another world who has been introducing himself with a courtly bow of his smooth, shiny head to incredulous passers-by in this town all week— in any sense be regarded as real? Will *both* candidates be real? Will *both* be make-believe? Here is a theme worthy of the great Pirandello. Nearly all of his plays, it may be remembered, are about whether we are who we are pretending to be. What is truth? they ask. What is fable? And, for all one knows, who is Ruth? Where the hell is Mabel? To return to the Warrington by-election.

The surprising news perhaps after this first week of campaigning, is that the people rather like Mr Jenkins. That does not mean a majority will vote him in. The one opinion poll so far strongly suggests that they will not. Rather, it means that he is seen as a figure above and outside politics, like the Queen. Certainly, he is seen as a less contentious and 'political' figure than, say, the Duke of Edinburgh.

How else can folk explain the extraordinary Jenkins carry-on? That incomparable voice, beside which Sir John Gielgud sounds like rough trade! That distinction of manner! People may not know precisely for what he is distinguished, but it must be for something. 'Roy Jenkins, a miner's son . . .' began one of the campaign leaflets. True, certainly; but only in the way that it is true to describe Mrs Jacqueline Onassis as the widow of a Greek merchant seaman. It simply does not do justice to Mr Jenkins' position in café society.

Nor was it really necessary for the leaflet to brandish Mr Jenkins' sole proletarian credential. Those who wrote it must have assumed the Warringtonians to be inverted snobs. This seems not to be so. They like an aristo. They see characters like Mr Jenkins engaged in idle, brittle chatter with groups of bejewelled bosoms, in the salon scenes of series like *Edward VII*. He's the one to whom some heaving duchess exclaims: 'You're so *clever*, Lord Melbourne.'

Sadly for Mr Jenkins, he is engaged in Warrington in politics. And politics is something which the people associate with less graceful figures such as the Labour candidate. He goes under the blunt, utilitarian-sounding name of 'Doug' Hoyle. He is short, grey-black-haired, has a small moustache and is somehow both round and compact, so that he resembles, as Alice Roosevelt Longworth said of the hapless Governor Dewey, 'the man on the top of the wedding cake'. One suspects that, to the people of Warrington. Mr Jenkins is some sort of ideal vision. Mr Hoyle is your husband, or yourself, and you vote for reality.

Mr Jenkins has turned out to be much more famous among the people than many of us thought. It is because of the European Community. This has nothing to do with, say, his activities in the cause of European monetary union. It is to do with his activities in the cause of European money. He is thought to possess an enormous amount of it which, relatively speaking, is correct. But the local attitude to this is not what might be expected. 'What did you think of him?' I asked Mr Alexander Done, of Dickenson Street, after he had been approached by Mr Jenkins in the shopping centre.

'A gentleman, and an educated man,' he replied.
Why educated? 'Well, the Common Market.'
Was Mr Done in favour of the Common Market? 'No, detest it.'
What was this about Mr Jenkins and the Market, then? 'Well, he got paid a lot of money by it, didn't he?'
Did Mr Done disapprove of that, then? 'No, everybody's got to get what they can, haven't they?'

Mr Done was not untypical.

I rather warmed to this non-moralistic, rollicking, eighteenth-century attitude towards these matters, although I doubt if Mr Done's was the line of defence which Mr Jenkins would prefer.

It all goes to confirm a theory of the crusty Tory back-bencher, the late Charles Curran, who used to say that the British working class did not object to vast wealth provided it was of a random or windfall nature. What they couldn't stand were people who had worked for it. Mr Jenkins' fabled riches seem to be regarded as being in the same category as those of pools winners or the Aga Khan or of Lady Docker in the 1950s.

Here is a theme on which the SDP must build if they are to have any chance of winning here. They must convince the voters that Mr Jenkins is not too good to be true at all, but is a bit of a card—with even a touch of the rascal about him. Look at all that swag he got paid in Europe.

I have long seen him in that way myself, believing that over the years he has been rather spoilt by the quality press. He has been depicted as the courageous liberal, a man more honest than other politicians.

There is rarely much courage required to be liberal, outside places like the Soviet Union, South Africa or Haiti. That is not to say it is wrong to be liberal, just that it is not courageous. In the Labour Party, Mr Jenkins was often a consummate politician. At the Dispatch Box, he was invariably superb—but to be superb at the Dispatch Box requires a considerable measure of low-minded demagoguery designed to impress selected people. This is true of Mr Enoch Powell, seeking to impress the mass on immigration, but also of Mr Jenkins, seeking to impress polite society on race relations.

Meanwhile Mr Jenkins challenges Mr Hoyle to say who he is for: Mr Benn or Mr Healey. Mr Hoyle replies that he and the people of Warrington are interested in issues not silly challenges, but while he is about it, he challenges Mr Jenkins to say who he thinks should be SDP leader.

Mr Sorrell, the Londoner who is the Tory candidate, says he is concerned about, among other things, crime and immigration. There is not much crime in Warrington and hardly any immigrants. Still, Mr Sorrell seems content. Perhaps that is why. Mr Jenkins produces the saturnine Mr William Rodgers, who says that a vote for Mr Hoyle is a vote for Mr Benn. Mr Hoyle says he is not going to indulge in personalities, especially with a traitor such as Mr Rodgers.

Sir Harold Wilson

Sir Harold Wilson—slightly more hunched, hair now white rather than silver—emerged to go on a lyrical, slow, but dignified, journey through the last day of the Warrington by-election campaign. He gave a press conference at which, as is the prerogative of former Prime Ministers, he gently spread a little havoc for his party. Then he pottered round the town, being cuddled by voters. Mr Douglas Hoyle, the Labour candidate, would give him a squeeze every now and then and kept on addressing him as if he were a slightly ga-ga inmate of one of the old folk's homes on which Mr Hoyle had descended these last few weeks.

Turned sixty-five himself now, Sir Harold was perhaps happier chatting with the old folk. As senior citizens are wont to do they talked about their operations. No one was quite clear who had invited him, for he and the present Labour candidate—indeed, he and the present Labour Party—are not of the same persuasion. It was thought that perhaps he more or less invited himself. Old bruisers sometimes feel the urge to haul themselves back up between the ropes for a final lunge. Perhaps Sir Harold felt the old tongue itch at the prospect of one more press conference, one last evasive answer, just as it was in the old days.

So we found him at Mr Hoyle's daily campaign press conference. All campaign long, there had been a duel between ourselves and Mr Hoyle to get the candidate to admit he was for Mr Benn as Deputy Leader. The rest of Warrington had remained oblivious to this epic struggle, but none the less it was a point of honour among us to resolve it on this last day. 'Did Mr Hoyle agree with Sir Harold's recent remark that Mr Benn had immatured with age,' one asked, and sat back triumphantly. That had got him. He was in trouble now. Harold was right beside him. How would he get out of it, eh?

Mr Hoyle shot me a look of simple hatred. He cleared his throat for a long time, so that it sounded like a gargle. Or a death rattle? No! Suddenly, he recovered. Tony Benn? Not standing in by-election. Warrington interested in policies, not personalities. What mattered was Leader, not Deputy Leader, and Doug Hoyle was for Michael Foot. Mr Hoyle had won again. Your correspondent subsided, beaten, demoralized. Sir Harold stirred. 'Tony Benn?' he muttered. 'Now, Tony Benn was a good Minister . . .' Mr Hoyle nodded gratefully. '. . . a good Postmaster-General. He introduced lots of pretty stamps.'

Mr Hoyle stopped nodding gratefully, for he had remembered that Sir Harold was a master of irony. '. . . . everyone in this town should remember that Tony Benn introduced the Queen's Award for Industry.' Mr Hoyle started nodding again. '. . . he wanted to call it the parliamentary award for industry, but it had to be the Queen's Award because she's the fount of honour, I told him stuffily . . . as far as Mr Benn is concerned, he has no following in the Parliamentary Party.'

Mr Hoyle, about to be one of Mr Benn's followers in the Parliamentary Party, had stopped nodding some time before, and was generally more relaxed when Sir Harold devoted his attention to Mr Roy Jenkins. 'Roy Jenkins? . . . tended to knock off at seven o'clock . . . a socialite rather than a socialist . . . The SDP? It's not a party, it's a clique or a click, as they say up 'ere. As for Dr Owen and Mr Rodgers, I never thought of them as Cabinet calibre . . . perfectly good junior ministers. Jim took a different view. I had retired by then—voluntarily—which is a very unusual thing in politics.'

Past glories now intruded into the shabby little committee room into which we were all crammed. There was one night when the whole government machine was working late, Sir Harold continued. Time of the seamen's strike in '66. He had sent out for fish and chips all round, 'for which I got knocked in the press for doing some kind of gimmick. Mind you, if I hadn't intervened that night, we could have had a six-month strike.' In comparison with such tales of encounters on the high seas long ago, the puny Warrington by-election seems to be far away.

Sir Harold was asked about his opposition to the next party leader being chosen by an electoral college. It was a constitutional issue, he said. The Queen may need a Prime Minister immediately after an election. It could be a time of crisis. Sterling. That sort of thing. She shouldn't have to wait for Labour choosing its leader. But he was not the right man to ask, because he did not know much about such matters. What could explain this unprecedented flash of modesty? Soon we learned. It was because 'I've very little experience of the party not being in power.'

With that wicked thrust at Labour leaders subsequent to him, who had lost an election or looked as if they could lose one in the future, Sir Harold, winner of four out of five general elections, brought the discussion to a close and resumed his place in history.

Politicians in Dublin

'I tend to agree with Seamus: it could be a hung Dail,' cried the experts to one another at increasingly frequent intervals as the television election night wore on—like a circle of the country's famously-shrewd farmers assessing some defective bullock.

On the face of it, there was no reason why it should sound any odder than the corresponding, British 'hung parliament'. But muttered by the Republic's indigenous psephologists and political scientists—who despite their essentially urban trade are still nobby-faced men with crinkly, sandy hair: very Irish—it did sound rather rural.

93

That in itself created the incongruity. For all these bucolic-looking, and sounding, types were exchanging their pungent opinions amid the whirling technology of a modern Irish election night. Although it would present fewer problems for a Continental visitor, or for Miss Enid Lakeman of the United Kingdom's Electoral Reform Society, the Republic's voting system is for a Briton ragingly complicated.

This gives the television graphics people the excuse for constant, spectacular effects designed to confuse the issue still further. Green, red and blue skyscrapers rise on the screen, then fall victim to some electronic earthquake. That is the rise and fall of the respective Fianna Fail and Fine Gael share of the first preference votes. Some red space invaders arrive on the screen and are immediately smashed to bits. That is the fate of the Irish Labour Party.

After some hours of this the novelty wears off and an Englishman yearns for the simple pleasures of our own BBC swingometer, or for our old-fashioned, steam-driven, yet comfortable Professor Robert McKenzie—who, as a matter of fact, was Canadian, but no matter. (Incidentally, disregarding all national bias, I think it is fair to say that the Republic's Robert McKenzie—Professor Basil Chubb, of Trinity College, Dublin—was, on this showing, inferior to Britain's. At one stage he was asked to comment on some minor point, and replied that he had nothing to say about it. Our McKenzie was never known not to comment about anything connected with an election. Faced with the silence of this wretched Chubb, one's heart swelled with patriotism.)

Being very much a believer in symbolism, I saw—in all those leprechaun accents and faces amid all that electronics—a symbol of modern Ireland. It is a glossy, smooth country of a kind to be found all over Western Europe and Scandinavia, swarming with fat men from Brussels in dark suits, but a country in which there are traces of the Gaelic-speaking, superstitious nation of de Valera's misty imagination—traces such as the still romantically inefficient telephone system.

The most evocative symbols are the bright, shiny notices in public buildings in which some lengthy, undulating Gaelic phrase is to be found alongside brutishly-shortened English. Thus the lilting *Leithris na bhfear* comes out, in the modern language, as the purely-functional 'Gents'.

Dublin itself is the supreme symbol. In his book, *Cities*, in the early 1960s, Mr James Morris (as she then was) could write of it: 'There stretches across Dublin, to an extent almost forgotten in most of

Western Europe, the dingy blight of poverty. . . . They will tell you that the Irish actually *prefer* to be poor.' It is not so now. Dublin is reminiscent of the London of the late 1950s—a fine old town, which has taken a certain amount of punishment from property speculators and modern architects, but which is still wonderful to look at and is riding the surge of a relatively recent affluence.

Mr Haughey emerges as a Harold Macmillan figure, the father of a jolly spending spree intended to win him an election. Shops bearing the legends of affluence—Laura Ashley, Sabena, Lancôme, Panasonic—heave with commerce in Georgian streets named in both English and Gaelic. The Gaelic names were put there after independence. 'Otherwise,' as Dominic Behan irreverently wrote, 'how would folk know where they were going?'

It is a suitable setting for the amiable bribes and counterbribes of a modern election. Come the Friday night, when the results were to be announced, and the newcomer had to decide how to assess the situation, one resolved on a battle plan: lengthy attrition in front of the television, with sudden forays into various taverns about the town, interspersed by increasingly frequent dashes to the *Leithris na bhfear*.

On the screen, no vote ever seemed to be conclusive. We would go over to Cork or Donegal. A returning officer would announce that, for example, W. B. Yeats had got such and such a total, and seemed to be top of the poll. But now they were going to have another count in which some of his votes were going to be distributed among, say, Sean O'Casey, J. M. Synge and Oliver St John Gogarty. Back in the studio, Professor Chubb or some other expert would explain that nothing should be read into any of this. After all, people may be voting tactically in order to do down the H Block candidate, Rory O'Mayhem, or ensure his eventual victory, as the case may be. In any case, it looked like a hung Dail.

One hurried out into the town. A colonnaded building loomed up. This turned out to be the Post Office—the centre of the 1916 rising, the fabled building in which, to hear them tell it later, half the population of the country was to be found at the relevant, heroic time. 'Bobby Sands RIP', said one of its graffiti. But this was matched by the more reassuring: 'Sandra Kelly loves William Malone'. One hailed a cab to go to one of the pubs visited by Leopold Bloom in *Ulysses*: the one in Eden Quay by the Liffey. It was an office block. But there was a pub near by. It had a disco and served campari with cherries on sticks, but it would have to do.

The drinkers were marvellously Irish—friendly, flirting,

expressing friendship with England, puking. Every now and then one of them would fall down the stairs. 'Is it always like this on election night?' one asked. 'No,' was the reply. 'It's always like this on a Friday night.'

Back in front of the screen there was still no progress. A raven-haired female Cabinet Minister was being interviewed in Gaelic, for the coverage had an alarming tendency to switch in and out of languages. Suddenly, the interviewer changed to English: 'Do you think your high profile hurt you in this campaign?' High profile? The dispiriting thought crossed the mind: perhaps even in Gaelic interviewers now use image, scenario, syndrome and confrontation.

It was difficult to work out which party were the nobs and which the yobs. An Irish colleague explained that anyone who said 'turteen tousand' instead of 'thirteen thousand' was Fianna Fail or Labour. On the other hand, Fine Gael, the nobbier party, was more sympathetic to Labour. Back into the town. Some professional daughters of the night presented themselves in O'Connell Street. I had recently read that Sir William Rothenstein had said of Gogarty: 'He is an intellectual aristocrat like Yeats. . . . He has a genial tolerance of barmen, drunkards and whores, unrelated to the conventional left-wing sympathy for the bottom dog.' So I engaged these fallen women in genial conversation about first preferences and the like. One of them expressed regret at the defeat of a certain politician. 'I thought he was great,' she said. 'Sure, but what was he like as a politician?' said her colleague. It was time to get back to the screen. Mr Seamus Brennan of Fianna Fail was forecasting: 'I think we'll get in by the skin of our teet'.'

In Conference

The round of the party conferences presents a unique opportunity to compare and contrast the different parties' styles. In 1981 the Liberals came first . . .

Liberals gathered together for the annual assembly, held in Llandudno this year. * * * Time was when the entire nation paid attention to the Liberal assembly, and knew all the names. Asquith! Lloyd George! Norman Scott! Rinka the Dog! There were giants in those days. We shall not see their likes again. Nonetheless, the assembly is this year attracting more publicity than at any time since those sterling days when so many of its prominent figures were helping police with their inquiries. The looming pact with the Social Democrats, the promise of the opinion polls that Liberals will once again sit in a Cabinet after the next general election, has changed everything. It is fitting, then, that this year's assembly is meeting in a town much associated with previous Liberal excitement. No, there was no particular dog which was done to death by a hired shotgun. Nor is the town noted for talkative male models. So the rich tapestry of Liberal history is not entirely represented here. But, as the local Liberal prospective candidate, Mr Roger Roberts, told the assembly: 'This is Lloyd George country.' So there is no telling what went on.

People in these parts really can say that Lloyd George knew their fathers, and there is no doubt that he knew quite a few of their mothers too. Welcoming us, the mayor, Councillor White, treated Lloyd George's famed sociability as a sort of local natural resource. The town had been in Lloyd George's constituency, the Mayor explained. 'He could charm the wings off an angel,' he said. 'Or, alternatively, he could charm their pants off,' he added with a wicked, municipal twinkle. There was much applause.

But was it consistent with the attitude towards these matters of the modern Liberal Party? On the book stall was to be found a copy of a pamphlet entitled, simply, *Women*. Aha! one thought, Lloyd George's subject.

The work was written by a certain Ruth Addison, a prospective candidate and herself a woman. It contained a passage about the 1960s idea of woman as a 'dolly bird, a fun toy for men to use and discard, all mini-skirt, no bra and the Pill'. If only Lloyd George, who died in 1945, had lived on to the 1960s, one reflected. There is no telling what leadership he could have offered. But perhaps this was not the conclusion which one was supposed to draw.

In the absence of the terrible old chauvinist himself, the assembly was due to hear a speech by his daughter—the liltingly-named Lady Olwyn Carey Evans, DBE. But she was prevented by an indisposition from appearing. Instead we heard a message from her endorsing the pact with the SDP. Most of the delegates interpreted this as meaning that any doubts about the Alliance could be safely abandoned. By association, Lloyd George was for it. *** Everyone was excited. Those few who were not excited by the prospect of the Alliance, were excited by its dangers. Every delegate was in his place as the debate got underway beneath the television lights.

The assembly is being held in the town's fading but still charming art deco cinema, the sort of building depicted in Sunday colour magazine articles. At the midpoint in the elegant curve of the stalls circle, with photographers hovering in the aisles to record their every reaction, sat Mrs Shirley Williams and Mr Jenkins, like the Queen and the Duke of Edinburgh.

The historic motion advocating the Alliance was moved by Mr William Wallace. Despite the change he was proposing, he himself was a figure in the tradition of the old Liberal Party: hardly anybody had ever heard of him.

'This is not the new Jerusalem. It is only the promised land,' he warned. Later in his speech, however, he assured us that Liberals could work with those true defectors from other parties 'who have seen the light on the road to Damascus and turned back towards Jerusalem'. This raised important issues of biblical scholarship and, unless there was a Jerusalem bypass, the Galilean motorway system. If Jerusalem was the ultimate destination, so much so that none of us had yet seen anything other than a glimpse of its promised hinterland, how come that those Labour defectors had been there already, having turned back towards it on the road to Damascus? Did they include Mr Jenkins? Was Jerusalem the same as Brussels?

Though most speakers were totally committed to the Alliance, there were a few doubters. Mr Derek Morse, of Chester-le-Street, made the important point that not all right-wing Labour politicians were as deodorized as people like Mrs Williams and Mr Jenkins.

Mr Morse reacted with horror to a certain Mr Michael

O'Halloran, MP. He is the old-fashioned Irish machine politician who, in a swirl of allegations and denials about old-fashioned Irish voting practices, has just left Labour and joined the social democrats—to the SDP's horror. As the debate wore on, the wretched Mr O'Halloran rapidly became, in the eyes of the assembly, the most lethal potential ally in the land with the possible exception of Mr Jeremy Thorpe.

A Liverpudlian councillor called Mr Mahon began his speech with: 'An Italian philosopher once said that nothing was more difficult, more uncertain, more perilous, than the attempt to create a New Order.' Did we have to import Italians to provide us with quotations like that? Have not we got enough out-of-work British philosophers who could have built clichés as good as that?

Still, it was a joyous debate, even if it marked, as an Italian philospher no doubt once put it, the end of an era. * * *

To make their new allies from the Labour Party feel at home, the Liberals presented them with a big split on defence. The Social Democratic observers were undoubtedly aghast. Nobody had told them that the Liberals did this kind of thing too.

On the other issues, the party's activists were determined, despite the fact that the Liberals are now grown up and may be in the next government, to carry on as usual. A woman with leaflets solicited me outside the hall offering to let me indulge in site value rating. I explained that I had been coming to Liberal conferences, man and boy, since the days of Andrew Gino Newton and I had long ago resolved never to find out what site value rating meant. That way, it would always be something to look forward to. She said it would only take a minute. That did not sound particularly good value—or good value rating. I made an excuse and left.

But once inside the hall, there could be observed, draped over the balcony, a banner proclaming 'Rate site value only'—a catchy slogan, one must admit. There must be another point of view. Otherwise presumably we would already have site value rating. Furthermore, it sounds the sort of thing which could cause trouble— bringing into being organizations like Rock Against Site Value Rating.

On to the defence debate: it was formidably impassioned. The standard of speaking, and the knowledge displayed of the intricacies of the subject, seemed to be far higher than at a Labour conference defence debate. There was less of the maudlin detail about the effect of radiation on babies lipsmackingly indulged in by Labour students of the issue.

An exception was Mr Paddy Ashdown, the prospective candidate for Yeovil, who led the forces which defeated the leadership's pro-cruise-missile defence policy. A fine, sincere speaker—but one whose rhetoric was something so shamelessly sentimental that he made Mr Frank Allaun sound like Bismarck. He began his speech with: 'The town of Yeovil lies in the Somerset hills.' As if we did not realize it, he explained at length that nuclear weapons would do an awful lot of damage if dropped on Yeovil—worse damage, one suspected, even than would be caused by the site value rating. On and on he went about Yeovil. One always suspected that Mr Brezhnev had it in for the town. The Slavonic races have traditionally been anti-Yeovil—a legacy from the Ukrainian-Somerset War of the late nineteenth century, sparked off by riots following the victory of the Ukrainian cricket team at Weston-Super-Mare.

'Fellow Liberals, the time in this hall is now 10.35,' chirruped the incorrigible Paddy. 'In Moscow, it is a few hours earlier, in Washington a few hours later. But over all of us and over the whole world there is a different kind of time, in which there are no time zones—the time, measured in minutes to midnight, between now and the nuclear war.'

There is also Liberal Cliché Time, observed in alternating British seaside towns every autumn.

The party's more bourgeois figures fought back. Mr Richard Moore, a Euro-figure, made a magnificent scornful speech. ***He invoked a forthcoming meeting of European Liberal leaders at which, if the anti-nuclear people won the vote, Mr Steel would be embarrassed. 'He has to go to Rome next week to meet Spadolini, to meet Genscher, as a minister in a future British government,' he pleaded. Mr Moore's belligerence, and his playing upon loyalty to Mr Steel, rather enraged the anti-nuclear faction. They seemed prepared even to sabotage the Steel-Spadolini summit. There were heckles. The vote was taken amid high excitement. The leadership lost: girls in jeans and wearing badges happily jumped up and down.

Then the assembly went on to discuss 'the arts, artists and the community'.

'You may not realize that this party has not attempted to produce a comprehensive policy on the arts since 1927,' said Mr Christopher Green, of Hereford, leaving one to ponder on what line that comprehensive arts policy of 1927 had taken towards expressionism, atonalism, Picasso's murky period, Joyce's *Ulysses* and the other

100

artistic issues of the day on which Lloyd George was known to be an authority.

Followed by Labour . . .

One of the duties of Mr Alex Kitson, this year's conference chairman, who told delegates earlier in the week that he had once played youthful football with his compatriot the late Mr Bill Shankly, was to announce the score after yesterday's big Labour v Nato international. It was another day of shame for England, but Mr Kitson did not seem to mind. Perhaps that is because he is Scottish. The conference had to vote on resolution 33, which recognized: 'That the threat to our future arises directly as a result of United Kingdom membership of the North Atlantic Treaty Organization', not, military strategists will note, directly as a result of Soviet Union membership of the Warsaw Pact.

Mr Kitson is a genial soul and a left-winger, if that is not a non sequitur. He called for a vote on a show of hands or possibly a show of knives. 'That's carried,' he briskly announced. We were out of Nato. Mr Kitson was over the moon. But suddenly there were cries from the right-wing unions for a ballot. An affronted Mr Kitson demanded to know if his ruling was therefore being challenged. He is from the Transport and General. Well, in the disinterested supervision of tests of opinion, the Transport and General is not exactly the same as Mrs Lakeman's Electoral Reform Society. So there were cries of 'Of course!' That meant Alex had temporarily to come off the field so that the proceedings could be resolved by Dame Judith Hart, the Deputy Chairman.

She is legendarily a rough player. In her Roedean-type accent— so different from Alex's refined Central Scotland—she soon terrorized the conference into a ballot. Late result: Britain back in Nato. The Left lost by millions of union votes. Mr Kitson was as sick as a parrot, but he did not show it. It was an honest mistake. He's a footballer, not a mathematician. Until then, he'd been playing a blinder all week.

Since his accent enlivened the TUC at Blackpool recently, when he brought some notably incomprehensible fraternal greetings from the Labour Party to that gathering rich in impenetrability, some of us had been determined to make him still more of a star this week. Apart from his unaccountably mislaying British membership of the Western Alliance for a while, he has been an excellent chairman, exuding a sort of menacing charm. To someone who reached the rostrum without being properly called, Mr Kitson genially cried on the first day: 'Git doon. Git doon. I'll decide who gits called to the roost room. Ah did nay call yew.'

He is creative with it. Calling the next speaker at one stage in yesterday's Defence debate, he rasped: 'Julian Moustache.' This did seem at the time a somewhat camp name for the rather rough-looking fellow who advanced on the rostrum. But then it was explained to one by a Scots colleague that what Mr Kitson had said in his graceful way was: 'Yew in the moustache.' This delegate proceeded to announce himself as Mr Cyril Hewins, but by then one preferred to think of him as Julian. *** 'I come from Epping Forest,' exclaimed Julian, which might have been interesting information had he been the Stag at Bay or a peeping Tom. *** Because of the Tory cuts Epping had lost its Memorial Hospital, he said, 'but if we have a nuclear war we won't have time to build a Memorial Hospital!'

Reasonably enough this argument went unchallenged even by the staunchest right-wingers. These included Mr Brynmor John, MP. Mr Kitson did not call him to speak in the Defence debate. This was understandable. He's only the Party's Defence spokesman.

As the debate drew to a close there were shouts and mutters of protest from the MPs' enclosure at Mr John's non-calling. It was difficult to sympathize with him. Being the Defence spokesman in the Labour Party is rather like being the resident chaplain in a bordello. ***

Conference had to decide, among other things in a busy day, who should write Labour's election manifestoes. A still more important question perhaps is who should read them. Normal people, such as a majority of Labour MPs and successive leaders of the party, do not need the stimulus provided by this sort of lurid, occasionally violent literature. But a minority in our society, as was all too evident by some of the disturbing cases on view yesterday, are unable to lead such fortunate lives.

What the conference should have established was whether such sad people could somehow be *helped* by being shown, under suitably controlled conditions, such material for hour after hour. None of this is to deny that it degrades women. But is not censorship also an obscenity? *** The issue in the debate yesterday was: should the drafting of the manifesto be fixed up, as at present, by the Leader in consulation with a few cronies, MPs or right-wing union villains; or should the fixing be by the National Executive Committee, interpreting the democratic wishes of the annual party conference—in short, by the mob.

Mr Foot favours the villains, Mr Benn, the mob.

As the conference chairman, Mr Kitson, explained at the outset of the debate, we were deciding nothing less than a constitutional matter or, as he pronounced it, a constitutional mutter. (Readers will be relieved to learn that that was positively our last-ever reference to the fact that Mr Alexander Kitson speaks with a Scottish accent. Furthermore, nearly everyone agrees that he has been a great chairman. He is ever-ready with a friendly greeting for every delegate coming to the rostrum, even if it is sometimes to get back where the delegate came from. He is quite simply Alexander the Greet.)

As the debate proceeded, a continuous, irritated constitutional mutter arose from the seats reserved for MPs. These seats form the conference's maximum security wing. In them are incarcerated men—and occasionally women—who are, on the whole, shunned and hated by the rest of the conference for what they have done in the past.

Delegates from the constituency parties went one after another to the rostrum to make it clear that they simply did not trust those MPs not to do it again—commit another moderate manifesto, that is, with all the attendant distress that causes.

A left-winger called Mr Kelly told the conference that one old lag, Mr James Callaghan, had actually *taken out* of the last manifesto, on the strength of nothing but his own authority and some sort of fantasy that he was the Leader of the Party, a conference decision to abolish the House of Lords.

Mr Callaghan's behaviour was generally regarded in the hall as being the action of a psychopath. He, and others like him, must never be allowed to prey on society again. Another left-winger called Mr Geoff Edge titillated the conference by openly admitting: 'I confess I am a former member of the Parliamentary Labour Party'—the sort of thing which, in socially conscious television documentaries, gets the speaker's face blacked out.

Mr Edge, haltingly but movingly, explained that since losing his seat at a general election, he had tried to lead the life of a normal, decent extremist. Drawing on his own past, he told a harrowing tale of how, one time, the first he knew of the manifesto on which he was fighting an election was when he received it through the letter-box. At this, looks of loathing were directed at the MPs' gaunt quarters.

Suddenly, one MP—Mr Giles Radice, who is doing long-term porridge for the safe Labour seat of Chester-le-Street—was allowed out for a turn on the rostrum. He looked as if he came from a middle-class home. He had a young, fresh face. No doubt all sorts of indignities had been visited upon him in Parliament. But it was the left-wing delegates at whom he directed his pent-up frustration.

'It's time to call off the campaign against MPs,' he cried (One suspected that this Radice was the sort of still dangerous, but clever MP who had done an Open University course and could therefore write letters, full of social science patter, to the quality newspapers—convincing the gullible that he was no longer depraved. Other incorrigible parliamentarians go in for poetry and painting.) He pleaded for an understanding between MPs and the rest of society. There was no need to distrust them as they went about their task of writing the manifesto, he claimed.

'We sink or swim together,' he added, in a phrase probably picked up from Durkheim or Max Weber. ***

The closing session consisted of those final Labour conference rituals which, even for an opponent of socialism, always have a curiously moving quality: 'the Red Flag', 'Auld Lang Syne', the chairman's farewell address, the translation of the chairman's farewell address from the Glaswegian, one last, nostalgic row over whether a frightful young man in tee-shirt and jeans had a right to put a point of order virtually after the conference had ended, and a closing debate accusing the police of brutality. As an ultimate sentimental touch, Mr Benn declined to link arms with the front row and joined Bennites at the back of the platform.

This final session, then, shows the Labour Party at its best. It must never be forgotten that, whatever they say, the things that divide the party are much greater than the things that unite it. Labour may have had its moments of unity, gleefully exaggerated by the media, but the fact is it left Brighton in a shambles. That is as the participants would have wished it. That kind of thing is what brought them into the movement in the first place. So, as it always does, the annual Labour conference had a happy ending.

When the last session got under way, Mr Alex Kitson, the chairman, brought to a climax a personally triumphant week by reading out a list of lost property which included a set of false teeth. Either that, or he was announcing the first prize in one of the party's numerous fund-raising competitions. Going, going, gone: a pair of false teeth, knocked out of the mouth of Mr Kinnock by Mrs Beckett at the Tribune meeting only two nights before, slightly soiled but still usable. Or a favourite pair of the chairman's own false teeth which he had worn throughout his fifty years in the Labour movement, which once belonged to Keir Hardie, who in turn was entrusted them by Annie Laurie, the actual mashers through which Kitson's Caledonian comments had reached a bemused English nation on television all week. But the teeth went unclaimed.

And so to the debate on the inner cities and the role therein of the constabulary. Mr Mike Petrov, of Streatham, moving the relevant motion, said it was not anti-police and neither was the party an anti-police party. This was undoubtedly true. Indeed, many members of the Labour Party strongly believe in the police even to the extent of being in favour of a police state.

But in a heart-warming display, delegate after delegate came to the rostrum to put in a bad word for the British bobby. Mr John Scott, of Lancaster, said he was probably unique at the conference in that he was a retired police officer. We must hope that he was not right about this and that the conference in fact had been infiltrated by large numbers of under-cover members of the Special Branch. Mr Scott assured a delighted audience that 'while this is a generalization and there are many people who are not racially prejudiced and not politically prejudiced, the great majority of the police are'. He was a great success with the delegates, very much their kind of copper.

Mr Sydney Bidwell, MP for Southall, thought that the answer was for the police, who he said were drawn from the working class, to form a free trade union and affiliate to the TUC. He did not explain why joining the TUC makes people less violent. Presumably, during the resultant go-slows, policeman would hit people more slowly.

But Mr Bidwell did not think this alone would be enough. He also called for more 'multi-racial, multi-lingual police'. But again he did not prove that more Gujarati-speaking Rastafarian rozzers would be less likely to be brutal. Are the peelers less violent in the West Indies or the sub-continent? Do Hindu Dixons disperse the latter region's frequent communal disturbances with an amiable but firm cry of: 'Move along there please'? Don't they just open fire, or wade in with sticks? More research is needed here.

The debate proceeded with the traditional mention of alienation, monetarism, unemployment, the absence of crèche facilities and all the other reasons why Britons have historically taken to the streets to loot and pillage. Who can forget the burning down of Jarrow in 1930?

Soon it was time for the singing and the final scenes of disunity, but not before the tee-shirt and jeans had tried to raise one last point of order. This gave the chairman, Mr Kitson, one final opportunity to tell someone to get lost. The chairman also explained to the affronted delegate that in any case it was time for the chairman's farewell. The delegate left the rostrum with a nostalgic shout of: 'Well, all right, if the conference prefers to listen to those facetious platitudes.'

Mr Kitson has never been guilty of a facetious platitude in his life. For one thing, it does not bear thinking how he would pronounce it. With characteristic good humour, he mused on the fact that all week the press had been making much of his Glaswegian sound. There was only one problem. He was not a Glaswegian. We knew that. But we like to think he is one of nature's Glaswegians.

'My accent will never change,' he rasped. 'I have seen too many accents change.' This produced a burst of applause. A Labour annual conference thus ended on a note of class rancour and the implication of the continuing, ever-present danger of class betrayal. That was somehow as it should be.

Then to Perth, for the first SDP conference . . .

So mankind has seen for the first time the new rank and file in British politics. Who are they? What do they look like? Do they mean us any harm, or are they simply trying to make contact with us?

Well, they seemed to know our language. They had learnt it from radio broadcasts. They seemed also to come from a civilization far in advance of our own, for everyone among them was polite to everyone else, especially when a speaker disagreed with another. In dress and general appearance they were extremely normal. This, therefore, makes them Britain's first ever political party made up of normal-looking people. The effect was deeply eerie. I don't know what's going on up here, but I don't like it. Of course it could turn out that, as is widely suspected, most of them are aliens from Planet Quango or other taxpayer-financed unheavenly bodies. But for the time being, we have no way of knowing.

Picture a gathering entirely bereft of all the wondrous and varied creatures who inhabit a British party conference. At the Tories, there are young strangulated-sounding merchant bankers with pink noses, watch chains and either no chins or several each. There are girls from Esher, eight feet tall, named Fiona ffrench-Leave or whatever. At Labour's, there are people in denim romper suits who have heads like those of the crazed cardinals in the work of

Mr Francis Bacon, and the men are sometimes frightening too.

But the visitors to Perth from another world looked collectively like a firm's outing from one of the target constituencies such as Reading or Basildon, picked out by the party's numerous psephologist members for its utter consistency with every new social norm. This does not automatically bode well for the future. Politics has never been an activity engaged in on any great scale by normal people. Inevitably, the leaders of social democracy will be engaged in the disasters, betrayals and reversals that must, not always through anyone's particular fault, follow any electoral triumph they might have. And all these strange normals might start to behave even more abnormally and dangerously than the people in the other parties who are used to disaster and who are abnormal and dangerous in the first place, anyway.

For this first national conference, Perth may be thought a somewhat extreme location for the moderate party. But over the week, the conference will gradually move south, like the out-of-town run of a musical or a play. We will be going to Bradford before ending up in London. *****

The more southerly Social Democrats reached Perth on what is now the most famous train in politics since the one that Lenin was sealed into in order to start the revolution. Photographers piled on board at Euston and got British Rail catering personnel to hold aloft the claret to be consumed. Wisely, Mr Roy Jenkins, acknowledged leader of the dominant Claret Tendency in the otherwise Pink Party, took the aeroplane up and thus denied the SDP's enemies this further proof of his Bacchanalian tendencies.

Handicapped by the good will of much of the British press, then, the Social Democrats finally opened their conference in the grey-stoned City Hall in the otherwise deserted streets of a Scottish sabbath. For one suspects that the party is more threatened by its friends than its enemies. It must struggle against a massively sympathetic and fair coverage. Mr Benn has shown that to have the press against you is a tremendous advantage for a politician. It enrages and galvanizes his followers, giving them a focus for that disinterested hatred which is at the heart of so much of politics.

But for the Social Democrats the situation is still worse. Several journalists of the distinguished opinion-forming variety seem to have actually joined it. Several were in evidence yesterday. We will not mention their names. If there is one thing that these people thrive on, it is publicity. Still more will probably appear as we reach the opinion-mining areas of the south, where men and women toil away at the word-face: hacking out vast articles on the need to implement the Brandt Report or the folly of doing without an incomes policy.

Historically, journalists have on the whole made lousy politicians, as is proved by the cases of President Warren G. Harding, Mussolini, Mr Michael Foot and Mr George Gardiner, MP. Churchill and Mr Nigel Lawson are dazzling exceptions in this as in all other things. But these were the sort of dangers which lay much concealed for the infant party. Agreement and unity swirled all around us. Mr Mike Thomas MP did, however, disagree with Professor David Marquand about the desirability of allowing the leader to be decided by the MPs rather than by the rank and file.

A delegate called Mr McCall observed appallingly of their dispute: 'May I say what a pleasure it was to hear arguments put forward with such tolerance and sympathy for each other's point of view.' It looks ominously as if this is going to be the Goodie-Goodie Party.

Mr Jenkins made the major speech. May one hazard, without wishing to deny its distinction or give any comfort to those forces which are polarizing our political system, a constructive criticism? (After a while, you see, it becomes contagious.) One's point is that Mr Jenkins's phrase 'We have even pricked the bloated bladders of complacency which for so long have cocooned the two big monopoly parties' was surely a bit of a cement-mixer of a metaphor. One does not know what Mr Jenkins does with a bladder, but one can be sure that he cannot cocoon anything with it. Later, Mr Jenkins spoke of 'the bitterness and internecine warfare which breeds bludgeons in the Labour Party'. Unless bludgeon-breeding is a speciality of Perthshire husbandry, the feat is surely biologically impossible. But may I say what a pleasure it was to hear the different parts of mixed metaphors getting along so well together.

We are writing from Perth shortly before boarding the now legendary train that is carrying the Social Democratic Party conference from city to city: the Flying Moderate.

The intention is that we should put in for two days at Bradford. Probably no train has ever before travelled directly between Perth and Bradford. What possible reason would it have had for doing so? British Rail could, therefore, be about to pull off the most spectacular feat in even its disgraceful history: the loss of an entire political party. Can our railwaymen do it? Previously BR has confined itself to losing such relatively unobtrusive, or unimportant items as Nato tanks, giraffes, and envelopes containing the life savings of little old ladies.

We shall see what happens.

The Gang of Four will be on board. One of them, Mr William Rodgers, has all the authority of a former Minister of Transport. That should be enough to end us up in Torquay. Either that or you will never hear from any of us again. We shall become a ghostly political party wandering, for the rest of eternity, the railway system of Britain: whiling away the endless ages with our own splits, leadership struggles, and 'quite uncalled-for' personal attacks. Perhaps like Wagner's Flying Dutchman we will be allowed, under the terms of the original British Rail curse, to step on to land every seven years—returning to our endless voyaging unless we find a majority of voters faithful to us unto a general election.

But perhaps with the journey about to start, one is simply getting nervous. After two days locked up here with all these moderates, one's old brain is going. It will be all right. We will get to Bradford. Whereupon, further fears and fantasies take over the mind. Perhaps this impending journey is not Wagner at all, but Agatha Christie, filmed by Hitchcock. Four important and ambitious politicians, a dozen unimportant, ambitious politicians, and hundreds of strange grass roots are all thrown together by circumstances on a long train journey.

It is *Murder on the Moderate Express* or, in deference to the reported train-missing tendencies of Mrs Shirley Williams, *The Lady Vanishes*. There is a poisoned bottle of claret. Any bottle of British Rail claret will do for that. Suddenly the train is cut off by a dense fog caused by the fact that Mr Rodgers is repeating the somewhat detailed economic speech he made in Perth yesterday. One of the Four disappears. Or perhaps all Four. Each of us has a motive. So does each of them.

No, all will be well. It is often forgotten, each time we lose a few in the occasional disaster, that British Rail transports without mishap thousands of politicians a year. But the time for departure is drawing close. Out of the window of the Station Hotel one can see that the fatal train has drawn into Perth's southbound platform. An inner voice is saying: Don't set foot on that train. You have the evidence of the sinister goings-on these last two days in Perth: you'll be bored to death. But one has no choice. In haste, one must recount the final hours in Perth.

They debated industrial policy. Mr Rodgers was the main speaker. Introducing him, Mr Mike Thomas, MP, said: 'All of us are proud to be a colleague of his in the SDP.' Mr Rodgers replied: 'Mike, thank you for those undeserved remarks.' If we lose

Mr Rodgers on the train, Mr Thomas will come under immediate suspicion.

Mr Rodgers's economic policy was a veritable compendium of clichés. He called for a 'genuine partnership between government and industry'. Why did not anyone think of that before, we all mused. He had a four-point plan, or possibly four plans each consisting of various sub-points inside the original one—the Rodgers Cube. He included a gas-gathering pipeline for Scotland, coming presumably from the North Sea, through possibly Bradford. There was also talk of laser beams and microchips.

He urged the electrification of railways, though one thought he said the electrification of people on railways, for even then one was obsessed by the subject of that train. Any minute now and we will get the Channel tunnel, one suspected. In a passage about Europe, we got 'the Channel tunnel could encapsulate what we as a party want'.

Later, he said: 'Anonymous bureaucratic nationalized industries must go.' One has never understood what that means, since they never say that nationalized industries as such must go—just anonymous ones. Does it mean that we would get nationalized industries with comfortable, reassuring names like Phyllis and Beryl? *** It is time to set out. Some of us may never see Bradford alive, which raises the whole question of whether Bradford is ever alive. You shall be kept informed.

Well, powered by one of the gleaming 'Debbie Owen' class of locomotive, the Social Democratic Conference Special—'Spirit of Croydon North-West'—reached Bradford from Perth, defying all those faint hearts who said the journey was impossible.

We got in a mere hour and a half late. Some turbulence around Hartlepool, or perhaps in the buffet car, had probably caused the delay. Bradford coped with the emergency magnificently. Long before our unexpected deliverance, all hope that the train might be found had been abandoned. The search for us had been called off. It had been assumed that, like so many trains before whose fate British Rail had hushed up, we had disappeared into the mysterious Ilkley Triangle.

Yet suddenly, in the early hours of the morning, Bradford had to cope with one former Chancellor of the Exchequer, one former Foreign Secretary, one former Minister of Transport, numerous MPs, scores of ranks and files, and dozens of us professional observers of politics, some of the latter in a distressed state, all putting in at the city's main railway station, hard by the Royal Victoria Hotel.

Once we had safely arrived, there were emotional scenes among the passengers, as indeed there had been throughout the voyage. Members of my own profession behaved as we were trained to do at such times. Some sank to their knees to kiss Bradford soil. Others tried the same thing with the female night staff of the Royal Victoria Hotel. Others just sank to their knees and stayed there.

And yet, by yesterday morning it was as if the night storms had never been. Peace and repose returned to Bradford: the Social Democrats were holding a debate on the economy. ***

It is proving to be an extraordinary week. The highlights so far? Well, one doesn't like to single out anyone in particular, but some of those young expert contributors to the various debates on regional planning and economics will one day reach Brussels itself to bore for Europe. ***

Yesterday the Social Democrats' enthusiasm for hearing the same thing over and over again in various cities had not diminished. All week speaker after speaker has risen and been applauded for announcing, 'We *will* break the mould of British politics.' Whereupon, a few speakers later, someone forecasts. 'We will break the *mould* of British politics,' and he still gets a big hand—leaving nothing for London later in the week, except: 'We will break the politics of British mould.' *** They are defiant about being the Boring Party. Mr Tom Ellis, the MP for Wrexham, referred to the fact that 'the newspapers have complained that we are dull, sober, earnest. But there is a particular thing about dull, sober, earnest, well-intentioned people. It is simply, we mean what we say.'

Mr Ellis then lapsed into a wind-up to the debate on regional policy, which was all the things he had described. Suddenly, Dr Stephen Haseler, a leader of the Social Democratic Alliance—the extreme wing of the Boring Party—enlivened the speech by falling off his seat on the platform. Resigning so soon, Doctor? His critics have always said that that man would do anything for publicity. They had long hoped for the Fall of Stephen Haseler. But the doctor climbed back to his seat of power and, like the rest of us, slumped intently through Mr Ellis's speech.

Deep in the debate on the regions there was at last proof that the moderates are finally producing some decent extremists. A Mr Guy Somerset spent nearly all his speech denouncing bureaucracy and people who want to organize us all, but ended with the announcement: 'What we need is a rural land strategy.' ***

London at last. The collapsible conference chugged bibulously south. Some of us required a certain amount of realignment as we emerged into the drizzly night around King's Cross. There had been some trepidation as to how the Social Democrats would be received, after their provincial run, by the flower of cities all.

In Scotland and the English provinces, the party had aroused much interest among a populace not satiated on novelty. Men would inquire whether Mr Roy Jenkins spoke like that in real life. Women would hurry to the Oxfam shop to don the new Shirley Williams Look. But London represents sophistication. How would the Social Democrats be received by all those violet-sellers named Liza, pearly kings and Household Cavalry who, according to the British Tourist Authority, make up the London electorate?

Londoners are not always at their most honest when receiving visitors. They often tend to assume that anyone coming out of one of the city's rail termini with suitcases has never set foot in the place before. Important moderates, swept by taxi from King's Cross to their homes in such Social Democratic strongholds as Holland Park or gentrified Kentish Town, no doubt heard the lovable Cockney cry at the end of the journey: 'Twenty pounds fifty on the meter, guv'nor, plus VAT and windscreen wiper depreciation.' *** We reconvened yesterday morning amid the wrought iron, stone staircases and endless tiles of the Central Hall, Westminster, a vast version of one of those magnificent pre-1914 public conveniences still to be found in the Strand. This school of architecture—George V Lavatorial—was peculiarly suited to the altered tone of yesterday's proceedings.

After Perth and Bradford we were in a world more pompous and self-important. A complete change had come over the conference. In Perth, the rank and file seemed to be largely drawn from the disaffected right-wing Labour lower orders. Salt-of-the-earth types, with a reassuring touch of dandruff. They were not in politics to become personally important or powerful. In Bradford, it is true that we were joined by rather more of those megalomaniacal academics. But in London, such figures seemed to become the dominant group. There was an atmosphere of determined ambition. For as well as all those solid citizens, and some noble souls, the party has attracted many men, and some women, for whom it represents opportunity, power, freebies.

Being essentially metropolitan figures, not many of them made the journey north. But now they milled around the echoing corridors. In comparison, the Gang of Four are benign figures. Yesterday they probably peered out with some distaste at the party which they were creating: Mr Jenkins, the most melancholy of them, no doubt reflecting that this sort of thing is inseparable from politics. The conference debated, among other things, the need for devolution, as well as education and the form the party constitution should take. Mr David Marquand, the former MP, spoke excitedly about the need to do away with bureaucracy. But, as in debates on the subject all week, any specific proposal he made tended to involve quite a lot of the hated stuff.

The party is in favour of incomes policy, but it is also aware that large, important-sounding organizations are unpopular. So Mr Marquand denounced something called the 'corporate state', which he defined as 'barons from the TUC locked in embrace with barons from the CBI'. How then would his non-baron-embracing incomes policy work? He did not explain. Instead, he rhapsodized about the need for small businesses as if this had been the cause which he himself had most identified with all his career. Instead, he had gone off to work for the most legendary bureaucracy of all: Brussels, which meant his name is virtually Marquango. ***

On to Blackpool, for the Conservative Party conference

Blackpool Revisited. Let it be said at the outset that, on the strength of this first part, this year's Conservative Party conference is fully living up to the advance publicity as the most treacherous and generally troublesome for years.

Nothing much has yet happened. But there are all sorts of latent, unspoken passions—hinted at, just below the surface, and all that. The cast is huge, including three million unemployed and Conservative Prime Ministers past and present. All the merchant bankers are called Sebastian.

At a lunchtime fringe meeting Mr Norman St John-Stevas gave a brilliant cameo performance as the outrageous aesthete Mr Norman St John-Stevas, who diverted and scandalized a whole generation and is a character believed to be loosely based on himself. He said that the Tory Party should be led by Disraeli, if one understood his message correctly.

The setting for the conference was perfectly observed—a rainy, freezing Blackpool in October. The baths in the hotels were as rare as ever. Plates full of abandoned, soggy chips awaited you on the coffee-stained, Formica-topped tables of the cafés and snackeries. The conference, then, is going to be compulsively watchable.

The proceedings began with the traditional religious service. A local C. of E. divine called on God for some assistance: 'We ask that debate may serve to improve our policies.' Leaving Him out of it for a moment, this naturally drew attention to the plans for the improvement of policies lately put forward by Mr Edward Heath, who was sitting at the far end of the platform. Soon an appalling duty devolved upon Mr Heath.

This year's Mayor of Blackpool was more than usually talkative. Giving his welcoming address, he observed that the illuminations were not only the most popular tourist display in this country 'but probably in Europe'. Having vanquished, as rival attractions to Blackpool, the Eiffel Tower, the Colosseum and the Parthenon, his worship went on to intervene in internal Conservative politics. It was Mrs Thatcher's birthday, he announced. He then led us in 'Happy Birthday to You', an electric organ suddenly emerging for the purpose. All rose. Mr Heath had no alternative but to rise as well. All sang the dirge. Mr Heath had no alternative but to join in. Was there no indignity which the Conservative Party would spare this man?

Mr Heath, victim of this ultimate dirty trick, moved his lips dutifully—but soundlessly, like a Muppet. The mayor, however, was not finished. He next announced that it was his birthday, too. The organ wheezed into action again. All rose. Mr Heath gave his bothersome burgomaster a look of dignified hatred, but had no alternative but to rise again. This time the lips did not move. There were some things the country should not demand of him. The mayor finally left us in peace.

It was time to get one's sociological bearings for the Conservative conference of 1981. For the conference is not changeless. The changes, however, are almost imperceptible year by year to all but the trained eye. This year's chairman was a trade unionist called Fred. One suspects that trade unionists called Fred are still among the most unpopular people in the country, but presumably the Central Office people who decide such matters as chairmanships know what they are doing.

Mr Fred Hardman turned out to be one of those large, comfortable men, like the self-made father in *Room at the Top*, whom the North supplies in such vast numbers for plays, films, and novels consumed mainly by the South. He seemed somehow symbolic of a slightly less frivolous, vaguely more earnest tone which the conference has this year.

Some of the traditional conference cries were still sounded. Young

114

women, catching up on the latest developments in modern Conservatism, could still be heard calling to one another: 'Did Jessica marry Desmond in the end or did she go off with that frightful American?' But, sadly, there seemed fewer of them this year. The SDP could be making inroads here.

The grass roots could undoubtedly be heard, if it is horticulturally possible to hear a root. The right-wing *Free Nation*, which was being vigorously distributed, had a lead letter from Dr M. V. H. Denton, of Elstead, taking the view that hanging was 'barbaric and degrading', and that the answer was gassing or other suitable drugs. A bit of a softie, eh? But he added: 'As a retired anaesthetist I am perfectly prepared to act should my services ever be required.'

With Dr Denton chillingly on offer, the conference launched into a debate on law and order. After rather emolient discussions on housing and Ireland, the law-and-order offering was in the pictures-que traditions of the party.

Mrs Edwina Currie, a councillor from Birmingham, held up a pair of handcuffs. A frisson of excitement ran through the house. One confesses that one was a little aroused oneself. Those handcuffs were for dealing with criminals, said Mrs Currie, excitingly. 'I am not concerned with prisoners' welfare,' she explained. 'Perhaps I should be. But I'm not.' This was an understandable point of view. On the other hand, it was a little odd coming from Mrs Currie because, as she also explained, she was a member of the Birmingham parole board.

Mr Brian Silvester, of Crewe, demanded that all Tory candidates should be in favour of capital punishment. Otherwise they should not be candidates. *** Mr Mike Truman, of Brentford, had an open-neck shirt, was young and denounced racialism in the party. Probably for all three reasons, in roughly equal measures, he was booed tremendously.

It was left to Mr Shakir Hussain, of Ardwick, to restore more traditional Tory values. He praised the police in the summer riots and denounced 'the leftist loonies and Bennies' who were not really in favour of good community relations.

The term 'Bennies' perfectly caught the essentially harmless fatuity, one thought, of those more normally referred to by the more impressive-sounding 'Bennites'. If Trotsky's followers had been called 'Trotties' and Marxist-Leninists had been known as 'Lennies' they might have caused much less trouble.

Mr Whitelaw, the Home Secretary, gazed down on the debate like a sad St Bernard. Winding up, he struck a careful balance between punishment and reform. He received a sitting ovation. Changes there undoubtedly are this year, but in some respects the party is the same as ever.

A former leader of the Conservative Party went on the rampage in a decaying, run-down area of inner Blackpool causing thousands of votes-worth of damage to the Government.

Unemployment was the main reason. Mr Heath has been unemployed since 1975. Some work was found for him on the Brandt Report—an imaginative scheme designed to provide useful employment for out-of-work international statesmen. But such short-term public works can be no substitute for a government of one's own.

Moreover, the situation has been aggravated by years of Central Office harassment and brutality against him. Yesterday the powder-keg finally snapped, as the saying goes.

Mr Heath did not see the day's events in the above terms. He thought he was making a constructive contribution to debate. A lot of Conservatives agreed with him, though not the majority. And there is no doubt that if you see the situation from their point of view, no harm was done—quite the opposite. Whatever the rights and wrongs, Mr Heath's presence, whether in or out of the hall, has dominated the conference so far. This situation has been taken so much for granted that it is worth remembering how unusual it is in the Conservative Party for a former leader to be anything other than loyal or dead.

We all watch Mr Heath to see when he applauds, for how long, and for whom. His motives are the constant topic of our chatter. He may deplore this, and insist that it is policies which he is all about. But it is all inevitable.

As for the rest of the proceedings, the aptly named blunt professional Northerner who is this year's conference chairman, Mr Fred Hardman, is proving a superb performer. The conference chairman is often an ingratiating, Wodehousian swell, genuine or feigned, with some such name as Richard Handley-Davenport-Fanshaw, MBE, later Sir Richard.

Such chairmen grovel even before Under-Secretaries winding up on pensions, and dare not terminate the speeches of the local government windbags. Mr Hardman is a chairman of vision and imagination. 'Thank you very much, that was very interesting. We should continue this some other time,' he suddenly boomed in the middle of an expert speech on European agricultural policy.

Mr Hardman was equally courageous, even with some of the

female councillors during local government and rating reform. He will be one of the few conference chairmen to deserve his knighthood.

Aside from Mr Heath, the speech of the day came from Mr Peter Walker, the Minister of Agriculture, Fisheries and Food, winding up on agriculture. To hear him tell it, he had done almost as much for agriculture as fertilizer. 'We have improved the whole zest of marketing. The British apple is now on the offensive,' cried this Montgomery of the market gardens. 'It is the French who are now defending . . . We are taking the biscuit to Europe on a massive scale. British sweets are being chewed and devoured on an unprecedented scale throughout the world—I hope accompanied by British toothpaste and British toothbrushes.'

By now he was delirious: 'We are actually selling spaghetti to Italy, bulbs to Holland, brussels sprouts to Brussels . . .' Brussels sprouts to Brussels! A certain sleight of hand there, surely. Any minute now and it would be freezers to Chile. He swept on. Where would it end? French polish to France! Spanish fly to Spain! Here was a man capable of bringing dash and excitement to the activities of the beloved old Min. of Ag. and Fish. A touch of Churchillian grandeur, too. He referred to it as 'The Ministry over which I have the honour of presiding.'

Mr Heath's first speech was at a lunchtime meeting organized by the Conservative graduates. It is an error to assume that his speeches are gruff and humourless because he knows no other way. He can make jokes if he wants to. 'Please don't applaud,' he told the conference when he arrived on the rostrum for his second speech later in the day. 'I haven't got very long and it may irritate your neighbour.' It is just that usually he prefers the heavier touch. There is a kind of dogged integrity about that. No one could say that he is a product of slick public relations. He scorns linking passages and graceful elisions from one subject to another. Interest rates (disastrously high). Salt talks (more needed). British nuclear deterrent (needed, but also a thing which has to be justified to idealistic young people: task for leadership). Educational vouchers (terrible idea: will split party: split country, too: alienate teaching profession: never get through Commons anyway: Sir Keith Joseph a complete no-no). World leadership (not enough of it about).

In the hall later, before a vast crowd, the rostrum besieged by photographers, the television lights blazing, his stuff was tauter. He was respectfully listened to as he protested about high interest rates and unemployment. But then he claimed that world leadership was 'paralysed'. This was widely taken as a reflection on the British team taking part in world leadership: the woman sitting directly above him. There were tense catcalls. Mr Heath changed the subject. He remained impressive, but he began to ramble. There were cries of 'Time'. He resumed his seat amid a respectful, but cautious ovation. ***

Disraeli suddenly started running neck and neck with Mr Heath as the most controversial figure at this year's Conservative Party conference.

The issue was: 'Whose side is Disraeli on, Mrs Thatcher's or the wets'?' A modern party conference is thus being asked to take seriously a man whose ideas were designed for a former age. Disraeli's are rather old-fashioned as well. Until mid-week, Disraeli had been a prominent figure at the wet fringe meetings. He turned up in the rebellious speeches of Mr Heath and Mr St John-Stevas and he was a hovering presence in that of Sir Ian Gilmour.

Yesterday the rank and file at Blackpool rose to acclaim the annual conference performance of *Hair*—the right-wing speech by Mr Michael Heseltine, the Secretary of State for the Environment. But this year the hair was short and the speech left-wing. No matter. None of them noticed. His standing ovation was the same as in previous years. Not for nothing are the Tories known as the Stupid Party.

Proof that the speech was left-wing was that, halfway through, Disraeli arrived in it. 'It required great courage when Disraeli first talked of one nation,' Mr Heseltine said. (Actually, it required nothing of the sort: Disraeli just put the phrase in one of his novels.) 'But he led the Tory Party through the great traumas of his day because he, in advance of his time, had the vision to lead in his time.'

It would have come as disagreeable news to Disraeli that it was traumas through which he was leading the Tory Party. He thought he was leading it through elections. He found that tough enough. Most elections he lost.

Poor Disraeli. As he would have told Queen Victoria: 'It was bad enough being in Blackpool, ma'am, a resort whose debaucheries and intemperance I could not possibly delineate in your blameless, regal presence.' But he was also marooned in the middle of a speech by this genial vulgarian, Mr Heseltine, full of such modish patter from the urban studies think tanks as: 'Authority became more and more remote. Great hospitals, panda cars, housing estates, tower blocks, comprehensive schools—they were the symbols of life that became more institutionalized and impersonal.'

What was this infernal babble about comprehensive, towering pandas in institutions. ma'am? Your servant confesses that he was quite at a loss. That is how it has been all week for Victoria's favourite prime minister. Shunted from Heath to Heseltine, by way of St John-Stevas, he has found himself associated with incomes policy, selective reflation, expanded apprentice training schemes for the inner cities, special help for all disadvantaged groups, and the general rubbishing of panda cars.

So we can be sure Mr Heseltine thinks Disraeli was a wet. The Secretary for the Environment, for all his gifts and prodigious energy, is not a man of originality. He is content to accept the prevailing view in these matters. But suddenly, in mid-conference, came the annual Conservative Political Centre lecture delivered this year by the pro-Thatcher Mr T. E. Utley, of the *Daily Telegraph*, an itinerant, jobbing Conservative philosopher. His subject was of course Disraeli.

His message was: 'Hold everything, folks! Disraeli was one of us'— though one concedes that Mr Utley might have expressed it more elegantly than that.

'Inside and outside the Conservative Party today, the crusading, moralizing, universalistic sentiments of Gladstone seem to me more in vogue,' said the lecturer. 'Let us make no mistake: Disraeli regarded these sentiments as a load of cant, and I cannot even swear that he would have endorsed much of the international idealism which marks the rhetoric of some of the most justly-revered leaders of our party today.' So, in the graceful way favoured by the more upmarket Tories, Mr Utley was inciting Disraeli to beat up Mr Heath over the Brandt Report. Moreover, according to Mr Utley, Disraeli was a roaring racialist—although again the lecturer phrased it more respectably. He quoted Disraeli as saying: 'All is race, there is no other truth,' and inquired: 'What would Mr David Lane have to say to that?'

To all of which the reader might understandably object: 'Disraeli! Schmizraeli! What does it matter so long as he loved his old Queen? What has it got to do with the Tories today?' The answer is that all Conservative splits are conducted in code. Unlike in the Labour Party, no one blackguards anyone directly. The wets have cornered the market on Disraeli, one of the few non-boring Tory prime ministers of antiquity. Hence the counter-offensive of Mr Utley, a friend of the Prime Minister.

LATE DEVELOPMENT: the current issue of *History Today* has an article by the historian, Mr John Vincent, entitled 'Was Disraeli a failure?', and argues persuasively that he was. So disregard above, both wet and dry.

And, finally, the Communists

With the final day yesterday of its three-day congress, Britain's Communist Party ended the round of party conferences. Indeed, many of its members, if they had their way, would end the round of parties—not just the conferences. But that is a separate matter.

The congress was held in the town hall of the London Borough of Camden. So a brief guide may be helpful to the significance of the venue. It was a Camden resident who made the occasion possible: Karl Marx. Shortly after his arrival on our shores, he lived in two rooms in Dean Street only a mile and half away from the hall—admittedly, within the jurisdiction of the Tory-controlled Westminster Council, though in the rougher part: Soho. But later, after getting a job as London correspondent of the *New York Herald Tribune*, Marx, like so many upwardly-mobile, radical, media employees, moved on to Kentish Town. That makes him a citizen of Camden. In fact, his ideas inspire much contemporary Camden Borough Council policy.

Aptly, he is buried in the borough. Over his grave is a monument in his name. Several million other people have also been buried in his name in such places as Katyn, which is within the jurisdiction of the Soviet Union rather than the London Borough of Camden.

Unfortunately, Marx would not have been allowed to take part in a contemporary congress of the British Communist Party because of his opinions. He was, for example, a male chauvinist, probably fathering a child on the housekeeper like any wicked Victorian Sir Jasper. On race he was something of a Powellite—though, in a letter to Engels, he favoured the view that 'races too weak to master the new conditions of life must give way' rather than the more liberal policy of repatriation.

Happily, the old brute was unable to be with us these last few days, so all the speakers spoke well of him. Translated into Conservative conference terms, at a Communist congress Marx is a combination of Burke, Disraeli, Churchill, Lord Thorneycroft and whoever is Tory leader at any given moment.

Translating the congress into Labour terms, the Communists were this year rather to the right of the Labour conference, since there was quite a lot of adverse criticism of the Soviet Union for going into Afghanistan. By 157 votes to 115, the congress voted in favour of Soviet withdrawal. So the party's Wets had the upper hand. These included most of the executive and the general secretary, Mr McLennan.

He would have been incapable of uttering the words attributed to his tremendous predecessor, Harry Pollit, on being asked by Mr Stephen Spender in the 1930s how best a poet could serve the cause. ('Go to Spain and get killed. The movement needs a Byron.') General secretaries of the party have declined since that golden age.

Mr McLennan was fluent and reasonable in tone on nearly everything. On foreign affairs he confined himself to denunciations of Mr Reagan and Mrs Thatcher rather than praise of the Soviet Union. Tacticians assured one that this was because of the party's desire to ingratiate itself with CND and the Peace Movement as well as being, of course, because of that Wetness which is seeping in everywhere these days. The pro-Afghan-invasion forces were led, however, by one's traditional idea of a Communist orator: Mr Tom Durkin, from Brent branch—white-haired, burly, open-neck-shirted, romantically proletarian, bellowing, Irish.

He roared defiance at the anti-Soviet states on the Soviet Union's borders who were constantly threatening it. As they had done ever since 1917 when, as he reminded us, fourteen capitalist states, plus Winston Churchill, gave trouble. 'Many of us would not be here today if it hadn't been for the titanic struggle and sacrifice of the Soviet Union in ridding the world of Nazism,' he added, prudently omitting mention of those who were not there that day as a result of the Soviet Union's pre-1941, titanic alliance *with* Nazism.

Mr Mick McGahey, of the Scottish NUM, turned out to be a moderate on Afghanistan—if not on Scotland, whose coalfields he periodically closes down. He thought the Soviets should not be there—in Afghanistan, that is, not Scotland. But what angered him most was any suggestion that this was disloyal to the Soviets or worse, as some speakers had unpleasantly hinted, that it was to equate the Soviet Union with an aggressive power such as the United States.

Feminism was intruded into most debates by young women wearing the standard liberated boiler suits and badges. But there were plenty of older women in sensible shoes carrying tea and sandwiches to the platform. Marx would have understood that.

By-elections

We retread, step by step, the more interesting byways in three by-elections which were to 'break the mould' of British politics. All were caused by the death of the sitting Conservative MP. First, in October 1981, Croydon North West:

Mr Edward Heath campaigned for the Conservatives in the Croydon North West by-election, and said nothing.

For Mrs Thatcher, it could have been a lot worse. He might have said something. But it would be an error to assume that his visit was un-newsworthy. On the issues, Mr Heath silent is as interesting as Mr Heath talkative, as well as easier to understand. His seminal silences yesterday on the subject of Mrs Thatcher were the most definitive public statement so far of his position on the matter.

Mr Heath appeared in support of Mr Butterfill—who sounds like a crunchy item of confectionery advertised disgustingly on TV, but is in fact the Conservative candidate. They had lunch in a pub and then advanced through the saloon bar for a Meet the People tour.

Some lunchtime drinkers called out. Mr Heath pressed on towards the street. As always, he preferred an Avoid the People tour. Mr Heath is not at his best with people. A TV crew asked him to turn back and engage a citizen in conversation. He agreed.

'What are your policies?' said the voice of the people at the bar. 'Yes,' Mr Heath replied slowly—or rather, 'Years.' The average citizen repeated his question. 'He's the candidate. It's him you're voting for,' said Mr Heath, placing a hand menacingly on Mr Butterfill's shoulder. 'I thought we were voting for the Government,' said the typical voter. 'You vote for them as well,' Mr Heath replied. He made the 'them' sound like the title of a horror film—them as in *The Thing!* But it was the most whole-hearted endorsement Mrs Thatcher was to get all afternoon. . . .

We left the pub and advanced on the rest of the electorate. Mr Heath and Mr Butterfill wandered up and down the High Street for a while in the middle of a tight pack of cameramen. A couple of times they all piled into a small grocery shop. Other times they would waylay passing housewives. Considering the difficult situation in which he found himself, Mr Heath was good-natured, showed none of his fabled quick temper, and even seemed at times to enjoy the proceedings. And there was no doubt that for him it *was* a difficult situation. He believes this Government to be disastrous, but the remorseless rituals of the Conservative Party, with its emphasis on unity, compel him to put in at least a token appearance at this by-election.

None the less he managed to convey an impression of distance from it all—as if, in his cashmere coat, arms at his sides like a Burton's dummy, he was simply being borne along, possibly against his will, by the tide of cameras and microphones. A passerby would recognize him and shake his hand. The talking would then be done by Mr Butterfill, whom Mr Heath would introduce as 'the candidate'. This was just as well. So distant did Mr Heath seem, so impatient is he with verbal nuances at the best of times, that any attempt at the exact name would have been bound to come out as Mr Butterscotch, Mr Buttermilk, or Mr Butter-Mountain, a fellow-European.

Eventually we found ourselves in a Betjemanesque suburban idyll called Briar Avenue. We all charged up and down a couple of gnome-infested gardens shaking hands with convinced Tories. A woman said she was voting Conservative because of Mr Ken Livingstone, the hated left-wing leader of the GLC whose name parents use in these parts to frighten disobedient children. 'I must say, Livingstone's a great help,' Mr Heath observed as he moved on. 'Where did they find him?'

Another woman hurried out of Number 33 with an autograph book for Mr Heath to sign. She had an SDP-Liberal poster in her window. 'I'd vote Conservative if they got rid of Mrs Thatcher,' she said. Mr Heath had no alternative but to reply that he was not interested in personalities but in issues, and that in any case, while he had his differences with the Prime Minister over certain matters there was no question of, as the woman put it, 'getting rid of her.'

After an hour and a half it was time for Mr Heath to go. He turned and waved to the photographers. One pressed forward in the hope of getting an exclusive silence. Instead, he observed that Mr Butterfill was a good candidate, 'Very good on the doorstep.' Was Mr Heath predicting a Tory win on Thursday? 'I don't make predictions,' he said as he lowered himself into his car which made off away from the clamour of the hustings.

At Tory campaign headquarters, it was explained that Mr Whitelaw had come to meet privately some people referred to as 'the minorities'. The Home Secretary is said to be very good with them. There is no doubt that this is true, for Mr Whitelaw is good with everyone except certain recalcitrant Conservatives.

Cloistered with the ethnic minorities, his goodwill no doubt swirled and heaved uncontrollably. Conservatives are for an independent Cyprus, he would probably be assuring the baffled, but still courteous Sikh representatives.

As for the Rastafarians, he had had the honour of commanding some of them in the war; marvellous little men who absolutely terrified the Japanese; the Labour Government should never have disbanded the Rastafarian Regiment.

APOLOGY: Mr Heath was quoted in this space yesterday as having no alternative but to reply, to a woman voter of Croydon who said she would vote Conservative if they got rid of Mrs Thatcher, that though he had his disagreements with the Prime Minister, he could not possibly agree she should be got rid of. There originally followed a sentence to the effect that this may have been what he had no alternative to reply, but reply it he did not. For he simply remained silent. Under the First Law of Journalism, this was the sentence which was inadvertently lost somewhere in transmission. So the passage, as published, was a serious allegation against Mr Heath of loyalty to Mrs Thatcher, which allegation I unreservedly withdraw. I apologize to Mr Heath for the distress it must have caused him.

Something interesting has happened at last.

Not Lord Goodman himself could find a smear worthy of the name in this unhealthily polite contest, one had mused in the comatose depths of the constituency the other day. But one should not take the Lord's name in vain. For one thing, to do so tends to cost thousands. Yesterday, in its closing hours, there came an unscheduled guest appearance from the face that launched a thousand writs, the man who put the junk in injunction, the greatest solicitor since Cicero: Lord Goodman. Two housewives had allegedly made certain remarks to two Liberal canvassers about Mr William Pitt, the Liberal/SDP Alliance candidate, in his capacity as chairman of a local residents' association. Whereupon, astoundingly, both women received through their letterboxes a terrifying letter from Messrs Goodman Derrick and Co—a letter of the kind that Lord Goodman has unleashed to bludgeon mighty newspapers and giant corporations down the ages.

The document's existence was discovered by the Labour Party which yesterday reproduced it in 5,000 leaflets warning voters, immortally, that if you tell Mr Pitt to get lost you might receive a letter from Lord Goodman. The pamphlet ends triumphantly: 'Stan Boden, your local Labour candidate, doesn't need a top people's lawyer. His door (47, Eversly Road) will always be open—whether you want to deliver bouquets or brickbats.' The pamphlet omits to mention that Lord Goodman, as public figure, was largely invented by the Labour Party. But no matter. At this stage, we must proceed warily. For at the name of Goodman every pen shall cower. It must be emphasized that everyone mentioned from now on is a person of unblemished reputation, total integrity, and personal freshness, except if Messrs Goodman Derrick and Co say they are not. Furthermore, there is not a jot or tittle of evidence for any suggestion to the contrary—or jit or tottle, tittle or bottle. There is not a scintilla, whatever that may mean, of any other evidence. It is all a farrago of untruths, and indeed, a fandango if required. (Lord Goodman's prose style is infectious on these occasions.) The letter demonstrates once again that Lord Goodman has no peer as an exponent of the legal-pomposo school of English.

'Dear Madam,' it begins. (A little impersonal, that, but it is probable that, just as with a Bellini or a Veronese, not all of the letter comes from the hand of the master himself, but from lesser members of the School of Goodman. That opening may have been the work of Derrick.) 'We act on behalf of Mr William Pitt,' the document continues. (All his life, the history-conscious Lord Goodman has regretted that he has never been able to write that sentence. Another ambition achieved.) 'It has been drawn to our attention that on the 17th October you made certain allegations . . .' Some of the phrases are rather dead, admittedly. More work by Derrick, one suspects. At this point a colleague has reminded me that Derrick is dead. That would explain it. None the less, experts would agree that the work is still priceless. For one after another the familiar phrases roll out. 'Our client strongly refutes these allegations . . . without prejudice to our client's rights . . . in respect of allegations already made, we are instructed to inform you . . . proceedings . . . forthwith . . .' It is all there. A masterpiece, albeit a minor one. The work ends with a tremendous, overwhelming, life-enhancing: '. . . including, if necessary, injunction proceedings to prevent you from repeating these allegations.'

Asked to comment yesterday, one of the recipients, Mrs Joyce Adams, understandably observed: 'When it arrived I couldn't believe it.' But she added: 'I'm not frightened,' which is more than can be said of the present writer. None the less, one will hazard the protest that things have come to a sad pass when you cannot slander a by-election candidate to a couple of his canvassers without there thudding through your letterbox a missive from the most numbing notary in the history of the British legal system.

Victory to Mr William Pitt

Mr William Pitt, the victor of Croydon NW, took the oath and his seat in the Commons.

For by-election victors this is always an embarrassing process. Get elected at a general election, and you simply swarm in with all the others, many of whom will be fellow-newcomers—a few bound for fame, a few for disgrace, most for obscurity, all perhaps for varying kinds of disappointment. But the by-election victor must appear at the Bar of the House, with two sponsors from his party, at the end of questions and statements: peak viewing time, the chamber full. At a call from the Speaker, the three figures must advance down the centre, bowing twice to the Chair, in full view of the rhubarb-rhubarb of the two great parties in the state plus Mr Dennis Skinner who is a Commons Uproar in his own right.

Mr Pitt and his sponsors, Mr Beith and Mr Penhaligon, slipped unnoticed into the Chamber during the Home Secretary's statement on the West End bombing. They waited at the Bar. Here, then, was the first elected member for the Alliance that could alter our politics for ever. Those years of 'community politics', all those broken pavements and vandalized telephone boxes, the failed attempts to get elected to Croydon Borough Council and the GLC, the lost deposit, the threat that Mrs Shirley Williams might cheat him of his inheritance; somehow, against all augury, it had all led to this apotheosis. If he is a historic figure, he had the first qualification, being totally unimpressive. The Commons is stuffed with tall, silver-haired, distinguished-looking men of the utmost unimportance.

Mr Pitt, however, has what it takes for immortality. You would not notice him at the bus shelter unless, to make some point connected with community politics as Liberals are wont to do, he was clambering up it. Yet future students, studying the Britain of our time, may recognize his name while assuming that, say, Heseltine was the drink for night starvation. At this sublime moment yesterday, with his fair hair and ginger beard, and squeezed between his sponsors, he was a small teddy bear.

'Members desirous of taking their seats,' said a shout which appeared to come from someone with black stockings and garters, and sitting in a big chair. Aha! The Prime Minister. No, a pleasanter voice. The Speaker!

The most awesome moment in the life of Mr William Pitt was upon him. He and the other two began to advance. He started to look down his small, tubby body. Could it be that, on this of all days, odd socks had somehow found their way on to his feet? Had some vital strategic zip been left unfastened? Too late now. If it were the latter, any correction at this stage would draw even more attention to himself. He looked up and pressed on.

Soon a man with a wig and Bible was asking him to swear an oath. He felt at home now. He had seen this sort of thing on the screen. He got ready to promise to tell the whole truth and nothing but the truth. Wrong oath. Instead, it was one about pledging loyalty to our sovereign lady the Queen. Better oath, easier to keep.

The clerk passed him on to the Speaker who shook hands. Then Mr Pitt disappeared behind the Chair and shook hands with his leader, Mr Steel. A Labour Member, Mr Arthur Lewis, happened to be standing there. He extended a hand as a matter of course, and Mr Pitt shook it. Then Mr Steel led him back, the two picking their way across the extended legs of the Opposition front bench, towards that small section of the Liberal bench not occupied by Mr Cyril Smith.

Mr Pitt took his seat somewhere, it appeared, in Mr Smith's vast, right-hand jacket pocket. Thus, after the glare of by-election and oath-taking, William Pitt, community politician, entered what could be both parliamentary obscurity and political history.

Crosby was a respectable little-known suburb in the north of Liverpool until the campaign culmination in a by-election on 26 November 1981.

Mr Benn descended on predominantly middle-class Crosby's by-election campaign.

With Mr Benn among them, instead of merely a fictional spectre on the television screen, it was not a night for gentlefolk to stir abroad. None the less, Mr Benn pulled off the feat of discovering Crosby's hitherto overlooked Red Belt. For his two meetings were both crowded and near ecstatic. Men in jeans and overalls lined the walls of the two school buildings. Proletarian matriarchs tut-tutted agreement as Mr Benn denounced Mrs Thatcher.

Mr Benn made first for Seaforth. This is at the end of the constituency closest to the Bennite heartland of Liverpool. There he

128

was a folk hero. He had come to help Mr John Backhouse, the Labour candidate in the by-election. In the past, more timid Labour by-election candidates have been almost ready to put up road blocks around the constituency in order to keep away Mr Benn's help. *******

At an hour when most of the middle class were safely tucked up asleep in front of *Brideshead* the working class of Crosby was watching a real aristocrat, the brilliant, unpredictable, wayward scion from Castle Stansgate.

'This is m'third visit to Merseyside recently,' he told them, the 'm' third' striking exactly the right tone for one of his lineage. It was m'third as in m'butler or m'shirtmaker. His audience understood exactly what he was talking about because they had seen the upper classes carry on like that in those plays on television.

But for some odd reason they did not seem to think of him as being upper-class in the wicked way that, say, Mrs Thatcher is upper-class. Now of course Mrs Thatcher is not upper-class in any way. That only added to the surrealism of the meetings as this strange apparition from the South, Mr Benn, referred to 'us' meaning himself and the people of Seaforth, two entities which have on the face of it nothing in common whatever.

It is all because he tells them that their woes are caused by what he rather over-didactically referred to last night as 'the economic system which we have which is called capitalism'.

Mr Benn proceeded to indulge in a sort of McCarthyism in reverse. He saw capitalists under the bed. He seemed to believe the SDP was a capitalist front organization. 'They're getting their money from big business,' he revealed.

Whatever the rights and wrongs of all this, there could be no doubt that Mr Benn could generate an excitement of which only a handful of other politicians are today capable at public meetings—a handful which, irritatingly for him, includes Mrs Williams.

There was a sense of expectancy in the air as, at the first meeting, we waited for him to arrive through a lengthy filling-in from Mrs Gwyneth Dunwoody, MP. After ritual passages about what Mrs Thatcher was doing to employment, housing and the health service, Mr Benn had still not arrived. So she started to ramble aimlessly about too much advertising being allowed for cigarette firms.

The Labour candidate took a few more puffs and prudently stubbed out his cigarette. Shortly afterwards, Mr Benn arrived to great acclaim and started puffing his pipe.

Those of us who have started watching the Crosby by-election campaign in its second week have known some of the plot from hearsay.

The Tory candidate, for example, is the one who always gets the bad press. Mrs Shirley Williams is the star, and acts up accordingly. The Labour man is the youthful, sincere one with his whole life to look forward to and to whom something terrible, like a lost deposit, is obviously going to happen. All this one knew already. Like so many media stereotypes, distortions and trivializations, all this turned out to be broadly true.

The Tory, Mr Butcher, has reacted to his bad press by abandoning his morning press conferences, in order to spend more time among rush-hour rail commuters. Presumably, he gets on better with people when they are rushing on and off trains. ***

Part of his difficulty is that he has managed to get himself depicted as the under-dog, which is a considerable feat considering that he is defending a nineteen thousand majority. The issue of whether Mr Butcher is arrogant above and beyond the call of Conservatism must for the time being be left open. A Tory official explained that he is secretly rather agreeable. If so, his secret is safe with us.

In contrast, Labour's Mr Backhouse is so sincere on such matters as, say, Merseyside unemployment that, as with Oscar Wilde's reaction to Dickens's death of Little Nell, it would take a heart of stone not to laugh. At his press conference yesterday, Mr Backhouse swirled on and on about Merseyside unemployment, and one could not resist an inward chuckle at the culprits whom he excluded from blame: unions, minimum wage regulations, the grim reputation of some elements in Merseyside's labour force.

In all fairness, it cannot be said that Mrs Williams or the Tory candidate much emphasize such dark subjects either. Understandably. The labour force has votes in the constituency.

At her press conference, Mrs Williams was her fluent, knowledgeable self. But suddenly, as in a Victorian novel or a pastiche of one by Mr John Fowles, an incident in this woman's past returned to her respectable present.

This is not a reference to the boring old Grunwick picket line, but to a quotation brandished at her yesterday by Mr Alfred Sherman, who contributes both to the *Daily Telegraph* leader column and, from time to time, to the Prime Minister's speeches. Sherman the right-wing ideologue is as relentless as Sherman the tank.

Apparently, on the BBC's *Election Call* programme in the campaign of 1979, she was asked about forty-three Labour MPs named by the Social Democratic Alliance—whose members now serve with her in the Social Democratic Party—who had either spoken on platforms with Communists or contributed to Communist publications. The forty-three are the sort of people who the SDP today says have made necessary the formation of the SDP. According to Mr Sherman's BBC transcript, Mrs Williams had told the caller: 'Well, I know quite a few of the forty-three and I'm bound to say, if they're extremists then I am one, too.' *******

'I don't recall the quote, Mr Sherman,' Mrs Williams brazenly replied. She paused. Then she started talking quickly. She *had* fought on the Labour executive against extremists. She had fought for publication of the party's internal report on the Trotskyist Militant Tendency, she added. In such a fight one sometimes had to say certain things one did not always believe, she added—rather revealingly.

Another pause. Soon we hearers of the tale had an impression of a difficult time in this unfortunate woman's life. She was quite alone during the period in question. Mr Roy Jenkins had left her for Brussels. She was known as the Belgian lieutenant's woman. Who were we to condemn her? Speaking with girlish haste, she eventually blurted out: 'Since joining the SDP, I have not had to say a single thing I don't believe in,' which was jolly nice to know.

To be fair to all concerned in this unhappy history, it should be emphasized that when it all happened long ago in 1979, she was fighting an election at the time. On the other hand, that is what she is doing now.

Back to the Crosby by-election campaign for its final four days.

Both the Conservative and Social Democratic campaign staffs produced detailed figures showing that, according to canvass returns, a majority of voters had said they were going to vote for them. All of which caused one to ponder that, in the media, it is the politicians' untruths which tend to attract all the publicity. We seldom hear about those diligent, unsung little people who, year in and year out, without hope of personal advancement, lie their heads off: the voters.

Under the conventions of democracy, one is supposed only to find fault with the politicians, never with the voters. But the latter have always struck me as being just as devious a group. If yesterday's figures are correct, at Crosby the voters have fought what, even by rough and tumble by-election standards, has been an exceptionally dishonest campaign. They have been all things to all canvassers. Some voters have had no real policies at all. Moreover, they have consistently refused truthfully to answer the politicians' questions. No wonder Mrs Shirley Williams gets on so well with them.

For one suspects that when they lie to Tory canvassers they are lying even more than when they lie to Social Democratic canvassers. This being a deeply religious constituency, they do not lie so much to opinion pollsters. That is why the opinion polls have Mrs Williams well ahead.

This is consistent with common observation. Mrs Williams bustles up to a group of willing voters outside some shops as if she is also a woman who can't stop now because she's got some shopping to do. That is correct. She is shopping for them. Breathlessly, she finds time to tell them that there are no easy solutions, that these are terribly difficult problems, but that one thing is certain: neither Mrs Thatcher nor Mr Benn have the answers.

Policies do not much come into it. On the rare occasions on which they do, she hurriedly explains that it is simply not true what 'they' say she said: she *is* in favour of private education, private health, private enterprise and no doubt—if she were pressed on the matter—private grief.

A few seconds later she is gone—leaving the voters to agree how nice she is and how she looks older/younger/shorter/taller/thinner/fatter/more married/less divorced than on television. For it is as a television personality that she is principally known in these parts—not as a politician.

Perhaps this is because she is a woman. But then so is Mrs Thatcher and she is seen very much as a politician. Perhaps it is not enough to be a woman in politics in order not to be regarded as a politician. You also have to have an air of impartiality.

She is, then, a skilful and cunning politician. Certainly, this does not stop the voters, as well as saying they will vote for her, also telling Conservative canvassers that they are voting Conservative. But that only goes to show that they are skilful and cunning voters. Like Mrs Williams, their view is: why be specific and give unnecessary offence?

At her press conference yesterday, Mrs Williams denounced any new trade union reforms from Mr Tebbit which might lead to confrontation with the unions. Not that she was against reforms, she hastily explained—just ones which led to confrontation. But how did we know that hers would not lead to confrontation, since confrontation was what these things tended to lead to? She said hers would not because there would be more communication between management and work force. ***

Over at Tory headquarters, their candidate, Mr Butcher, showed the assembled press an egg. It had been thrown at one of his meetings, he said. Happily, it had been caught by a well-wisher—a young Conservative named Miss Brown.

How did we know it was the same egg? It looked like any other egg. Mr Butcher was rapidly regretting he raised the subject. 'I think it was Karl Marx who made some remark about the yoke of the workers . . .' His voice trailed off. We stared at him in silence. Quickly, he changed the subject to the unions. He blamed them for Merseyside's troubles. This is the truth. It is bound to get him into trouble.

Mr John Butcher, the Conservative candidate in the Crosby by-election, threw himself under the rush of commuters at one of the constituency's railway stations. After the opinion polls, it was the only way out. No doubt a coroner would rule that he took this course of action while the balance of his majority was disturbed. Another reason was his obsession with a woman.

'May I ask you who you're going to vote for,' he asked one commuter.

'Shirley,' was the reply.

Shirley! That fatal name. Mr Butcher was a happy man until he came into the clutches of Shirley. Every other ambitious young Tory, anxious to get into Parliament, would have nothing to do with her at Crosby. But Mr Butcher thought he could tame her. It was a decision which was to lead him to his present desperate situation.

Before all this happened, he was a chartered accountant not yet forty. He had been elected to Kensington and Chelsea Borough Council. He had been treasurer of the Bow Group. He had a light-brown, camel-hair overcoat. Life had treated him well.

Now he is threatened with the loss of what a man like him believed to be the most precious thing in life: a huge Conservative majority. All because of that cunning woman. 'Could I ask you why you are voting for Shirley?' he asked the commuter (a first-time voter named Janet, aged eighteen). 'Because I've heard of her,' Janet replied.

I suppose one should not feel sympathy for so distrusted a class as politicians but the sheer irrationality of democracy sometimes wins one to their side. 'Now that's interesting,' Mr Butcher said. 'You're voting for her because you've heard of her. Have you heard of me?'

'Yes. You put a leaflet through our door.'

So she *had* heard of him, one observed. Contrary to her first reply, she had heard of both him and Shirley. Why, then, was she against him? Was it because she did not like having things put through her door? As a reason for her choice, that would have been no less irrational than many of the other explanations being produced by Crosby's electorate for their impending decision.

Mr Butcher abandoned his questioning of Janet. He lacks staying power. He repositioned himself at the top of the station stairs in front of the wave of commuters from the next train. (We were on Formby Station in the second most staunchly Conservative part of the constituency after the town of Crosby itself.) A BBC camera crew hovered nearby to make him look ridiculous for some programme on the election. He co-operated.

Suddenly, commuters surged up the stairs. He was standing too near the top. So they did not have a chance to slow down before seeing him. Instead all they saw was this man in a light-brown camel-hair coat and a blue rosette suffused in a television light. One after another the commuters collided with his outstretched hand as if they were those little dots on the space invader machines.

'Hello, I am John Butcher, I am John Butcher, hello, hello. I am John Butcher. I am John Butcher.' He is not a particularly vain man as Conservative candidates go, but it did not seem to occur to him that people's first reaction might be to ask of themselves the question: Who's John Butcher? *****

The candidates had made the last speech, negotiated the last U-turn, slipped on the last banana skin, terrorized the last old people's home. Peace had returned to Crosby after three weeks. The by-election campaign was over.

The fight ended with one final atrocity. The 83,000 voters were due to be bombarded with leaflets even as they slept last night. The Tories were intending to put theirs through doors around midnight and the Social Democrats to follow at about 5 a.m. with a document cheerily beginning: 'Good Morning!' (They *would*.) With luck, these operations will have led to canvassers being mistaken for late-revelling husbands and hit over the head with rolling pins or appearing in court this morning charged with various nocturnal offences.

The closing forty-eight hours of the campaign produced Mr Michael Foot. His party's candidate, Mr John Backhouse, has no chance of winning. Nonetheless Mr Foot made the same speech he would have made in a marginal or in the House of Commons. This was partly because Mr Foot these days only has one speech. That does not mean that it is a bad speech, merely that it is by now a famous one.

134

It consists, for those readers who have not yet heard it, of half an hour about economics during which Mr Foot appears to be talking in his sleep. He hates economics. For the final quarter of an hour, however, he perks up as he explains how it is always Labour which has saved the nation at times of crisis. In that alternating blaring and whispering that is the basis of his oratorical style, he explains: 'We SAVED the COUNTRY in the SECOND World WAR'— presumably a reference to the fact that Labour voted against Chamberlain in the Norway Debate of 1940, rather than to the fact that it did not vote for conscription and other warlike measures in the years immediately before.

He rambles on, changing the subject, stalling for time. You can almost see that old brain debating which other historic crisis it should chance its luck with next as one of Labour's rescue jobs. Agincourt? Waterloo? Harold Wilson? On this occasion, he did get round to a second crisis. But it turned out to be essentially the same one. 'We saved the country at the 1945 general election. . . . That is, after the SECOND World WAR.' His speech was safely home. He sat down to polite applause. There were many young people in the audience who were perhaps hearing the well-loved speech for the first time. Hearing it thus must be like a young person's first acquaintance with one of the improving classics such as *Moby Dick*: unintelligible. Next morning Mrs Shirley Williams appeared for her last press conference. She was fresh, bright-eyed, confident, well-briefed, fluent— in a word, insufferable.

Victory to Mrs Williams

Yesterday marked the State Opening of Mrs Shirley Williams. She took her seat as the first member elected to Parliament as a candidate of the Social Democratic Party.

What a wealth of pageantry is conveyed by those simple words. Yesterday's was a strictly non-controversial occasion. All her public appearances are. Being one of the most senior members of the SDP she is of course not allowed, under the British Constitution, to make known her political opinions. As a result of this system, which has served the nation so well for almost an entire year, Mrs Williams and her friends win nearly all the elections.

Mrs Williams arrived at the Bar of the House. She was looking very smart. This meant that she had sacked Oxfam as her couturier. The new team had kitted her out in a two-piece which a female

135

colleague in the press gallery informed me was in French blue. That sounded vaguely improper for the representative of so religious a constituency.

By-election winners have to take their seats at the end of Question Time and ministerial statements. *** Members high and low came by to pay their respects. Mr David Steel, the Liberal leader, was granted an audience. Mr Stephen Hastings, a right-wing Tory, shook her hand. Mr Jack Ashley, for Labour, gave her a kiss on the cheek. She talked with Mr Ian Wrigglesworth, the member for Thornaby and a defector to the SDP. He is presumably the man who puts the wriggle in her policies.

The House was unusually crowded. People peered at Mrs Williams from all corners. The day's business alone could not justify such a crowd. It was Mrs Williams who had drawn it. The Peers' Gallery was full. That is always a macabre sight—resembling, as it does, a very up-market eventide home or some annexe to *The Times* obituary column, where the distinguished await their turn.

Prime Minister's Questions got under way. Mr Michael Foot, Leader of the Opposition, protested about the financial crisis affecting the British Museum. A suitable home should certainly be found for Mr Foot but this hardly seemed to be the most disinterested way in which he could go about it. Certain Tories interrupted him with vulgar cries of 'That's where you should be,' and so on. 'The barbarians opposite are not interested in great institutions such as the British Museum,' he said. That was true. To those barbarians, the British Museum is so old it ought to be in a museum. Mr Foot was right to rebuke them. Alas, he got nowhere with Mrs Thatcher.

Next, Mrs Williams had to linger on while Mr Willie Whitelaw put up the BBC licence fee and there was a long quarrel about the effect on old age pensioners. Mrs Williams would have noticed that our traditions had not changed during her absence since the last general election. For Mr Whitelaw produced a fine Willie-ism.

A Willie-ism, it will be remembered, is a remark similar to the one he made during the 1976 Common Market referendum when he accused the Labour Party of 'going around stirring up apathy'. Yesterday someone asked whether, in view of the anomalies, he would examine alternatives. With characteristic compassion, he replied: 'We are examining alternative anomalies.'

As soon as Mr Whitelaw sat down, Mrs Thatcher and Mr Foot had an excuse to leave and thus avoid viewing the Assumption of Shirley. But Mr Edward Heath stayed on, being prepared to sit through Mr Secretary for Transport on heavy lorries. Mr Heath has

136

no interest in heavy lorries, except one which might cause a vacancy in the office previously held by himself.

There came the moment awaited by all people of goodwill throughout the nation as well as by existing SDP MPs. Mrs Williams advanced between her two sponsors, Dr Owen and Mr Rodgers. The French blue looked wonderful. Dr Owen was wearing it too. Mr Rodgers looked a dream in Burton's grey.

Mrs Williams took the oath and passed out of view. Mr Heath left. He had not had such a good time since Mrs Thatcher's economic strategy collapsed.

And finally, the return to the House of Commons of Mr Roy Jenkins via an unlikely route which took him back to Scotland, the country which had played host to the SDP's first party conference. He was elected on 25 March 1982.

To Hillhead, to take in the by-election campaign. It is good to see it before it finishes. Any visitor getting into any fashionable by-election before the end of its run knows just enough about it to make it confusing.

He is like the man who has *not* seen one of those up-market knockabout plays which for months on end provide the analogies and metaphors in brittle London chat. The reader will know the sort of thing: 'You should have been at Dominic's leaving party. It was *pure* Tom Stoppard, just like in the scene where the tortoise catches fire on the philosopher's head? D'you remember?'

'Er, no,' some of us have to admit. That reply can be a bit of a dampener, so what I often do is allow it to be assumed that I am indeed familiar with the work. This saves many lengthy explanations. For it is always possible to keep one's end up because the details of these entertainments have a way of permeating the brain in a scrambled, but still usable form, even if you have not yet seen them. Thus, asked about Hillhead I have for weeks gone around confidently saying such things as: 'The Labour man's had to take off his ear-ring because he's a Bennite.' This seems to satisfy anyone listening. It is not entirely fraudulent, for I seem to remember something about the Labour man's ear-ring early on.

The visitor, then, when he arrives, may be watching a tale, the ending of which he is unaware of. But he is familiar after a fashion with the plot until now. Mr Roy Jenkins finds it much more difficult than expected. Defying all precedent, the Tory candidate, Mr Malone, is no fool. Suddenly, the polls move against the SDP

Alliance. Mr Jenkins faces the loss both of the by-election and the leadership. He becomes demoralized. Meanwhile, through it all, there is still no sign of the Labour man's ear-ring.

That was the state of the plot at the start of the last act. Suddenly, there was a twist. Over the weekend the polls moved in Mr Jenkins's favour again. A telephone poll put him ahead while the latest, in the *Daily Express*, had the Tory less than one per cent in front—in effect a dead heat. Mr Jenkins could bloom again. He was not listless now.

'I never comment on polls,' he told us. But purely by chance he detected 'a movement' in his favour. That word 'movement' was drawn out to prodigious lengths—as if summoned up from the deepest recesses of his cultured tonsils—m-u-u-r-v-m-o-n-t—and accompanied by that shaking of the jowl and authoritative gesture with the hand indicating some gathering, unstoppable force of history.

The true Mr Jenkins was among us again. He was back on form—this much-loved, gracious figure who is to the liberal classes what the Queen Mother is to the rest of us. What evidence had he for the muurvmont, if it was not those polls about which he never commented? That presented him with a problem, but not for long. He stared upwards and called up an answer. I was so transfixed by it, having attended performances by Mr Jenkins since childhood, that I took it down afterwards from a colleague's tape recorder so as to provide the literary world with the authentic, unchallengeable text.

'What struck me very much was the spontaneity of the response in the shopping centres in all parts of the constituency,' began this dignified figure from whom Scottish shoppers have apparently been fleeing in awe for weeks, 'and the responsive waving primarily when we drove around making our noise.'

Note the magical term 'responsive waving'. People do not just go in for any old wave when Mr Jenkins hits the shopping centres.

They *responsively* wave, 'primarily', as is made clear in the text, when he drives around making his noise. What noise? the philistine might well inquire. It cannot be his muurvmonts. They would not be enough to get him a good round of responsive waves; quite the opposite. Inquiries later elicited the clarification that 'our noise' was the splendidly disdainful way in which the candidate referred to the SDP's theme tune, Aaron Copland's *Fanfare for the Common Man*. The common man referred to in this context, it should be explained, is not Mr Jenkins. Quite the opposite. It is he who is the fanfare.

In these final days of the by-election campaign, the energy problem has emerged as a key issue.

Mr Roy Jenkins regards his energy as a precious national asset that must be conserved. His Labour opponents are demanding to know how much of it, if elected tomorrow, he would be prepared to expend on Hillhead. The issue came to the fore as follows:

Mr Roy Hattersley, the Shadow Home Secretary, arrived on Monday and, addressing a factory gate meeting, reminded people that Mr Jenkins had represented a neighbouring constituency to his in Birmingham. Mr Hattersley implied that during those years Mr Jenkins had always taken care to husband his resources. But by yesterday's Labour press conference, the party was warning Hillhead of a massive lethargy crisis if Mr Jenkins won.

The issue, then, was whether, if elected, supplies of Mr Jenkins in Hillhead would soon run out? To the independent analyst, there seemed every possibility that this might happen. The more interesting question was: did the voters much mind if it did?

The evidence suggested that the voters were rather less priggish and high minded about the matter than the politicians. It was announced that Mr Jenkins, protruding through the open roof of a motor vehicle, would be drawn in some pomp around the constituency yesterday in a motorcade escorted by a detachment of halberdiers and pikemen up from the crack moderate regiments of London. Here was a chance to see whether Hillhead shared Labour's doubts about Mr Jenkins's devotion to them, and whether he was as ill-at-ease among the Scots as earlier reports would have it.

Well, it can be reported now that Mr Jenkins's state visit to several shopping centres occasioned scenes of widespread responsive waving. Every now and then he would stop and walk among the people. There was little hostility. What socialists never understand is that the citizenry has nothing against the traditional hereditary ruling class as such. To this it may be replied that Mr Jenkins is not a traditional hereditary ruler. But it is too late to start confusing people.

He was particularly devastating with older women. According to the *Daily Express* poll, Mr Malone, the well-behaved young Tory candidate, had rightly gathered up mass support among the females over fifty who are a huge voting block in this constituency. Yesterday Mr Jenkins seemed to look upon that as a challenge. With an unerring eye for his target, he singled them out for precision waving as he sped by. Nearly always, they responsively waved back.

When working the shopping centre pavements, Mr Jenkins, once he had trained his woman in his sights, would approach her, and engage her in fatuously polite conversation, bowing slightly from the waist, and sometimes making a graceful gesture as if to raise his hat to her, a considerable trick considering that he was not wearing a hat at the time.

This last gesture would consist of simultaneously raising the hand and lowering the head. And what a head! An egghead, certainly, but a Fabergé of an egghead—shining, exquisitely crafted, full of delights.

'I'm a dyed-in-the-wool Tory, but he's a marvellous man,' Mrs Margaret Graham, of Churchill Drive, replied when I asked her for her opinion just after he had worked her over. She added: 'He has held some of the most important jobs, and he has deported himself in them very well.' How Mr Jenkins would have approved of the idea that he 'deported' himself. For that indeed is what he does.

I left Mr Jenkins, deporting himself about at the Jordan Hill shops, and made off in the direction of the harsher more real world. The impression was clearly left that the voters of Hillhead regarded Mr Jenkins as a merciful relief from that world. They probably did not much care whether he would spend much time on their problems. Indeed, it might spoil the whole point of him if he did.

The city is riddled with Bennite social workers to do that sort of thing. The Labour candidate, Mr Wiseman, is presumably one of them. He, however, denies it. Denies being a Bennite or being a social worker? Both. 'I've been called a Bennite and I'm not,' he told us yesterday. 'Tony Benn isn't either. He was once in favour of the Common Market . . . Nor am I a social worker. I'm a community worker.'

It has been, by all accounts, a joyous campaign and it is no disservice to the other principal candidates to say that this is because of the presence of Mr Roy Jenkins.

Mr Malone, the Tory, some thirty years Mr Jenkins's junior, manifestly has more knowledge of 'the issues', including the national ones, than Mr Jenkins, with weary decades of issues stretching back behind him, can nowadays muster. But somehow, it is right that Mr Malone should know the details that Mr Jenkins should not. For this is Jenkins: the Last Phase; the period when the finished man is known to us all and we judge him by what he would *be* in office rather than what he would do, which is in the case of any politician largely unknowable in any case. Nothing would go exceptionally right under Mr Jenkins's rule. But nothing would go exceptionally wrong, either, and it would all be done with some aplomb.

140

The Hillhead voters sense this, which is why, though his opponents have convincingly demonstrated over the past week that his attitude on the issues is indistinct, his rise in the opinion polls has gathered momentum.

Perhaps the voters are tired of issues. And politicians are to be enjoyed for other reasons. There is what might be called, for want of a better term, their carry-on; the props, gestures and mild absurdities which make them stand out from lesser, greyer, figures.

When Mr Jenkins is carrying on, the tone is raised, the atmosphere is sweeter. That is why this by-election, whether he wins or loses it, has been a success. Our attitude to Mr Jenkins is very similar to that of the old ladies of Hillhead. We just like to hear him talk.

Yesterday was the traditional eve of poll rally of clichés, the day when all candidates detect a 'late swing', or 'scent victory' or are 'quietly confident'.

Such phrases are of course quite separate from the Royisms which give us so much pleasure. But we none the less like to hear them from Mr Jenkins's cultured tones and distinguished, quivering jowls because from such a source they sound as new. The interest of his final press conference, then, lay in seeing how many we could coax from him.

As soon as he arrived, we knew he was going to carry on. 'My reaction in shopping centres, in what I would regard as nodal areas of the constituency, has been very striking,' he drawled. Nodal areas? So he could still produce a new Royism on the last day.

Later research in a dictionary revealed that 'nodals' were 'great circles of the celestial sphere, especially the orbit of a planet or the moon'. There were few of those in Hillhead, so we opted for the secondary meaning; a meeting-place of roads unless he meant, with that distinctive voice of his, noodle areas, a reference to Hillhead's hitherto unnoticed Chinatown. It did not really matter.

'There is every sign of a substantial movement of opinion which has gone on and is going on, a real late swing.'

'At Crosby, you said you scented victory,' asked a colleague from the BBC, choosing the cliché that would give Mr Jenkins almost the full set. 'At Crosby, I said that, did I? Yes, I've been scenting victory for some time in this campaign,' he replied.

'We're not cocky, but we're quietly confident,' he added, achieving the full set. Whereupon, Mr Jenkins ended the press conference which could have been the last of his electoral career or the herald to that career's apotheosis.

But the memory of his campaign which lingers most was his reply to a persistent young man in a menacing leather jacket who had upbraided him in a nodal area about leaving the Labour Party. 'I believe in a fair society, which we will govern far more effectively than an extremist Marxist Labour Party, and goodbye.' That was Mr Roy Jenkins's election address to the voters of Hillhead.

Victory for Mr Roy Jenkins

Mr Roy Jenkins took the seat he won. And by exchanging warm greetings over the course of the afternoon with a baronet (Sir Ian Gilmour), a Tory back-bench knight (Sir Hugh Fraser) and the owner of part of Cumberland (Mr William Whitelaw), he demonstrated to us all that he was back among the simple folk from whence he had come.

Among them there was much quiet rejoicing. It is nigh on six years since he went away. His travels had taken him to Brussels, Warrington, Hillhead and Morgan Grenfell. But he had never forgotten his roots. Through all that exotic voyaging he had remained as insufferable as he was on the day he left the Commons in 1976.

Insufferable, that is, to those people who do not buy his act; such people include the entire Labour Party, the rougher half of the Conservative Party, and half the Gang of Four. This prejudice is not shared by us. When Mr Jenkins strolled through those doors yesterday, positioned himself at the Bar of the House, put his hands behind his back, swayed on the balls of his feet, and pointed his nose in the direction of the rafters, we knew it was the miraculous return of the golden age.

Before being invited by the Speaker to take his seat, Mr Jenkins had to stand for more than half an hour through exchanges involving Mr Rossi, Minister for Social Security, on the subject of the death grant, the sum paid by the State to the relatives of the recently-deceased to help to defray funeral expenses. Mr Rossi and his Labour critics—notably Mr Rooker, the permanently-hysterical social security spokesman—had a lengthy disagreement as to which party had over the years done more for the dead. Mr Rossi announced a 'consultative document' on the subject of who should qualify for the grant. 'Means test,' shrieked Mr Rooker.

Mr Jenkins continued to rock serenely to and fro, Sir Hugh Fraser came up to him and clasped him warmly about the shoulders. Mr Jenkins inclined his head in greeting, and whispered something in Sir

142

Hugh's ear. The knight laughed, patted Mr Jenkins on the shoulder and moved on.

Various Labour Members continued to rave about the Tory intention of 'discriminating' between people who receive the death grant (presumably they objected to the fact that you had to die in order to qualify).

Sir Ian Gilmour came by and paid his respects. Mr Jenkins beamed at him. Sir Anthony Royle, another back-bench Tory knight, exchanged a nod and a smile. The lower orders on both sides of the House kept their distance. Mr Whitehead, a Labour man with a beard, shook Mr Jenkins's hand. But he is a former television producer and, like nearly everyone in television, probably has a mistaken impression of where he stands in the social order. Mr Enoch Powell streaked past, ignoring Mr Jenkins. Mr Jenkins ignored him back.

Eventually, at the Speaker's call, Mr Jenkins advanced down the Chamber to take the oath flanked by the two Scottish SDP members who were his sponsors: Mr Robert Maclennan, and the man whose name resembles that of some African dictator, Dr Dickson Mabon.

The combined SDP and Liberal resources on the back benches managed to muster rather a good cheer. 'Another merchant banker,' cried Mr Dennis Skinner from the Labour Left. This was understood to be a reference to the hobby, which Mr Jenkins took up to while away the time on leaving the Commons, of collecting currency.

On taking the oath, Mr Jenkins passed behind the Speaker's Chair to be greeted by Mr Whitelaw. Meanwhile, as a foretaste of all those terrible Scottish Question Times yet to come, both Labour and Tory members pursued him with such cries as 'och aye' and 'whisky, not claret'.

Yesterday, within 24 hours of his return, he made the first intervention of his new parliamentary career. This occasioned a scene of almost uncontrollable excitement otherwise known as Mr Dennis Skinner.

The Prime Minister was at the Dispatch Box making a statement on, and answering questions about, the Common Market summit which she had lately attended. Every now and then Mr Michael Foot, the Leader of the Opposition, would rave at her on the subject of El Salvador. (El Salvador is not a member of the Common Market. But it was too late to let Mr Foot know that now. Why spoil an elderly gentleman's illusion of a lifetime?) For a few seconds in her statement Mrs Thatcher touched on the summit's call for peace all round in El Salvador. That was enough for Mr Foot. He seized on the subject with gratitude.

For, like most of us, he regards Prime Ministerial statements about Common Market summits as the most indigestible mass of detail to come out of Europe since the Diet of Worms. Again like most of us, the Common Market only arouses his interest when it periodically inspires something outrageous. The wine lake! The butter mountain! Or, in connection with Mr Jenkins's former salary, the money mountain.

So no one could blame him for latching on to El Salvador. At least it is all about things of which Mr Foot has direct experience in the British Labour movement: Marxist guerrillas, dubious elections, subversion. Merrily, he battered Mrs Thatcher for lending support to 'the gruesome fiasco of the election in El Salvador'. On and on he went about the wretched place. From his point of view, it was a much more romantic subject than the details of the EEC budget contributions. These he did address himself to for a while. But the difficulty there was that Mrs Thatcher was being as defiant towards the European powers as it was possible to be, short of troop movements.

Mr Jenkins sat through all this in a stupendously statesmanlike pose, draped across the Liberal bench. His chin was from time to time balanced in the palm of one hand, the fingers of which were somehow splayed across the face—several of them appearing, from a distance, to disappear up one nostril.

Eventually he rose. Whereupon there was a disturbance on the bench immediately below him. This disturbance went, of course, by the name of Mr Skinner.

A contrapuntal mutter arose from Mr Skinner consisting of money, the European Commission, people who do all right for themselves, and related symbols.

The Speaker intervened. Mr Jenkins resumed his seat. 'The hon. Member was shouting,' said the Speaker. . . . 'This House stands for free speech.' (It also stands for shouting.)

Mr Jenkins got going again. Alas, it turned out that he wanted to talk about micro-chips. Worse, he talked about micro-chips at prodigious length. At the word 'secondly' renewed civil commotion broke out on the bench below. Mr Skinner's friends, Mr Cryer and Mr Canavan, joined him in cries of 'too long', and 'What does he know about it?' This last was a fair point. From all we know of Mr Jenkins, he could not fix a light bulb, let alone a micro-chip.

'Get back to the gutter,' Mr Neville Sandelson shouted at Mr Canavan. (Mr Sandelson is a prominent moderate.) Mr Jenkins was still, as they say, heavily into micro-chips. But suddenly he broadened it out to Europe, micro-chips, and the Third World; perhaps because Mr Jenkins sees distant Hillhead as part of the latter. Mrs Thatcher thanked him for his interest.

As a punishment, the Speaker did not allow Mr Skinner to put a question until the very end of the exchanges. Mrs Thatcher seized on his routine anti-Common Market rave to accuse him of being 'an East European believing in East European economics.'

Whereupon, an affronted Mr Skinner rose to utter the phrase: 'On a point of order, I am not an East European economist'—a cry not heard in British politics since the great days of Lords Kaldor and Balogh.

Parliamentary Session

The House of Commons has a unique dramatis personae, *who take part in what often seem to the onlooker arcane rituals spread over the year. 1981/82 had its share of glory and reflection.*

Gazing down from the Gallery on the navy debate one had to accept that Britain would never again build those romantic, massive, ocean-going, impenetrable Conservative back-benchers.

There are very few genuine naval persons left in the party these days. Gone, for example, is Rear Admiral Morgan-Giles, once the pride of the Tory back-bench fleet. He was of the feared 1922 Committee class of destroyers. Until the last election, he was MP for Winchester—that boisterous, saucy, bustling port that bestrides the treacherous waters of the South Eastern stockbroker belt. In the saloon bar of the Jolly Investment Analyst, on his constituency's notorious seafront, many's the briny yarn he could tell of his engagements against Britain's traditional enemy: the Labour Party. And it was always a thrill at Question Time to watch him slip his moorings. With his massive firepower and reinforced skull, he would fearlessly boom away in the vague direction of his opponents.

Today he is a rusting hulk in retirement, aground presumably somewhere in Hampshire. Or perhaps, like the *Queen Mary*, he has been sold as a tourist attraction to some coastal resort in California. On the modern Conservative back benches, in place of vessels like him, there is a flotilla of public relations consultants and similar types. This was one of the reasons why this week's threatened Conservative revolt against the Government's defence policy dwindled into such a feeble affair. *** But the Old Right, though sadly depleted, remained. There was the inevitable Julian Amery. There was Mr Winston Churchill, who though only forty, is an honorary old buffer. The difficulty in listening to them is that they so much resemble those strangers who sometimes approach one in the pub and warn about Afghanistan and the sea routes, or insist the Government owes them gold bars. I am told that during the war such people would come up and explain that Stalin was about to change sides or that Hitler's tanks were really all made of cardboard. Still, it was good to see them powering away in convoy into the night.

One of the curious customs the House allows itself is the pretence—by all involved—that the monarch tells it what to do.

One hurried to the House of Lords for the State Opening of Parliament, but swiftly retreated to watch it on television, for you can't beat the real thing.

Our great state occasions, popularly supposed to go back centuries, were in their present form invented in the early 1950s by the late Richard Dimbleby, an ancestor of the present holder of the office of Dimbleby of State. Only the ancient craft of the television commentator can bring out one of the many strengths of the British Constitution: the fact that hardly anyone knows what is going on. Down a long corridor, on the screen at one stage, walked Black Rod—itself a name which begs many questions—preceded by a senior police officer. 'Hats off Strangers,' roared the policeman. 'That is the shout of "Hats off Strangers",' explained Mr Dimbleby. The crucial point here is that Mr Dimbleby offered no further explanation. That would have spoilt it.

Visitors to our shores sometimes assume that we understand our pageantry. Untrue. We vaguely know that Black Rod, though a man, wears black stockings and that he gets a door slammed in his face, usually at this time of the year. There our knowledge ends. Furthermore, none of us really wants to know more.

Was that policeman's cry directed at the strangers or at whoever was supposed to whip off the hats of the strangers? What were perfect strangers doing in a place like this in the first place? If we all knew the answers it might cause us to doubt the utility of our institutions. As it is, we could all supply our own explanations yesterday as the ancient ceremony and the still more ancient commentary moved on. 'There is the Lord Great Chamberlain with his white staff,' tolled Mr Dimbleby, leaving viewers all over Britain to assume some disability and to murmur, one to another, it's amazing how that Lord Great Chamberlain manages to get about.

'Baroness Young,' Mr Dimbleby continued, 'Chancellor of the Duchy of Lancaster, there she is holding the Cap of Maintenance.' Close-up of the cap being held on stick. Marvellous! Incomprehensible!

The Queen and other members of the Royal Family entered the House of Lords followed by some young men in breeches and a throng made up of people whom Mr Dimbleby announced as being, variously, ladies of the bed-chamber and aides de camp, some of whom looked camp indeed if they were the same as the young men in breeches, as who would not in that gear?

Having battered down the door of the Commons, Black Rod led in the MPs—the men among them in a riot of monochrome in their boring suits and dandruff. At this stage Dr David Owen, the leader of the Social Democrats in the House, made a sudden move. Already irritated at not being allowed to lay a wreath on the Cenotaph at the same time as the other party leaders, he barged in alongside Mrs Thatcher and Mr Foot. When they all reached the Lords to hear the Queen's Speech, Dr Owen, conveyed by that Barge of State, appeared on the screen in a prominent position. Only the fact that the Duke of Edinburgh got in first prevented him from occupying the throne next to Her Majesty. The Queen read the Speech and gave it to a venerable man who wore a full-bottom wig and an eiderdown. 'The Lord Chancellor returns the Speech to his purse and walks backwards down the steps,' Mr Dimbleby helpfully explained.

Later, in the Commons, Mr Foot made a speech denouncing the Speech, which was now in the purse of the man last seen walking backwards on television. Mrs Thatcher made a speech defending it. This was the purely ceremonial part of the day's proceedings, and was unsuited to television.

Mr Foot incurred some adverse criticism last week for going in for detail in last week's censure debate instead of relying on his trusty broad brush. But yesterday he redeployed the brush.

He talked of the need for reflation, but was happiest reminiscing about his visit to Moscow.

Mrs Thatcher's speech was slightly damper than usual. She spoke especially of government aid in industrial training. Mr Eric Heffer rose and, reasonably enough, said such aid was merely a reversion to Labour policy. She did not deny it, but merely said she hoped Mr Heffer would therefore support it.

Mr David Steel, for the Liberals, said he was not in favour of General Reflation, though left it unclear as to whether he was in favour of Major Reflation or Lance Corporal Reflation. The debate continues.

Day two of the week-long Queen's Speech debate was concerned with foreign affairs and defence.

Some Labour members expressed deep foreboding about nuclear strategy—our own and that of the United States, that of the Soviet Union seeming to cause them remarkably little concern.

One noted with relief that it was a Soviet, rather than an American, submarine which had violated neutral Swedish waters. Otherwise the debate would have been disrupted by left-wing back-bench disorder, as outside Professor E. P. Thompson and his hordes brought Central London to a halt. The cry would have gone up: how dare the United States launch this unparalleled act of aggression against Sweden; the world's first welfare state; the nation which invented the whole concept of abortion; the homeland of Dag Hamarskjold, Strindberg, Ingmar Bergman, and indeed Ingrid Bergman, as well as, while we are about it, Britt Ekland? (For the left is apt to throw in any old cultural name on these occasions.)

As it was, the Russians had done the violating and so the subject was never mentioned.

The Government deployed one of the most conventional of its weapons: the chief Foreign Office minister in the Commons, Mr Humphrey Atkins. This stretch of the debate was therefore an exchange between a very clever man, Mr Denis Healey, the Shadow Foreign Secretary, and a very ordinary man, Mr Atkins. When a very clever man debates with a very ordinary man on the intricacies of nuclear strategy, the result is inevitable. The ordinary one always wins.

The mistake the clever ones make is to assume that the rest of us do not realize that nuclear weapons are exceptionally horrible. They resent our refusal to be hysterical.

In Mr Atkins we have at last found our champion. It was his first Commons speech in his foreign affairs job. He was quite exceptionally dull. Quiet, polite, hesitant, no expert on the subject of East-West nuclear diplomacy, he was deeply concerned but clearly had no idea where it would all end—the world, that is, not his speech. That had clearly been written for him in the Foreign Office.

He knew for sure (and with relief) where that would end—on the last page, not a moment later. Painstakingly, he assured the House: 'We . . . do not believe . . . that they are . . . anything but dangerous.' He was referring to nuclear weapons.

But such was his resigned, rational tone, he could have been referring, since he was speaking on November fifth, to fireworks. Her Majesty's Government wished it to be known that, in releasing nuclear warheads, you should light the blue touch paper and retire immediately, he may well have been reading. A bucket of water and a quantity of sand should be situated close by.

No doubt we were all supposed to deplore Mr Atkins's lack of melodrama on this apocalyptic subject. But nuclear warfare has been the excuse for a generation of verbosity from the decades of passion of Mr Foot to the recent, less colourful, windbaggery of Professor Thompson. Mr Atkins came as a blessed relief.

In contrast, Mr Healey at various points confidently discussed the political situation in Nicaragua, Grenada, Guatemala, Honduras, Chile, South Africa—no doubt changing at Crewe at one stage, for all one knew, for one's attention tended to wander, so unrelenting was the expertise.

What his speech had most to do with, however, was the situation in the British Labour Party. That compelled Mr Healey to sound much more concerned about all those exotic places than he really is.

His expertise knew few limits. At one stage he found himself discussing the successors to Mr Brezhnev. 'They will be in their fifties,' he assured us. 'It is interesting that the generation of Soviet leaders in their sixties were killed in the Second World War'—many of them by one another. I bet though Mr Healey confined any disrespectful remarks to unnamed members of the American rather than the Soviet administration.

Mr Wedgwood Benn made his first front-bench speech since the general election of May 1979. The House was more crowded and excited than at any time so far this autumn. But it was also a solemn moment for the Labour Party. Mr Benn wore a light grey suit and brown shoes. Opinions may differ as to whether this was appropriate attire for him to wear while laying a wreath on Mr Michael Foot. But this he proceeded to do. He rose at 9 o'clock. By the time he sat down half-an-hour later he had committed a future Labour Government to renationalization of the oil and gas industries without compensation, import controls all round, price controls, wages uncontrols and much more of a leftish character.

Mr Foot, slumped on the front bench beside him, stared around the chamber—offering neither assent nor dissent amid the general uproar. He is only the leader. *** Mr Foot had invited Mr Benn to speak from the front bench during the section of the week-long Queen's Speech debate dealing with energy, presumably on the grounds that Mr Benn has an unnatural amount of it. Mr Foot's idea was that a Benn speech from the front bench was desirable on grounds of party unity. Mr Benn agreed. He used the occasion to unite the Bennites. He rose under the fascinated and horrified stare of two former prime ministers, Mr Callaghan and Mr Heath, plus any number of politicians on the Labour benches who want to be future prime ministers, including Mr Foot.

Mr Benn was in tremendous form. Within seconds he had covered the situation of the Anglo-Persian oil company, in 1914 (nationalized by Churchill; nationalization therefore patriotic); the subsidy and productivity figures of France, Germany and Belgium compared with Britain (worse or better, as the case may be, since his argument was rather complex); and the safety record of British Gas installation (you have a better chance of being blown to bits by capitalist gas installers rather than by the Gas Boards, assuming, that is, you can get the men from the gas board to call round).

Mr Benn accused Mr Lawson, the Secretary for Energy, of delivering British energy resources into the control of the dreaded multi-nationals. The Minister would be powerless to control them, he forecast.

'He reminds me of King Canute,' he added.

A pity that Mr Benn should have marred a good speech with yet another personal attack by a politician on the late King. The Moral of the Canute story is that it was the King who was the wise one. He commanded the tides not to come in order to show to sycophantic courtiers that there were limits to governmental power. He was an early Thatcherite. These constant attempts to depict, not the courtiers, but *him* as the idiot can only cause distress to his surviving relatives. *******

As always, the Queen's Speech debate ended with a wind-up by the Leader of the House. This is traditionally a knockabout occasion—a time for mangled metaphors and soppy similes.

The present incumbent, Mr Francis Pym, is no Willie Whitelaw. But after a routine onslaught on the Labour Party, Mr Pym closed with a passage about the SDP worthy of that grand master of mixing. He shouted above the din that this 'stale claret in new bottles is a confidence trick and a poisoned chalice to the Liberal Party. I say to them: don't mistake it for the elixir of life.' One had no idea what he was talking about, but it sounded delicious. 'It is a reckless and a half-baked idea,' he added in a final flourish subtly mixing the metaphor still further to encompass the kitchen as well as the wine cellar. As he sat down he was justly rewarded with a cheer from both sides of the House.

After Mr Benn's excesses of the night before, Mr Peter Shore, the Shadow Chancellor, had opened the day's debate. He likened the

Government's economic policy to (1) the mercifully abandoned Morgenthau Plan (named after the U.S. Secretary of the Treasury, Henry Morgenthau) for the pastoralization of Germany, and (2) the Soviet Union's laying waste of Manchuria's industry in 1945. Corrected result: *Wedgie* was the moderate.

Mr Shore stormed and raged amazingly for forty minutes. He— and Mr Benn at the end of the previous sitting—thus brought this seemingly interminable Queen's Speech debate to an uncharacteristically noisy final stretch. This was not the restrained, responsible, reasonable debate I joined as a lad all those days ago. But I like to think that it is the debate which has changed, not me.

Traditionally, on this last day of the debate, most of us are in no mood to listen to speeches. Throughout Mr Shore's remorseless performance it must have been difficult for many members to get a decent afternoon's sleep.

'The country is living through a tragedy the dimensions and consequences of which we have scarcely begun to grasp,' Mr Shore said. But he was only warming up. The trouble we were in was 'so deep as to be almost beyond our comprehension', apparently. It was 'on a scale which almost defies analogy and comparison in recent history'. Nonetheless he made the effort. That was how he got around to the Morgenthau Plan and Manchuria. One assumes that, outside the Commons, people were still going about their lives unaware that they were being pastoralized or their industry carted off by Russians. But Mr Shore was in a terrible state about it.*** Suddenly, he was raving about 'the alien philosophers, Friedman, and von Hayek.' He mentioned the *von* in the name of the gentle Austrian Nobel prize-winning economist with especially brutal emphasis, as in *von* Ribbentrop.

The thought crossed one's mind: supposing a Tory Member had used the adjective 'alien' to describe any of the *Left*'s savants—or indeed anyone including real aliens. There would have been uproar.

The further thought crossed one's mind: which side has got the highest number of alien economists anyway? Labour's bear such fine old-roast-beef and Morris-dancing names as Balogh, Kaldor, Engels, Marx. At least the supporters of capitalism can produce one with the name Adam Smith.

When a front-bencher is making a notably incomprehensible but learned-sounding speech his back-benchers always make out they know what he is talking about. This is especially true of the more slow-witted ones. Nobody wants to look a fool. So great is that desire, it is amazing that so many of them still do.

So the Labour back-benchers nodded sagely at that reference to Morgenthau, recognizing him instantly no doubt as one of those swine hanged at Nuremberg. And Mr Shore's mention of 'the obsessions, madness and theoretical nonsense of the Chicago school' was assumed to be a reference to Al Capone's poker game.

Mr Andrew Faulds, the Labour Member for Warley East, has been detained on the back benches without remission since what the self-righteous regard as a serious offence by him fifteen years ago which most decent people have long since forgotten (his election). But every now and then he is allowed out on the Opposition front bench. *****

Mr Faulds is Opposition spokesman on the arts. This is because, when he is not being an MP, he is a professional actor (or *particularly* when he is being an MP, he is a professional actor). Also, it is because he has a beard. In the Labour Party, beard is proof of a knowledge of the arts.

The Department of Education contains a Minister of State for the Arts. His job, presumably, is to cause the arts to flourish. That must be his job. Otherwise there could be no respectable reason for having a Minister for the Arts. Over the centuries, the job has been held by people with names like Lorenzo the Magnificent, the Duke of Urbino, Louis XIV and Mr Norman St John-Stevas. In our own time it is held by the more prosaic figure of Mr Paul Channon. That must be the reason why there has not been much good art lately.

A tremendous seriousness fell upon the House as soon as we reached arts questions on the order paper. It must have been like this in the nineteenth century when they reached questions about whether certain chasubles or mitres were legal or illegal in the Anglican communion. Just as you once had to be C. of E., or at least pro-God, today nearly everyone has to be for the arts.

'Questions to the Minister relating to the arts,' cried the Speaker, and for all one knew he might well have been using 'relate' in the modern Californian sense, as in: 'I really *relate* to the arts.'

Mr Faulds rose and proceeded to be stupendously statesmanlike, constructive and dignified in his inquiries to Mr Channon.

It rapidly emerged that Mr Channon's job had nothing to do with the arts, but was entirely to do with money. It was all about people who wanted to spend other people's money on the arts. Mr Channon, it seemed, had a large private collection of banknotes bequeathed to him by the taxpayers. He started to shower them on art galleries and theatres, encouraged by Mr Faulds and the rest of the House.

This arts terror reigned for fifteen minutes. For fear of being called a philistine, no Member dared get up and so much as hint that there was no connexion, either in aesthetics or economics, between artistic genius and the amount of Government cash spent on 'the arts'.

Mrs Renee Short, the Labour Member for Wolverhampton NE, lamented the decline in the numbers of provincial theatres. Everyone agreed it was terrible. Yet this decline had coincided with the era of subsidies to provincial theatres. This did not seem to trouble anyone.

Mr Faulds busied himself calling for reports and lamenting the delays in implementing the findings of various committees. ***

'Really, the House is anxious to see this report,' he said at one stage. 'Or at least the more cultured section of the House is anxious.' Various brutes on the Labour benches nodded agreement.

Mr Channon announced that an important Rubens was to be bought for the Courtauld Institute. Mr Faulds offered 'my heartiest congratulations', Mr Channon thanked Mr Faulds for the part Mr Faulds had played in bringing about the happy outcome. Over in the more cultured section of the House, the Labour aesthetes grunted approval, perhaps assuming the picture to be the work of the former chairman of the Coal Board, Alf Rubens.

*

Sir John Junor, the great editor and columnist of the *Sunday Express*, told a story on television to illustrate the Prime Minister's essential concern for her fellow humans. Like so many of Sir John's best anecdotes—for his intention is always to cheer us up—it depicted someone as the victim of total disaster. A meal was being served at Chequers. As is traditional, Wrens were waiting at table. One Wren was new. She dropped a portion of roast lamb over Sir Geoffrey Howe, then, as now, Chancellor of the Exchequer. Bits of meat and drops of gravy were all over him—including, as Sir John (with the master journalist's eye for detail) recounted with relish, his brown suede shoes.

The Prime Minister jumped up and rushed instinctively to the side of the stricken public servant: that is, the Wren. Mrs Thatcher put an arm around her shoulder, 'Don't worry, my dear,' she said as recounted by Sir John. 'It could happen to anyone.' What could be more humane? Sir John implied.

The story did not strike one as illustrating the Prime Minister's humanity at all. What it told us was that chunks of lamb and gobbets of no doubt disgusting stew landed on Sir Geoffrey and it turns out that anyone could have been responsible. It was the sort of thing that happened all the time, apparently.

Wrens are always going around befouling the Chancellor of the Exchequer, it seems. Presumably the Prime Minister sometimes joins in herself. He gets the stuff all over his brown suede. Some Wren gets the prime ministerial arm around the shoulder. That has been the story of Sir Geoffrey.

One reflected on the melancholy symbolism of Sir John's story as the Chancellor trudged loyally through yet another statement levying various imposts. It is Mr Heseltine, the Minister ultimately responsible for housing, who charges glamorously around Merseyside expressing deep concern and promising aid. It is the stew-bespattered Sir Geoffrey who announces the rise in council rents. This has long been the sad fortune of all Chancellors. There has not been one with consistently good news since the late Mr Maudling nearly twenty years ago, and he ruined the country in the process.

But Sir Geoffrey is the most perfectly cast in the role. There is nothing meretricious or demagogic about him. He is openly the bearer of bad news. The most rabble-rousing observation he made was: 'The outlook, in short, is for gradual recovery.' All the other post-Maudling Chancellors have been bad news men. But Mr Callaghan and Mr Healey used to wrap it up in much ho-ho-ho-ing and cheerful villainy, and Mr Jenkins used to deliver the message with such suavity that it was almost a pleasure to pay his taxes. Sir Geoffrey, however, just stands there at the Dispatch Box, announces his increases, and courteously replies to the Labour baying and general accusations of brutality. Those brown shoes which he always wears (if one may intrude a fashion note, they are called Hush-Puppies) emphasize his stolidity.

Yesterday's measures were of course perfectly mild. No great privations will be visited on the working class. That is traditionally done by Labour Chancellors. But parliamentary exchanges are not intended to take account of such realities. So Sir Geoffrey was assailed by the increasingly-prolix Shadow Chancellor, Mr Peter Shore, who has become a considerable exponent of outrage. 'I wish to ask the Chancellor six questions,' he rasped. Some Tories groaned. This gave Mr Shore an opportunity to get in additional outrage at any suggestion that so terrible a statement as Sir Geoffrey's did not justify six questions, 'Yes, six . . . six . . . six,' he raved. ***

The worldly-wise say that Mrs Thatcher will remove the good Sir Geoffrey as the election approaches and good news is required. What was all that about her humanity?

*

Members of Parliament, like most Britons, presumably regard the beginning of December as the start of Christmas, for there was already a touch of Yuletide ill-will in the air.

Mr Michael Foot, the Leader of the Opposition, showed some of his old aggressive spirit by denouncing in the most personal terms a candidate in the Bermondsey by-election which is expected in the New Year. Unfortunately it was the Labour candidate. Later there was a substantial row about housing arrangements in Norwich. Still later, following some Labour procedural sharp practice, there was a blundering Tory attempt at a sort of filibuster, just to remind us that Christmas is coming and the heads are getting fat.

But first, Foot. Or rather, feet first. For it was with some abandon that he jumped into trouble. For months, the Conservative newspapers had been telling him to take the side of the moderates in the constituency parties. There are no moderates in the constituency parties. That is the beauty of it from the point of view of the Conservative newspapers.

Yesterday he took their advice and hit out. When he had picked himself up off the floor, one reflected: is there nothing that will go right for this lovable figure these days? A man capable of getting bad publicity out of laying a wreath on the Cenotaph is a man from whom the Gods have mysteriously removed their favour.

The scene was Prime Minister's Question Time. An inquiry was directed at Mrs Thatcher by the defector from the Labour to the Social Democratic benches, Mr James Wellbeloved. But it was really intended to make terrible trouble for Mr Foot, who was sitting on the Opposition front bench in the way that lovable pensioners sit on benches all over Britain, without being bothered, in the sunset of their lives, by people like the menacingly-named Mr Wellbeloved.

Was the Prime Minister aware, Mr Wellbeloved asked, that the prospective Parliamentary Labour candidate at Bermondsey had called for 'extra-Parliamentary action to be taken to challenge the Government's right to rule'? This was, as we later discovered, a reference to a certain Mr Tatchell who is indeed the prospective candidate at Bermondsey. He is aged twenty-nine, a social worker, and (one is informed by Tuesday's William Hickey) a Gay Rights campaigner who, at the tenth world youth festival in East Berlin in 1973, hoisted a banner calling for solidarity with East German Gays, had it ripped down by his own delegation, and burst into tears. In other words, a perfectly normal member of the modern Labour Party.

Mr Tatchell had raved harmlessly about extra-parliamentary action in a totally unreadable and unread Labour newsletter. Mrs Thatcher solemnly expressed concern, Mr Foot rose. That was his first mistake. 'Since the matter has been raised, can I say, Mr Speaker, that the individual concerned is not an endorsed member of the Labour Party and as far as I am concerned never will be.'

This delighted those in the Parliamentary Labour Party who favour a strong line against extremists. That was all very well, but what about the other nine tenths of the Parliamentary Labour Party? From them there were visible expressions of concern.

So forthright were Mr Foot's remarks that a lot of us assumed that he had not heard the reference to Bermondsey and thought we were discussing the application to join the party by Mr Tariq Ali, the grand old man of 1960s extremism. Mr Peter Bottomley, a Tory back-bencher, made an attempt to find out who Mr Foot thought he was talking about.

Later, Mr Foot intervened to say that he had not intended to use the term 'not an endorsed member', but 'not an endorsed candidate'. So it was indeed the chosen candidate of the Bermondsey party who had been disowned.

Then, for some murky procedural reason, the Government whips tried to prolong, for two and a half hours, a half-hour debate on an alleged injustice done to a Preston police dog-handler. This was in order to prevent Labour forcing a debate on the previous day's economic statement. The dog-handler debate included a filibustering speech by the Tory back-bencher Mr Geoffrey Dickens. He achieved fame last summer as the hammer of the paedophiles and terror of the *thé dansant*. He is thus the second most famous Dickens in English comedy. He said he knew nothing about the dog-handler. There was no doubt a logical explanation for it all—Christmas.

*

Mr Michael Foot, last seen disappearing down an organ well in Hull, was trapped all afternoon inside the organization committee of the Labour Party yesterday. He eventually climbed out, insisting that he was unhurt. But at his age, and coming so soon after all his other accidents (particularly his becoming Leader of the Labour Party), the incident must have shaken him.

The organization committee was meeting in an upstairs room at the Commons. In the Chamber, though Mr Foot was nowhere to be seen, the troubles of the Labour Party and its leader were in everyone's thoughts. Labour Members gathered in twos and threes. Mr Willie Hamilton, whose constituency reselection vote ended in a tie at the weekend and who must face the ordeal again soon, was deep in conversation with Mrs Renee Short.

Mrs Short slowly shook her head in disbelief and horror as Mr Hamilton perhaps told her tales of what the extremists were capable of doing. There was something odd here. Mrs Short *is* an extremist. Mr Hamilton left. Mrs Short appeared to wish him luck. She turned and spoke to Mr Jock Stallard on the bench behind her, possibly retailing Mr Hamilton's sad story. We are none of us safe, they all seemed to be telling one another. It was a joy to watch.

Meanwhile, as always at times of national tragedy, life went on normally—or, in the case of the House of Commons, abnormally. Mr Dennis Canavan, a Labour back-bencher, was questioning the Solicitor General, Sir Ian Percival, about Soviet spies in the Foreign Office.

Mr Canavan always proceeds on the assumption that being a Soviet spy is one of the qualifications for joining the Foreign Office, and events sometimes conspire to encourage him in this belief. Routinely, he denounced 'the legal establishment's massive cover-up' of this latest evidence of spying. Equally routinely, the Solicitor-General told him that his allegation was 'as monstrous as it is absurd'. Everyone was satisfied.

Among later business on the order paper, the spectator had a choice between a Government statement on the Severn-Trent Water Authority or the second reading of the Local Government and Planning (Scotland) Bill. This was rather like the choice which convicted murderers have in the state of Utah between being hanged or shot.

This spectator opted for water. Mr Tom King, who labours under the handicap of being called the Minister of Local Government and Environmental Services, came to the Dispatch Box, and as he spoke of the Severn-Trent Water Authority, one heard the seductive, unmistakable, exotic lilt of the Quango. The Authority—which had been the subject of a Monopolies Commission report on whose findings Mr King was reporting to the House—had been set up by Mr Peter Walker. Mr King spoke of it as if it had been set up by

Simon de Montfort. He repeated the Commission's reference to 'the Authority's real achievements in its first seven years.'

One's instincts told one that since the Severn-Trent region had managed to get by without this Authority until seven years ago, it had probably been both unwanted and expensive those past seven years. But Tories in office tend to be beguiled and seduced by really powerful Quangos. Labour undoubtedly sensed it. But they are the party of Quangos. The SDP, in the form of Mr Robert McClennan, seemed to have no policy on water—except perhaps, Perrier Water, which is the sort of thing it would favour.

Mr Edward Graham, the Labour front-bench spokesman, limply said 'the image of the water industry could be improved'. Mr King said the Government would be studying the Commission's report. Would that Mr Foot were present to give a lead. Before he had any responsibilities he had confident opinions on even the most obscure and intractable subjects. True, he would have assumed that the Trent referred to was the one involved in the Council of Trent (1545–1563). But he would have sounded confident about the matter. Alas, as the late Sam Goldwyn once put it: 'We've passed a lot of water since then.'

*

Sydney Smith once said that every time there was a new book, he looked for an old book. To be candid, one has no idea whether Sydney Smith said anything of the sort. It is just that half the smart remarks ever made are customarily attributed to Sydney Smith. It may have been F. E. Smith, to whom are attributed the other half; or for all one knows, Cyril Smith, or W. H. Smith, or Harvey Smith, or my cleaning lady, Mrs Smith.

All of which is by way of being a preamble to the observation that every time there is a Big Debate, I look for a Little Debate. For, under the First Law of Parliamentary Tedium, big debates are always a disappointment. So it was with leaden hearts that we all assembled for yet another big debate on the economy. One searched on the order paper for a little debate, but there were none. The economy would be on all day.

Over at the Lords they had, among other things, the third reading of the Hops Marketing Bill and the Harbours (Scotland) Bill, but these were rather too epic for my purposes. No, the big debate on the economy it had to be. And soon, as so often happens, one's essential loyalty to the series took over. Parliament has had almost as bad a press as the BBC's 'Borgias'. There are complaints that all they do is stab one another, that the accents are all wrong, that Mr Edward Heath does not look a bit like that, and so on.

But yesterday's big debate could easily be confused with an interesting occasion. It was enlivened by speeches from Mrs Shirley Williams and Mr Heath. Admittedly, it was deadened by one from Sir Geoffrey Howe, the Chancellor of the Exchequer. But you cannot have everything. There were all the most famous politicians of the day sitting within a few feet of each other. As well as the present one, there were two former heads of Government, since Mr Callaghan was present for a while as well as Mr Heath. All it needed was Sir Harold Wilson and it would have been a full crisis of Prime Ministers.

Sir Geoffrey Howe spoke first and was, in the opinion of this observer, more or less right about everything. Moreover, any other conceivable Chancellor would be doing the same. Indeed, several already had. This will get Sir Geoffrey nowhere.

Sounding like one of those lead stories in *Pravda*, he broke the news that the steelworks at Llanwern was 'breaking production records week after week'. Somehow the Tories are now so demoralized that they believe none of it. But all Sir Geoffrey's statistics sounded plausible. There was this Jones the Stakhanovite breaking productivity records week by week in Llanwern. The Tories slumped on.

Mr Heath rose. As he spoke, Mrs Thatcher's face stared down at the notes she was making as if for the speech with which she would close the debate. She was not making a speech closing the debate. No matter. She had to find something to do with her face as Mr Heath spoke. On a distant back bench, Mr Enoch Powell listened intently. Here were hatreds of Borgia-like complexity. Mr Powell hates Mr Heath. Mr Heath hates Mr Powell. But he (Mr Heath) also hates Mrs Thatcher who hates him back. Mr Powell hates Mrs Thatcher as well. But that is not because she is Mrs Thatcher. She qualifies for it merely because she is Conservative leader. It is an ex-officio hatred; nothing personal.

Mr Heath was enjoying a great success with the bulk of the House as he denounced unemployment. Mr Powell was visibly growing angry. Mr Heath made some monstrously technical point about the Opec balances. He may or may not have been right, but that was not the point. Mr Powell intervened and asked an equally monstrous technical question. Mr Heath smiled. Mr Powell sat down with the observation: '. . . and the right hon. gentleman might as well take the grin off his face.' The whole House went: 'Ooooo,' and 'Pheeeeew.' For a second the two men were linked by bonds of mutual detestation. Mr Heath replied: 'The right hon. gentleman can ask a great deal, but it's too much to ask me to do that.' No one cared who was right about the technical point. Mr Heath had won his first game against Mr Powell in all the years of championship hatred they had played against one another.

*

Mr Humphrey Atkins, the Deputy Foreign Secretary, made a statement about what was going on in Poland. He knew no more than the rest of us about what was going on in Poland. One has had occasion in the past, in this space, to express gratitude for Mr Atkins's lack of exceptional intelligence. It means that he cannot be clever about the grave matters concerning war and peace with which he must deal. He can only confine himself to broad expressions of common sense.

In contrast, the Opposition Shadow, Mr Denis Healey, does have an exceptional intelligence. Yesterday he rose in reply to Mr Atkins's amiable platitudes, and talked knowledgeably about the extreme fragility of the Polish economy caused by the readiness, or otherwise, of Western banks to reschedule Poland's debts.

'Agreement has already been reached at technical level between the banks and governments concerned in such a rescheduling. It was due to have taken place during the next week or so,' he added, expertly.

In reply, Mr Atkins kept his nerve. He did not quite let on that he had no head for stuff like the rescheduling of debts. Indeed, he agreed with Mr Healey that it was an important matter. But one suspected that, like all non-brilliant people, he knew that there was only one matter of concern at the moment: would the Eastern villains invade? So he remained loyal to his platitudes. Like all decent Englishmen, his ignorance of Eastern Europe is probably encyclopaedic. From all over the House, Members put questions to him designed to demonstrate how much they knew about the place. Would he agree that the ban on meetings was a breach of the Helsinki Accords? Could he assure us that the Nato allies would act in unity? Would he oppose any reversal of the reforms of August, 1980? All this was hurled in the direction of a decent sort like Mr Atkins, who probably thinks that *Rude Pravo* is an improper Czechoslovakian comedian, or at best a defected male ballet dancer. One's heart went out to him.

You may inquire: what was the British Government doing making a statement about Poland in any case? What can the British Government do about Poland? You may further inquire: what can the British Government do about Britain? But that raises wider issues.

Mr Enoch Powell scoffed away at all suggestions that it was anything to do with us. The real answer to him was that the statement was being made because it was expected of us—as are all manner of illogical things in this life. But Mr Powell, another brilliant brain, has no time for that kind of reasoning.

Mr James Wellbeloved pledged 'the full support of the SDP'. One recalled that there had been a 'Clement Attlee' Brigade, drawn from the Labour Party, in the Spanish Civil War. Perhaps all those fat academics and junior managers who comprise the SDP would be forming a 'Debbie Owen Brigade' to come to Poland's aid. Mr Winston Churchill the Younger said Britain had once 'drawn the sword' to preserve Polish freedom. Mr Healey got up to say that the Member's grandfather had 'put Poland in the Soviet sphere of influence'.

The furious mini-Churchill got up again and said that under the Yalta Agreement, Stalin had agreed to free elections. He thus depicted his grandfather as a rather more gullible statesman than one suspects was the case. On his way out, Mr Churchill walked over to Mr Healey and called him a liar. *****

*

Mr Norman Tebbit, the Secretary for Employment, announced his new training and special employment measures. Labour Members proceeded on the assumption that the Tories were not genuinely interested in this sort of thing. Yet less than three years ago, Mr Tebbit was generally considered to be virtually unemployable. He used to hang about below the gangway, getting into scraps with that Dennis Skinner (Bolsover, Labour). Under the Thatcher training and special employment measures, he is now a Cabinet Minister. So it can be done.

Mr Tebbit is now the complete master of his craft. He moved through forty-five minutes of hostile questioning without encountering the slightest difficulty from his enemies—many of whom are on the Labour benches. Once he used to mutter well-turned, sometimes insulting, asides at Labour Ministers from his seat among a group of Tory right-wingers: the Chamber's notorious blue light district. Now, superbly well-briefed, he delivers alarmingly articulate replies to supplementary questions. One is getting a little worried about him. Sometimes he finds himself saying outlandishly respectable things such as, at one stage yesterday: 'If the hon. gentleman would allow me to finish I might be able to answer his question, which he has not had the courtesy to ask except from a sedentary position.' That came from a man who was once a master of the sedentary position: a man who could have written a whole Kama Sutra on the sedentary position.

The burden of yesterday's Labour complaint against Mr Tebbit's measures was that they did not go far enough. This is an infallible sign that they are not much different from what Labour would have done. There is, however, a school of thought which says that Labour would have done nothing, since when they were in office they only published a couple of White Papers on the subject. But we will be charitable and assume that yesterday they were simply being hypocritical. ***

'This morning I had a call from a lady in Salford,' was the somewhat conversation-stopping confession of Mr Frank Allaun (Labour, Salford East). At first one assumed that the exchange had begun with Mr Allaun exclaiming: 'I thought I told you never to ring me at work.' But it turned out that this lady from Salford was protesting in advance about Mr Tebbit's youth training scheme. She was concerned about the financial arrangements involved, Mr Allaun said. They meant that young people were being virtually forced on to the scheme. 'She said it was like the Hitler Youth, and would lead to riots,' he excitedly added.

One tends to find that strange women who telephone one from places like Salford *are* apt to say rather distasteful things. Mr Allaun should have stalled for time while the police traced the call. But apparently he rather liked it, for he told the House that she was quite right about all that Hitler stuff. This cry of 'compulsion' was taken up by other Labour Members, particularly on the Left. They included Mr Allan Roberts, of Bootle. Every time he gets up, people are tempted to drag up the fact that he was the one who went on a delegation to Soviet-occupied Afghanistan and reported back that he saw no tanks. The temptation to drag that up has again not been resisted, for the incident is proof that being too left-wing can damage your eyesight. After Mr Roberts came out with 'compulsion', Mr Tebbit indulged in a welcome relapse into his days of unemployment below the gangway. When he wanted to see compulsion, he looked behind the iron curtain, he said—'to the places on which the hon. Member is an expert'.

A noisy complaint about delay in implementing the measures came from Mr Faulds, the Labour Member who is also a professional actor, or the professional actor who is also a Labour Member, or the professional actor who is always a professional actor. Mr Tebbit accused him of 'only acting up as usual'.

The Minister swiftly resumed his loftier manner, and rebuked a sedentary Mr Skinner for muttering 'stinks' in relation to Mr Tebbit's policy in general. On hearing the rebuke, Mr Eric Varley, the Opposition spokesman, muttered: 'That's what you used to do.'

*

Parliament returned from its recess, and at the start of the sitting the Chamber was cut off by Wales. A dense, impassable blanket of Welsh affairs was the subject of the opening Question Time.

Welsh Question Time is difficult to approach at the best of times. As a race, the Welsh seem peculiarly given to lamentation and to blaming their plight on others. That is perhaps what makes them so good in the chorus of the Hebrew slaves in their National Opera Company's revivals of Verdi's *Nabucco*.

But yesterday the fact that the House had been away for three weeks meant that there were enormous, pent-up reserves of their national despair to be loosed off in the direction of Mr Nicholas Edwards, Secretary of State for Wales, and his junior ministers. So Welsh Question Time was even more Welsh than usual. The Welsh Members, nearly all of whom represent the Labour interest, sighed and moaned their way liltingly through their well-loved chorus, the central theme of which is that the Principality's unemployment, housing problems, relatively low educational achievements, infant mortality, and snow (some of the subjects touched on) are all caused by English Tories.

The Secretary of State for Wales was reasonably rational in dealing with all this. But, being a Tory, he is not really a Welshman. The Tories are short on Welshmen. At least his constituency, Pembroke, is in Wales. When they first had to fill the Secretary of State's office, after it was created by Labour in 1964, the Tories put in a man who sat for warm, emotional, Celtic, coal-mining Hendon, South.

Mr Edwards did his best. But his Opposition shadow, Mr Alec Jones, was the real thing. 'What has happened in the last fortnight is something few people in Wales have seen in their lives,' he bewailed. That was presumably a reference to snow.

That sort of shameless exaggeration is what we expect of a Welsh politician. It is what we, the English public, go to Welsh Question Time for. The Secretary of State replied: 'Responsibility for dealing with emergencies in the first instance falls primarily on the local authorities,' which is not the right tone at all.

We moved on to Welsh education. And Mr Jones could be heard sorrowing over the fact that under the Tories 'Nine hundred less teachers are engaged in Wales.' If one might make an élitist, grammatical observation, what he meant was nine hundred *fewer* teachers. But, no doubt because of the English Tories at the time, Mr Jones endured certain educational disadvantages in early life. According to his *Who's Who* entry, he was forced to earn a living as a teacher.

Welsh Question Time continued without let-up. Experts said it could go on for days. Matters were not helped by the fact that Members taking part tend to be called, in the case of the Member for Caernarfon, Dafydd when they could just as well be called David or, in the case of the Member for Caerphilly, Ednyfed when they could much more easily be called Edna, though the Member for Caerphilly might object to the latter simplification on the ground that he is a man.

*

Members debated an Opposition motion headed: 'Higher Fuel Bills Following Extreme Weather'.

The Labour Party had presumably thought it was about time it condemned extremism. A search went on for a form of extremism which did not command substantial support within the party's ranks. That left only extreme weather. The motion should be seen in the context of the endless search for Labour unity. *** Mr Christopher Price, a Labour back-bencher, produced at Question Time the subject of a man who got sent to prison for writing a cheque 'on the carcass of a dead rat'.

Mr Price said the man wrote the cheque on the dead rat to draw attention to his rat-infested property. A cheque written on a rat was legal tender, Mr Price insisted. In fact, it was legal tender to write a cheque on 'any substance, however distasteful', he assured us. We all did it all the time, we were left to assume.

The thought occurred that perhaps the man therefore went to prison, not for contempt but for passing a forged rat. Or perhaps there were not enough rat carcasses in his account to cover the sum. One was sure there was some such logical explanation.

Mr Price produced another man. He got sent to prison for not standing up straight in court. At this a Tory voice muttered: 'Quite right.' The eye searched the Tory benches for the mutterer. He would have to be someone devoid of ambition and not one of those Tories always trying to get written up by the liberal prints as one of the more compassionate Conservatives. That narrowed the search down to Mr Anthony Fell. One's apologies to Mr John Stokes, who was also present, if it was he.

Replying to Mr Price on the rat cheque issue, the Attorney General said: 'The only one I know about involved toilet paper.' Also, the other man was sent to prison not because he would not stand up straight, but because he would not stand up at all. This clarified the situation all round.

Returning to the debate about extremism in the weather, could it really be that there was still a Victorian cult of death flourishing among small savers? Were folk being denied a decent burial because they were having to spend their funeral savings on fuel bills on account of the Tories' £300 rule? Hardly anyone believed a word of it. But the idea cheered up the Labour Party no end.

The desire of the British Railways Board to introduce 'flexible rostering' met with determined opposition, and ultimately strike action, from the train-drivers' union, ASLEF, whose members were concerned at the idea of changing working conditions which had been established at the end of the First World War.

For the second day running, and third time in a week, Mr Leslie Huckfield, the Labour Member for Nuneaton and an Aslef-sponsored back-bencher, rose at the end of Question Time. He unsuccessfully sought an emergency debate in order that he might put the union's case in the present rail dispute.

Mr Huckfield is therefore the only Aslef-driven service which at present can be relied upon to run. Every afternoon these days, no matter what the weather, the Nuneaton Flyer, one of the famed Vested Interest class of locomotive, leaves the back benches.

But each afternoon, in the great traditions of the union he is proud to serve, the service is subject to some unavoidable delay. The Speaker always refuses to grant the emergency debate.

Furthermore, there are always natural disasters which impede the journey. These take the form of various Conservative back-benchers. Yesterday, for example, Mr Robert Adley, a Tory back-bencher, after the Speaker had spurned Mr Huckfield yet again, demanded:

'Is it in order for *Hansard* to contain every day a one-sided account of this dispute when nobody has sought, rightly, to deal with the case from the other side?'

The short answer to Mr Adley's question is: yes. The outlawing by the Speaker of one-sided arguments would lead to the end of parliament as we know it. But the Speaker put it more gently. He said he was looking into the procedure for the use of emergency debates. 'I intend to use my discretion when it is necessary,' he added darkly.

Mr Robert Atkins, the Conservative Member for Preston, North, rose on a point of order to point out that according to the MPs' register of interests Mr Huckfield was sponsored by the Transport and General Workers' Union, but also represented Aslef in the House. Did that not imply a conflict of interest? Mr Huckfield intervened to say that both were included by him in the register of interests. Furthermore, both unions thought it was all right, we gathered.

What is it in Mr Huckfield's background, we asked ourselves, that made him so sought-after a champion of the proletariat? A glance at *Who's Who* revealed that he had followed the craft of lecturer in economics, so perhaps it was his experience of unskilled labour.

The Speaker observed: 'In the last parliament I had occasion to comment then about the necessity of not abusing our emergency debate procedure'—a remark which amounted to the threat of a national shutdown of the entire Huckfield service. The public should watch announcements in this space to see whether Mr Huckfield runs in future.

Elsewhere during yesterday's proceedings, Mr Clement Freud, the Liberal unsuccessfully seeking leave to bring in, no doubt for some fell purpose, a Bill making it unnecessary for the Speaker to be elected to the House, quoted 'Marshal Clemenceau'. The difficulty here was that Clemenceau was never a marshal. Indeed, he was not even a soldier. Mr Freud may have had in mind a chap named Clemenceau who was the doorman at the Playboy Club, but he probably was not even a Frenchman. Furthermore Mr Freud, perhaps distracted by Mr Dennis Skinner's heckle of 'get back to t'roulette wheel', forgot to add the punch line of the quote. So the military figure he was thinking about during his speech must have been General Chaos.

*

Yesterday saw the debate to which Opposition MPs of all parties had been looking forward for more than two-and-a-half years, the one about the three million unemployed. But first some travel news: for the first time in three days, a speech by the Aslef-sponsored Mr Leslie Huckfield (Nuneaton, Labour), was cancelled yesterday. Throughout the dispute, Aslef has, for humanitarian reasons, maintained this essential service. Mr Huckfield has puffed his way out of the back benches at the end of question time. You could set your watch by him. But yesterday, come departure time, and we, the long-suffering public, were let down. No Huckfield in sight. Had he allowed himself to be intimidated by Tory protests that he was abusing the procedures of the House? Or was it that, in a sharp escalation of its tactics in the dispute, Aslef was not even prepared to run its MPs? You will be kept informed.

*

Sex shops were the subject of the main debate yesterday. Earlier in the day the Common Market reared its ugly head. But first, in response to reader demand, the latest details of the availability of the tireless Mr Leslie Huckfield. Non-Huckfield-users should be reminded that he is the Aslef-sponsored Labour back-bencher who regularly gets up and, disguised as someone asking for an emergency debate on the rail dispute, manages to make a small speech in defence of the Aslef case before being refused the debate by the Speaker. Mr Huckfield was again the only Aslef service running in the whole of Britain yesterday. It is a proud record. He will be getting his long-service gold watch soon.

Mr Huckfield's speech departs at the end of Question Time. Unfortunately, no sooner had he got under way yesterday, than he encountered a certain amount of vandalism on the line from Mr Tristan Garel-Jones, the Conservative Member for commuter-intensive Watford, where feeling against Mr Huckfield must be running high. Every time the service has run, some Tory or other has got up to complain to the Speaker that it is an abuse of the procedures of the House. Each time the Speaker, though with no great enthusiasm, has allowed Mr Huckfield to proceed on his journey. But Mr Garel-Jones had devised a new way of delaying the run. He had remembered that, though still the Member for Nuneaton, Mr Huckfield had managed to get himself adopted for the safe Labour seat of Wigan. On both sides of the House it is considered by many to be bad form to change constituencies in this way. The general view is that there is nothing wrong with looking for a safe seat, provided you have already lost an unsafe one.

'On a point of order, Mr Speaker,' Mr Garel-Jones asked: 'The hon. Member has been referred to as the hon. Member for Nuneaton, but should he not be called the hon. Member for Wigan?' This was simply another Tory attempt to bring chaos to the whole Huckfield network. Mr Garel-Jones was just hitting the public. It was sheer bloody-mindedness.

The Speaker briskly told Mr Garel-Jones that that was not a point of order. Whereupon, the 3.45 Huckfield, changing at Wigan, rose from the Labour back benches.

Mr Huckfield, in accordance with tradition laid down since the beginning of the dispute, applied for an emergency debate on 'the failure of the British Rail Board to honour its agreement to pay all railwaymen a three percent increase from January of this year and the consequences for industry and the travelling public'.

Mr Huckfield's very formal manner recaptured some of the pomp and grandeur of the industry which will be fondly remembered by older readers. He is a reminder of an age when men were proud to work on the railways, when station masters wore bowler hats incessantly, when children fancied that the very rails on which the train travelled were repeatedly spelling out the name of their destination. We romantics in the gallery fancied we heard the rails carrying Mr Huckfield along, reverberating with their message of 'we're going to Wigan, we're going to Wigan'.

But angry commuters on the Tory back benches began to take the law into their own hands. Mr Huckfield was menaced with cries of 'sit down', 'shut up, for God's sake', and 'we've had enough'. Inevitably the Speaker once more refused him his debate.

On the Common Market and sex shops, Mr Dennis Canavan (Stirlingshire West, Labour) sought leave to bring in a Bill to close down the former. His proposed measure withdrawing Britain from the EEC was defeated by 212 votes to 110. Later one went into the debate on the Government's plan to license sex shops, though improperly dressed, for one lacked the customary grubby raincoat.

The premises were denounced in all parts of the House. 'Sex shops regard women as objects and not as rounded personalities,' said Mr Roland Moyle (Lewisham East, Labour), though some of us were under the impression that sex shops regarded women solely as rounded personalities. Mr Timothy Raison, the Minister in charge of the Bill, referred to 'the pornography industry'. There was no pornography-sponsored Member to put the industry's case. Sex awaits its Huckfield.

*

Conservatives and Labour, at the height of the debate on the Government's trade union reform Bill, at last satisfied the demands of moderate folk and stopped attacking one another. They attacked the moderate folk instead.

The latter were represented by Mr William Rodgers, of the SDP. He rose to put his party's official policy on the Bill, which is to vote for it. This policy has caused a revolt among the working-class rank and file of the parliamentary Social Democratic Party: Mr Eric Ogden and Mr John Grant. (Mr Ogden, before his election as Labour Member, was a miner. Mr Grant worked at the wordface as a Fleet Street industrial correspondent.)

This split, following as it did the opinion poll at the weekend which showed a fall in the SDP-Liberal Alliance lead over the other two parties, had raised Tory and Labour spirits enormously. They set upon Mr Rodgers the moment he rose. He began by regretting that Mr Norman Tebbit, the Secretary for Employment, and Mr Eric Varley, the Shadow Secretary, had indulged in the 'old-style cat and dog fight' in the speeches they had made opening the debate. This priggish attitude enraged the two brutish factions facing each other across the Chamber. *** 'I am happy to encourage them to behave in the traditional way,' Mr Rodgers added, managing to be more insufferable still. This was a very bad Government, Mr Rodgers argued (Labour cheers). On the other hand, that did not mean that this was a bad Bill (Tory cheers). Furthermore, he had no time for Mr Tebbit (silent cheers from between roughly a quarter and half the Cabinet).

Mr Rodgers launched into a detailed discussion of what was wrong with the unions. In particular, he thought there was a lot to be said for people being required to contract into paying the political levy. Mr Frank Haynes (Ashfield, Labour) started to contribute a second opinion. 'Did ya say that when ya were on the Government front bench?' he rasped.

Mr Haynes kept this up rather admirably for some time. Suddenly, Mr Rodgers made the error of saying: 'I want to be honest with the House.' At this, there was much ribaldry, particularly from Mr Haynes. Mr Rodgers told him to listen because he might learn something. 'Carry on. I'm learning all the time,' observed Mr Haynes.

'I'm a recent convert to this kind of legislation,' Mr Rodgers continued, amid renewed ribaldry. Whereupon, Mr Haynes muttered something unparliamentary. Mr Arthur Lewis (Newham North West, Labour) was unsure whether many of us had heard it.

So Mr Lewis repeated it. Being a considerable parliamentarian, however, he devised a way of doing so without either getting into trouble with the Speaker himself, or being disloyal to his colleague Mr Haynes.

'Mr Speaker, is it in order, even if it might be true, to call someone a "twister"?' asked Mr Lewis on a point of order devious even by his standards.

The Speaker replied that he had not heard what 'the hon. Member for Mansfield,' had said. Mr Haynes rose. 'I'm the Member for Ashfield, not Mansfield,' Mr Haynes explained.

'I hope that's *all* the hon. Member is saying,' the Speaker replied in his most censorious, 'wet Sunday in Wales', tone of voice.

Mr Ian Mikardo, of the Old Left, rose on a point of order. (That was all we needed!) It could not be out of order to call anyone a 'twister' because that was an honoured, occupational term in the textile industry, Mr Mikardo helpfully explained.

'Everyone must speak for his own industry,' the Speaker commented with a slight hint of impatience added to the Welsh.

(Though he may well choose to depict himself as some sort of humble handloom weaver when the mood takes him, Mr Mikardo has no known connexion with the textile industry—which was yet another agreeably surrealist touch to these exchanges.)

By now, people had rather lost interest in Mr Rodgers' views on the reform of the unions. These views may well have been admirable, but long may men of ability, moderation and knowledge fall foul of the likes of Mr Lewis and Mr Haynes in the British House of Commons. Otherwise they would be even worse.

*

Transport and road safety were the subjects of yesterday's main debate. So beforehand, to put us in the mood, a Conservative back-bencher asked Mrs Margaret Thatcher to ease the tax on whisky.

Mr David Myles, the back-bencher, a tenant hill farmer who represents Banff, is one of the few Tories with a Scottish accent, most of the others tending to speak in the simple, picturesque, rude tones of the wild Kensington-Chelsea border country. That is because the few Scottish Conservatives in captivity tend to be far more up-market than their English colleagues. Mr Myles, however, is the real thing. So, for long stretches, he is incomprehensible.

At Prime Minister's Question Time, he gurgled and rumbled his way through a lengthy reminiscence of the time when Mrs Thatcher paid a visit to a whisky distillery at Glen . . . Glen . . . Glen. Members consulted one another. Glen where? No one seemed to know. The up-market Scots were probably no help. It could have been Glenn Miller for all they knew. Mr Myles continued happily on his way. 'Will she recall the visit she made to the Glen-gurgle distillery . . . taxation . . . jeopardize jobs . . . malting, blending and bottling plants.' He ended with a rousing call to Mrs Thatcher on behalf of 'the doyen of the drinking trade'. This was taken by many of us at first to be a reference to some exceptionally bottled back-bencher. It turned out to be a reference to the whisky industry itself.

Mrs Thatcher, conscious of the drinking-class vote, was quick to assure the House that taxation on whisky was lower under her Government. The Labour Party was unsure whether to deny or deplore this. Traditionally, Labour Members are unclear about where they stand on whisky, though in the headquarters hotel bar at the party conference some of them do not stand on it at all. So some Members denied Mrs Thatcher's claim, others deplored it.

The questioning turned to the subject of Sir Freddie Laker. Here was a subject on which Labour Members could agree. Sir Freddie is something of a lad; despite his present troubles, he manifestly enjoys life; and he is a folk hero of the working class. So Labour Members loathe him.

Mr John Rathbone, the Conservative MP for Lewes, asked for a two-month extension of the Laker company's air operator's certificate and route licences. Mrs Thatcher prefaced her reply with the observation: 'I can well understand the hon. Member's concern. As he knows, I'm a Freddie Laker fan.' This was regarded on the Labour benches as hilarious, preposterous, incipiently Fascist and so on. It took some time for the laughter and ironic cheers to die away. The Labour Party was now in a thoroughly good mood. Not only had someone's business collapsed, but that someone was liked by the Prime Minister.

Nothing could take away from Sir Freddie the fact that he brought cheap travel to millions, the Prime Minister added amid further Opposition hilarity. Mr Robert Cryer, Keighley's Labour Member, shouted that Mr Ken Livingstone was also trying to bring cheap travel to millions. Actually, Mr Livingstone is trying to bring cheap travel *paid for* by millions. But no matter; Sir Freddie's fall had given a lot of simple pleasure to the Labour Members which it would be churlish to deny them.

In the end, it is probably simply a question of manner. The

Labour Party is simply not at home with people like Sir Freddie. If he had managed to close down his airline by calling it out on strike he would be more popular with them; it is just a question of the right way of going about things. Labour Members are far more at home with their Shadow Minister of Transport, Mr Albert Booth, who spoke in the transport debate and launched an attack on the Government's modest proposal to privatize parts of the National Bus Company. Albert Booth! The very name suggests solidity, lack of risk and the static concept of transport. 'Hi, I'm Albert, fly me.' No, it doesn't sound right. 'Booth Airways.' Definitely not. Here was the sort of provider of transport with whom the Labour Party could do business.

*

Prime Minister's Question Time being an occasion on which anyone can raise virtually anything, Mrs Thatcher yesterday challenged Mr Foot to say whether he backed the activities of Aslef. Taking up the challenge, Mr Foot immediately replied by demanding whether she backed the activities of El Salvador. Mrs Thatcher struck back with a reference to the support being given to Aslef by Mr Albert Booth, the Shadow Secretary for Transport. Mr Foot retorted with a reference to her support for the El Salvador policy of President Reagan. These exchanges went on for some minutes amid Tory cries of 'What about El Buckton?' and Labour ripostes about American imperialism. Not only did the two parties disagree about the policy, which is perfectly understandable and indeed essential, but they could not agree about the subject.

This congestion occasionally happens during the rush-quarter-hour of Prime Minister's Question Time because it is permissible for a Member simply to ask the Prime Minister to list her engagements for the day. This allows the Member to ask her about virtually anything by the device of requesting her to find time during her day to consider the subject. In supplementary questions other Members can use the same tactic. It is an admirable system.

Yesterday she listed her engagements at the request of Mr Robin Squire, the Conservative Member for Hornchurch. Mr Squire rose and asked Mrs Thatcher to deplore Mr Booth's support for the terror-backed Aslef régime which was threatening the stability of Hornchurch and the whole Essex sub-continent.

Mr Booth had said that the Labour Party was backing Aslef, according to Mr Squire. Then, in a masterly demagogic flourish intended to appeal to the passions of the crazed commuters of

Hornchurch, Mr Squire said that a lot of other people would 'like to get behind Mr Buckton, albeit with a different aim'.

Mrs Thatcher replied by placing herself at the head of the struggling masses of the First World as epitomized by the oppressed commuters of Hornchurch. 'Many commuters are making heroic efforts to get to work,' she told the House. Her remarks were a reaffirmation of the historic links that had always existed between the Conservative Party and the peoples of South-West Essex.

Feeling against Aslef—and its lackey, the Labour front bench—was now running high on the Tory side, as it is in the country. No wonder, when he rose, Mr Michael Foot preferred to talk about El Salvador.

El Salvador is a matter about which the Government, let alone the Opposition, can do nothing, It therefore suited Mr Foot's purposes yesterday to perfection. He protested about the murders being committed by the El Salvador junta and sought to suggest that the British Government was somehow among those to blame. Mrs Thatcher replied: 'With regard to the first part of the question, it is a matter for Acas.' As a matter of fact, neither in the first nor subsequent parts of his question, had Mr Foot talked about Acas. He was talking about El Salvador. Mrs Thatcher was presumably still thinking about the Hornchurch Member's question.

'There will be elections on March 28,' the Prime Minister added. 'Other countries are being invited to send observers.' Free elections in Aslef? Never! But it turned out she was talking about El Salvador. Mr Foot rose once more and said the event of March 28 would be 'a murderous farce'. Agreed, but one must hope that the strikes will be over by then.

*

Mr Teddy Taylor, the Conservative Member for Southend East, and Sir William Clark, that for Croydon South, yesterday demanded corporal punishment from the Home Secretary (for other people, presumably: nothing strange about those two, one hopes). Sir Albert Costain, Folkestone and Hythe's Conservative representative, put in a good word for castration (though only rapists need apply). And Mr Alan Clark, the Conservative MP for Plymouth, Sutton, protested to the Prime Minister about 'gangs of up to fifty young blacks looting shops in broad daylight'. On a more violent note, the House was menaced by a lobby organized by the ferociously-entitled 'National Pensioners Convention steering committee'.

But first, for enthusiasts for the age of steam, news of Mr Leslie Huckfield, the Labour Member for Nuneaton. It had been a long time since he had been taken out of his shed. He was the pride of the Nuneaton-Wigan run. Time was when he would steam out at the end of Question Time with those applications for an emergency debate into the rail dispute, and folk would hurry down to watch his pro-Aslef propaganda whistle past before he was ruled out of order by the Speaker.

Well, yesterday was Aslef's day of victory. And we enthusiasts of the Huckfield and District Railway Society organized a special run. Mr Huckfield came into sight during the routine Thursday questions to Mr Pym, the Leader of the House, on the business for next week. 'Is the Leader of the House aware that the settlement in the railway dispute provides a complete vindication of the position which Aslef has maintained throughout the dispute,' he began. Puff, puff, puff, went Mr Huckfield happily. And that was only his chest. 'As a result of the settlement, the British Rail Board has gained nothing that it could not have had last July,' he continued. 'Could the Leader of the House arrange for a statement next week on the future policy of the railway industry and on the future policy of the chairman?'

Mr Pym tried to fob him off with the usual patter of defeated Ministers after strikes, that it was 'a great mistake to talk about a complete vindication of anyone'. But no one believed that, least of all the exultant Mr Huckfield and his victims, the back-benchers of the commuter-front organization: the Conservative Party. The latter howled at Mr Huckfield as he sped by.

The rout of British Rail had demoralized the Tory back-benchers. Their morale slumped still further when, during questions to Home Office Ministers on the subject of rising crime, Mr Whitelaw and his colleagues were unable to offer corporal punishment to Mr Taylor and Sir William.

Mr Flannery, a Labour left-winger, shouted 'miserable re-actionary' and 'slave owner' at Sir William. It was perhaps to restore a less controversial atmosphere that Sir Albert advocated castration instead. He asked Mr Mayhew, the Minister of State, whether his attention had been drawn to a letter sent to the Home Office 'by a constituent of mine suggesting that rape is such a dreadful crime that castration is the only proper remedy'. Passions were running so high on the Tory benches yesterday, after Aslef's rape of Sir Peter Parker, that Mr Mayhew, a lawyer with a nice line in caution, replied that while sympathizing with the constituent's sense of abhorrence, 'I think there might be certain practical problems.' This seemed to reassure Sir Albert.

But virtually the whole afternoon was taken up with talk of muggings and thugs demanding money from old people—a subject only marginally less frightening for MPs than old people demanding money from MPs, which was the aim of that steering committee lurching round the building with a gang of determined old folk at the wheel. One terrified old age pensioner, Mr Michael Foot, felt it prudent to join the gang. Three times during Prime Minister's Questions he got up in an effort to prove that the pensioners were worse off under the Tories. Forewarned of the Grey Terror loose in the area, Mrs Thatcher came armed with a cudgel made of solid statistics. After their third exchange, she exasperatedly demanded of Mr Foot: 'The right hon. Gentleman has heard my reply. Which of the facts therein does he disagree with?'

Mr Foot has never been strong on facts. So wisely he replied from a seated position: 'All of them.'

*

A Conservative back-bencher accused Mr Dennis Skinner's election agent of having bought his own council house.

We were all stunned. It was an imputation of blasphemy second only to a suggestion that Mr Skinner himself could be capable of making so base a purchase. But it was awful enough. For here was an accusation that Mr Skinner, Bolsover's Labour MP, spiritual leader of Britain's millions of extreme, fundamentalist proletarians, was harbouring close to his person, indeed in his very entourage, someone who had availed himself of Conservative wider home ownership legislation.

The wretch who made the charge was Mr John Heddle, the Conservative Member for Lichfield and Tamworth. He did so in the guise of a question to the Prime Minister. A terrible scene ensued. For Mr Skinner was present, seated in the place below the gangway from which he had conducted his years of struggle against all bourgeois forms of government. Mr Heddle made his accusation against someone whom 'the hon. Member for Bolsover employs as a political agent'.

The Tory benches broke into cheers at this amazing news. Mr Skinner suddenly sat upright, chin held high—the whole effect being one of affronted dignity probably not seen in public life since the death of Queen Victoria. He rose. Alas, Mr Michael Foot rose at the same time. The Speaker called Mr Foot. Mr Skinner remained standing. He remonstrated with the Chair, though in the noise it was impossible to hear his words. The Speaker told him that that Question Time had only just begun, the implication being that once Mr Foot had spoken Mr Skinner would shortly have an opportunity to defend himself against a charge which, if left unanswered, would destroy the faith of Mr Skinner's humble followers throughout the length and breadth of Bolsover and even further. But Mr Skinner could not possibly wait that long. Eventually, his words reached us. It was as if he was appealing to us in the gallery to send reassurance as soon as possible to the demoralized masses.

'I 'aven't *got* an agent,' he shouted.

He resumed his seat. Mr Foot began to put some rather tedious questions about the Budget. Mr Skinner shouted to him across the gangway to refute the awful charge. 'I am sure my hon. friend can look after himself,' Mr Foot inadequately commented. Eventually, from the Chair, came the cry of: 'Mr Dennis Skinner.' Mr Skinner rose once more. Drawing on all his authority, he ruled: 'Is the Prime Minister aware that I haven't got an agent, and that the person referred to is no longer on the executive of the Bolsover constituency Labour Party?'

From Mr Skinner's words—and like all great mystics he tends to speak in parables—it was clear that there *had* been someone who had made an evil purchase, someone (darkly described as 'the person referred to') with a recusant desire for, say, his own chiming door bell or privately-owned plastic garden gnome. But he was '*no longer on the executive*'. What a wealth of damnation was contained in those simple words.

Mention of which brings one to Mr Frank Haynes, the Labour MP for Ashfield, who, on a point of order, later reminded the Speaker that the Chair had last week rebuked him for using the term 'What the hell!' In that case, asked Mr Haynes, why had not the Speaker rebuked a Tory who had said that Western European countries involved in the Siberian gas pipeline had 'sold their souls to the devil'? The Speaker simply repeated that references to trips to hell were not approved of by him—or presumably by Him.

Mention of hell led naturally to the committee stage of the Canada Bill. Dante, author of the standard guide book to hell, missed a trick by not including in one of the innermost circles those whose punishment was to listen for all eternity to Mr Enoch Powell explaining during the committee stage why the Canada Bill was a paradoxical absurdity.

Mr Powell and the all-party opponents of the Bill have mounted a filibuster. Their aim is to speak for the rest of eternity. There will therefore be a more detailed account in this column later in eternity.

*

A Welshman appeared in the Commons after an affray late last Thursday involving drink. He was Nicholas Edwards, aged forty-eight, who gave his occupation as Secretary of State for Wales. 'I wish to make a personal statement,' he said. The statement was about what he described as 'an incident' during a series of interventions at the end of the debate on Welsh affairs last Thursday. 'I would like to apologize to the honourable Member for Rhondda for suggesting that he might have been drinking, a suggestion which was unjustified and which of course I withdraw,' he said. 'I would like to apologize to you, Mr Speaker, for making your task more difficult by a remark from a sedentary position that was out of order.' What was out of order? The remark or the sedentary position? From the sentence, this was unclear. No matter. No Minister should be held responsible for his syntax. This is one of the first principles of our legal system. Long may it remain so.

Where was I? Ah yes, Edwards in a sedentary position. To continue. 'I hope,' said the defendant, 'that St David's Day is an appropriate moment to make amends.' Edwards was wearing a daffodil in his left lapel.

The Speaker accepted the apology. Mr Edwards was allowed to go. Being a Welshman, the Speaker may have noticed that daffodil. Perhaps it is a code among the Welsh, like certain signs are among Freemasons. But one prefers to think that Mr Edwards was simply being given a chance to start a new life. For no man should be blamed for what he does in a sedentary position.

Presumably, the case arose out of a complaint from the Shadow Secretary of State, the Member for Rhondda, the one accused of being drunk. The Welsh are said to be a suspicious race. Let us hope he took the right course of action. Certainly, had he kept quiet about the incident, hardly anyone would have known about it, as a Welsh affairs debate late on a Thursday evening is not peak viewing time. Furthermore, like most Welshmen, the Shadow Secretary is named Jones. It could have been any one of them. Still, Mr Jones seemed happy as Mr Edwards sat down yesterday. Next case.

That turned out to be Mr Gerald Kaufman, the Shadow Secretary for the Environment. He appeared to be driving under the influence of ideology. He demanded an emergency debate on the proposed tour of South Africa by Mr Geoffrey Boycott's cricket team.

The essence of Mr Kaufman's argument was that the tour was

wrong because it was to a part of Africa where whites oppressed blacks. It was not clear whether he was equally opposed to tours in parts of Africa where blacks oppressed blacks which is most other parts. One suspects not. That is not the Labour Party's tipple. Still, Mr Kaufman sang happily away at the Dispatch Box about members of the hated tour 'selling themselves for blood-covered krugerrands'.

The Speaker declined the emergency debate. But Mr Kaufman had registered another success. **✱✱✱**

In March, a cricket tour of South Africa caused a flurry.

'Maggie Fury at South Africa Cricket Tour' said a headline in the *Sun*. Other morning newspapers had variously described the Prime Minister as dismayed, and concerned and angry. Some of us went into Prime Minister's Question Time, then, with foreboding, being dismayed and concerned at her anger. For that is not what we regard her as being for. We like her fury to be directed at the great liberal causes. But it turned out that all was well. Throughout the exchanges she bore the rebellious cricketers' action with marked composure. She preferred to dwell on the importance of allowing citizens of a free country to travel where they liked. This, for a minority of us, is the true issue. So the Maggie Fury at South Africa Tour was presumably that day's page three girl, a descendant perhaps of the pop artiste of old, Billy Fury. ('Maggie's ambition is to travel. She will be in South Africa for the cricket tour.')

It was an historic Question Time. Mrs Thatcher presumably entered *Wisden* by becoming the first Prime Minister to bat steadily through an entire Commons uproar without once supporting the Government. The pedantic may object that she is the government. Well, not always. All the evidence suggests that she regards the government as a vast force with a life of its own. It is entirely made up of such uncontrollable phenomena as Sports Ministers who have no alternative but to denounce cricket tours of South Africa, and various spokesmen who have to put it about that she is 'concerned' about such visits to forbidden lands.

For these purposes, she tends to include the official Opposition, much of the press, and the BBC as part of the government; certainly the SDP is included, indeed she probably sees it as the permanent government.

But, like Mao Tse-Tung, every now and then she generates

cultural revolution against the régime over which she nominally presides. Such an occasion was yesterday. The right-winger Mr Nicholas Winterton, the Conservative Member for Macclesfield, rose. He is co-author of a Commons motion congratulating the errant cricketers. He has a loud voice, as befits a man who bullies for England. He demanded that Mrs Thatcher defend the principle that 'any law-abiding citizen of this country has the right to travel where he wants to'.

Some of us more delicate souls might have preferred that our cause be championed by a more *verligte* figure than Mr Winterton, but one cannot always choose one's allies. Matters were not helped by the fact that Mr Winterton is burly, blond, and has a military background.

Mrs Thatcher replied that all citizens were free to travel and no restrictions would be placed upon them. With that, she sat down. There was no condemnation of the tour. It was in this not entirely subtle way that she revealed her lack of fury. One assailed oneself for ever having doubted her. The Labour benches were enraged. Actually, they were delighted. What one means is that they made out they were enraged. Mr Foot rose. He denounced Mr Winterton's motion as 'deeply humiliating to the House of Commons'. He urged her to condemn it. She rose again and repeated that citizens were free to travel. If they were restricted, 'We would no longer be a free country.'

Mr Foot got up again and condemned the Tory motion. Mrs Thatcher returned to her theme about freedom. Some Labour Members shouted at her to condemn the tour. 'Say it, say it,' said others, taking up the cry. She did not. Mr Foot and Mrs Thatcher continued their exchange on the same lines as before. Two Tory wets, Mr Hector Monro, the former Minister for Sport, and Mr Peter Bottomley, did condemn the tour. This intensified the Prime Minister's lack of fury.

The other *Wisden*-type fact to be recorded is who was the first Labour back-bencher to shout 'racialist!' and after how long into Question Time. (Mr Martin Flannery: five minutes.)

*

Mr John Carlisle, the Conservative Member for Luton West, managed to draw the House's attention yesterday to the suggestion that Mr Denis Howell, the Labour spokesman on sport, has been on a football tour of the Soviet Union through it all—the 'all' being the cricket tour of South Africa.

Mr Carlisle and other *verkrampte* back-benchers such as Mr Nicholas Winterton (Macclesfield's Conservative MP) and Mr Tony Marlow (who sits for the same party for Northampton North) have been trying to intrude this priceless, immortal, glorious piece of information into the Commons uproar all week. But such are the rules of order and the haphazard way in which details get into Commons exchanges it sometimes takes days for the rest of us to grasp a point. 'Where's Denis Howell?' these useful Tory brutes have been crying to no effect for some time. Still more obscurely, Mr Winterton demanded from the sedentary position at one stage earlier in the week: 'Tell us about Aston Villa.' (Only now do most of us realize that Mr Howell is apparently visiting the Soviet Union with that famous football club, the Shadow Minister for Sport being a Birmingham Member.)

The Labour benches have been in a moralistic trance all week ever since Mr Gerald Kaufman launched the uproar with his memorably awful phrase about cricketers 'selling themselves for blood-covered krugerrands'. And all the while Mr Howell was travelling amicably in a land which practises several forms of separate development, not least that between the rulers and the rest of the population. Are the Villa getting a share of the gate? Has Mr Howell drunk so much as one tincture of free vodka? If so, there's rouge on these roubles, as Mr Kaufman would put it.

Enormously heartened by Mr Howell's own goal, the Tory back-bench hard types nodded with approval through another classical Thatcher innings yesterday on the issue of the tour. The very first question was on the subject. Mr Jack Straw (the Labour MP for Blackburn) denounced her previous 'mealy-mouthed' and 'half-hearted' batting on the issue: a reference to her memorable overnight stand at question time last Tuesday. Did she now condemn the tour? he demanded. 'Yes or no.' The Prime Minister replied that she stood by 'the Gleneagles agreement'. This has been her tactic throughout the bowling, for hardly anyone can remember what the Gleneagles agreement was. But by yesterday she had become hampered by an irritatingly unequivocal condemnation of the tour by Lord Carrington, the régime's *verligte* Foreign Secretary. So yesterday she went on to say she shared the opinion of Lord Carrington that 'this tour is perhaps a mistake'. (Actually he put it rather more strongly than that.) Mrs Thatcher almost mumbled those words.

It is clear that she hates the whole controversy. Labour started raging. The loyal Sir William Clark (the Conservative Member for Croydon South) tried to change the subject. Mr Foot rose. 'To return to the cricket tour,' he began and rambled into a question which contained the prying phrase 'does the right hon. lady agree with the Foreign Secretary', the correct answer to which is: very rarely. 'The right hon. gentleman cannot have been listening,' she told Mr Foot, assuming a world-weary air. 'I endorsed the Foreign Secretary on this matter in my last reply,' which really she had not. Suddenly, Mr Winston Churchill (Stretford's Conservative MP) bored in with a barrage balloon of loyalty consisting of: 'May I congratulate the Prime Minister on taking the initiative among oil-producing nations to procure a sharp downward trend in oil prices? This provides not only Great Britain, but the industrialized world with the opportunity to break into what Iain Macleod called the virtuous circle in which . . .' There was almost no end to this tremendous conversation stopper.

*

Mrs Renee Short, the left-wing Labour Member for Wolverhampton North East, demanded the overthrow of the British parliamentary system of eating. She asked the representative of the catering sub-committee to 'encourage the provision of low-cholesterol meals in the House'. Her outburst came only a few days after the prospective Labour candidate for Bradford North, Mr Patrick Wall, demanded that a future Labour Government be prepared to overthrow the rest of our ancient institutions such as, presumably, Mr Michael Foot.

Mrs Short's remarks are bound to cause a tremendous row among the overweight, self-indulgent and contented MPs who make up the majority of both main parties. Mr Joe Dean, Labour Member for Leeds West, the representative of the catering sub-committee who answered Mrs Short's question, obviously had no enthusiasm for her violent cause, but such is the power of the middle-class health extremists who are out to take over the country, he thought it prudent to humour her. 'I can give the hon. lady an undertaking that we shall look into the question,' he said.

Mrs Short told him that, while the dangers of full-fat butter were now widely known, many people were unaware of the dangers of full-fat milk. Mr Dean reiterated his assurance that the matter would be looked into. To Tory approval, he added: 'The final outcome may have to be decided by the economics of the situation,' a principle which, if applied by Labour MPs to issues in general, would mean the end of Labour Party policy as we have known it.

Mrs Short's initiative—with its implied threat of muesli, and thin, uncreamy milk—was seen as a move to undermine Parliament by making MPs as miserable as the rest of us, bludgeoned as we are by pro-health propaganda. Mercifully, Mr Alan Clark, Plymouth Sutton's Conservative MP, changed the subject. He complained to Mr Dean about the idea that Members' spouses should be allowed to come into the refreshment rooms at all hours. He had no objection to their being on the premises, but he thought they should stay in the corridors 'rather than disturb our traditional ways'.

Mr Dean pondered his reply. He is a ruddy-faced, Northern engineer. He just *looks* unliberated. He agreed that Mr Clark had a point. 'Members' wives with children might come,' he added, 'and I could see no end of trouble.' In Mr Dean, the *Guardian* women's page will presumably be claiming another victim. In Mrs Short's eyes, Mr Dean had been saying all the wrong things. To satisfy her, he should have promised not just spouses in the smoking room, but crèches for the offspring. Being in favour of watery milk and low-cholesterol food, she is bound to be pro-crèche. Though there is no logical connexion they always go together.

Mr Frank Dobson, Labour MP for Holborn and St Pancras South, raised with the Speaker the proposed appearance of President Reagan in Westminster Hall. He and the rest of the party, especially the Left, seemed to be against. Was this because America was the world's biggest cholesterol-producing super-power? Hardly, for it is also the world's biggest jogging power. The Speaker quietened Mr Dobson by saying that he knew nothing about the visit, but would look into it.

Another matter which would be looked into was whether Stanley Baldwin or Ramsay Macdonald should be the subject of the next statue in the lobby, according to Mr Francis Pym, the Leader of the House, answering questions. It was the sort of subject to enrage Mr Wall and the Militant Tendency, not that they tend to be strong on bourgeois history. Macdonald, an enemy of the working class! Did he not bring in the high-cholesterol hamburger?

The death of Lord Butler, better known to most as 'Rab', in early March 1982, was marked by a tribute in the House on 10 March.

Members listened in silence yesterday to the Prime Minister, the Leader of the Opposition, and others paying tribute to Lord Butler, and then in uproar to Mr Leon Brittan, the Chief Secretary to the Treasury, paying tribute to the Budget. This is the sort of thing which enrages the high-minded public most about Parliament. In saloon bar, golf club, launderette, and indeed senior common room, the tedious cry goes up: how can they be all dignified one minute and then turn the place into a bear garden the next? For some reason, 'bear garden' is the analogy most used, as if we all know about bear gardens from direct personal experience. Yet it is one's understanding that bear gardens are illegal, even in the North of England.

It is unlikely that Lord Butler would have objected to yesterday's sequence of events. He seems to have been a realist, rather a melancholic one at that. He passed virtually a lifetime in Parliament. He knew it to be all too human a place, and one of the things about being human is that you have to contemplate the sublime sometimes and the ridiculous most times. So he would not have been the least put out by the fact that his sublime obsequies were followed within minutes by a ridiculous, but marvellous, uproar about whether Mr Brittan has misled the House over the proportion of tax to be paid by people in the lower and middle income brackets as from the next financial year.

'Sublime' may be putting it rather too high to describe the obsequies. But they were of high quality. And there were illuminating nuances. For famous politicians, as well as being people, are also myths, or code words or symbols, especially departed politicians. They are used by other politicians as part of the contemporary struggle. Thus Lord Butler is used by opponents of Mrs Thatcher— Tory, Labour and Alliance—to symbolize a supposedly more 'civilized' Conservatism which the present Government is said to have abandoned. 'He was the original wet,' Mr Foot confidently assured us yesterday. If there were Tories like this newly-deceased statesman conducting this present Government matters would be different: this was the inference which Mr Foot wanted us to believe. It was all harmless nonsense. For later one's hand strayed to the cabinet in the library where is kept *Hansard* for all eternity and from which there can be no appeal.

It was thirty years ago, almost to the day. Mr Gaitskell, then the Shadow Chancellor, was deploying the Opposition case against the then Mr Butler's first Budget. 'It will please the right-wing press, for it is a party Budget. It may even reassure some of the more right-wing critics of the right hon. gentleman [Mr Butler] in his own party that a Tory progressive is not really so terribly dangerous after all . . . stripped of all disguises, it is a lamentable move to take from poor people and to give to wealthier.' The explanation is simple. The literary and theatrical conventions which govern debate do not permit a Labour spokesman to praise a Tory Chancellor's compassion, except when he is safely retired or dead. No harm was done by yesterday's tributes. But it is important that we draw no conclusions from Lord Butler's career about what Mrs Thatcher and Sir Geoffrey Howe are doing at this stage in theirs. The Prime Minister herself delivered a well-modulated tribute. Later, Mr Brittan claimed that taxpayers at all income levels were going to be better off under the Budget. Labour spokesmen leapt up to deny it totally. Mr Brittan insisted.

Uproar! Suddenly, Mr Ridley, the Financial Secretary, was noticed having slipped away from the front bench to consult the civil servants kept in a pen in a dark corner of the chamber. Labour pointed at him *en masse*. Mr Ridley remained deep in complex chat with a plump-faced young pen pusher, no doubt a quadruple First in some Higher Nonsense or other, who was illustrating his points with gestures indicating scales and tables which must have confused Mr Ridley's mind very satisfactorily. Here was proof of Derby's famous assurance when Disraeli, pleading ignorance of the subject, at first declined the Exchequer: 'They give you the figures.' Mr Brittan plunged on with his speech.

Lord Butler would have enjoyed yesterday, being a man who relished both a good batch of tributes and a few colleagues in difficulties.

*

James Callaghan, a 69-year-old retired Inland Revenue officer of Cardiff South-East, was yesterday questioned by Mrs Margaret Thatcher about a series of murders in the late 1970s when he was allegedly Britain's 'Mr Big'. He succeeded the notorious Sir Harold Wilson, who was Britain's 'Mr Little'. Looking directly across at Mr Callaghan during noisy exchanges on the law and order issue, Mrs Thatcher told the House: 'Murders were greatest during the lifetime of the last government.' Mr Callaghan pleaded not guilty to all charges. Reporting restrictions were lifted. The entire Labour Party offered to act as character witnesses on his behalf, which was more than could be said when he was Prime Minister.

Giving evidence, Mr Callaghan said that 'serious crimes, offences recorded by the police, of violence against the person, burglary, robbery, handling of stolen goods and criminal damage declined each year when I was Prime Minister'. So Big Jim, this man who terrorized a nation, had decided to deny it all. It was his last amazing gamble. He'll never get away with it, we all told one another. 'He's innocent, it's a frame-up, OK?' a woman shouted from the public gallery. (Well, all right then, perhaps it was Mr Dennis Skinner. Or perhaps I imagined it.) The Speaker said that if there was a repetition of such behaviour he would clear the court. Furthermore, this was not a court of morals. (Or at least, if the Speaker said nothing of the sort, he should have said it.)

There was then a sensational development in the case. In a complete reversal, Mr Callaghan said that serious crimes not only 'declined each year when I was Prime Minister', but 'have gone up each year since'. And he waved the Home Office document containing the statistics that would prove his innocence. So it was Mrs Thatcher who had presided over the most murders.

This ending was contrary to the most fundamental principle of crime fiction. This is the rule that the police officer must never be the character who turns out to have done it. Otherwise it is just cheating. Yet here we had an ending in which the detective-figure, Mrs Thatcher, was the one responsible for the most murders. Any of us could write crime fiction on that basis. It is simply a matter of making the least plausible or most respectable character into the villain. It was all as wretched as *The Mousetrap* in which, you will recall, the murderer is the one who everyone believes is the policeman. The Speaker, who I assume writes the scripts of all these Question Times, was simply not trying yesterday, brilliant though he usually is.

Mrs Thatcher, still seated and rummaging among her notes, made as if she was going to deny the terrible evidence that Mr Callaghan held in his hand. But as he sat down he remarked: 'Despite what the right hon. lady said in her election speeches, neither she nor I has any influence at all on those statistics.'

Mrs Thatcher arose amid colossal Labour derision. She hesitated and once more pillaged her notes. Suddenly, she opted for candour. The situation was that desperate. 'I am grateful to the right hon. gentleman for the last comment which is obviously correct. I cannot reinforce what I said about the number of murders, I was thinking about something else. I will therefore give the House the relevant statistics of which I was thinking, which I had in mind, although it was not all about murders . . .' Last night the entire Home Office was helping the Prime Minister with her inquiries.

Wartime

The agenda for the spring of 1982 appeared to offer entertainments to suit all tastes. We were promised guest appearances from the Pope and President Reagan; on the domestic front there was a Royal pregnancy, and for those interested in foreign affairs there would be the World Cup.

All these innocent amusements were overshadowed by the invasion, by Argentina, of the capital of the Falkland Islands, Port Stanley, in the early hours of 2 April, and the despatch of the Royal Navy (curiously, known now as 'the Task Force') on Good Friday.

5 APRIL   Outside: the sunshine, breeze and pale blue sky of a London spring; inside, for three hours on Saturday, the House was swept by storms not seen in this place since (ominous and, pray God, inapt comparison) Suez.

A huge queue had formed for the public gallery. The motive above all was no doubt curiosity. But there was also an air among the queuers of quiet, well-ordered concern. Argentina's equivalent at times of national crisis is the vast Buenos Aires rabble on behalf of whose depraved passions eighteen hundred Falkland Islanders have been set upon. The civilized world will agree that we come best out of the comparison. Inside the Chamber, men whom we had long seen as Tory Party hacks or place seekers became people of independent mind and righteous anger.

It was clear that their feelings were genuine. Indeed, perhaps it was the previous timidity which was the pose: the sad, necessary requirement for getting into the House in the first place. On the routine exchanges about the economy which had made up the stuff of a British political career these twenty-five years, there could have been little point in expending true feeling. But here was a subject to engage the emotions. For three hours, all time-serving was suspended. How long it will last, we cannot say. But the Government had not bargained for such a mood as the debate got under way. Mr Pym and Mr Whitelaw sat huddled together on the front bench, heads down, occasionally whispering to one another: nature's party men, two former chief whips, professionals with half their lives behind them of string-pulling, elbow-squeezing, thwarting back-benchers who were 'unhelpful'. When they came into the Chamber on Saturday, they may even have thought the emergency debate to be a routine party unity job; the same sort of thing as a tricky law and order one. Must stop any witch hunt against Peter Carrington: must make sure enough back-bench speeches helping poor John Nott.

But it was not to be as easy as that. Indignation swept and roared around the Government. Mrs Thatcher sat transfixed. She understood the feelings involved all right. For a start, she undoubtedly shared them. Yet she was, at this opening phase of the crisis, still at the mercy of the experts who draft the briefs. When she said: 'Yesterday morning, at 8.23 a.m., we sent a telegram,' she adopted a heroic tone as if what was sent at 8.23 a.m. was a gunboat.

When Mr Enoch Powell reminded us that Mrs Thatcher had once gloried in the name of the Iron Lady, and when he added: 'In the next week or two the House, the nation and the Prime Minister herself will learn of what metal she is made,' she looked across at him, nodded slowly, and appeared to mouth something in agreement. ***

Throughout the debate there was a closing of ranks against what so many see as Britain's traditional enemy: its Foreign Office. 'Someone has blundered,' said Mr Cormack, a Tory. ***

With his crinkly black hair and shiny moustache, Sir Bernard Braine looks, if he will forgive the expression, like an Argentine. But he displayed a healthy hatred of them. 'The thought that our people are in the hands of these criminals makes an Englishman's blood boil,' he boiled.

Of Mr Nott we will say little, except that he is a self-confident, nimble debater who has never had much trouble at the Dispatch Box before, which only went to show how wretched was his brief.

Let us hope, for the sake of the Falkland Islanders and our fleet sailing towards them, that the Government fares better in the debates that lie ahead.

6 APRIL Members yesterday proceeded through a routine Monday sitting. But all knew that this was a Monday like no other for a quarter of a century. A British Government had put a fleet to sea in anger. A Foreign Secretary, previously considered unsinkable, was suddenly gone. [Lord Carrington had resigned on 5 April.] What the consequences of it all would be no one could foretell. Passion, noise, intrigues, betrayals—all lay ahead.

Meanwhile there was all this waiting. It would be twenty-four hours before the Prime Minister would appear for Question Time, two days before the Falkland Islands would again be the subject of the day's debate. Few could think of anything but that subject—few, that is, except those whose passions were equally engaged by the matter of Ireland, the subject of a statement yesterday from Mr Prior. None the less, there was a whole parliamentary day to be got through. Members asked questions on the usual maze of subjects, raised points of order, laughed, became irritable, occasionally made fools of themselves, just as on any other day. But there was a difference. There was an almost overwhelming air of tension.

The Prime Minister was absent throughout the proceedings. *** Mr Biffen, the Secretary for Trade, made a statement on the state of commercial relations with Argentina. Even at times of national crisis, the Tory back-bench lawyer, Sir Derek Walker-Smith, like Parliament itself, must go on. He hoved into sight to ask Mr Biffen a vintage question about 'playing in aid the doctrine of frustration, which is well-known in commercial law and international law'. Mr Biffen humoured him as best he could.

Mr Pym, at this time still Leader of the House, arrived on the front bench, where he sat slightly hunched, his wary little head darting looks around the chamber.

Sly Mr John Silkin, the Shadow Secretary for Defence, arrived and deposited his well-upholstered bulk opposite Mr Pym. All weekend he has raged against Mrs Thatcher, called for Cabinet heads, and breathed defiance at the Argentines. Rightly so. The Tory back benches have no quarrel with him for that. None the less, they could have been seen staring across at him with profound distrust, whispering to one another and at the same time pointing towards him. He was crafty enough to put in some small print, wasn't he? He didn't actually say he'd back us up if we have to start shooting, did he? If Mr Silkin, once the ships are in action, does find pressing reasons why he never really meant it to come to that, then he will have proved to be a scoundrel. But right now he is one of the men who have been proved right. He could be forgiven his look of satisfaction yesterday.

Mr Pym rose to answer some banal questions in his capacity as something called the Minister in Charge of Co-ordinating Information. *** A Labour man, Mr Dalyell, seized the opportunity to ask Mr Pym whether he was aware that 'as soon as the first shot is fired, they will be taking on the right, left and centre of the entire Spanish-speaking world'. The phrase was meant to inspire the rest of us with awe. But to most reasonable people it conjured up a world of rotating coups, juntas, generals with medals won for offensives in the torture chamber.

What was worrying the Tory Party benches at this moment was the possibility of opposition from the rest of the English-speaking world, in particular the Washington State Department and the British Labour Party.

7 APRIL   In between yesterday's Prime Ministerial Question Time and the previous one last Thursday, the world had fatefully changed for Mrs Margaret Thatcher, and the fact showed. She had about her an almost visible aura of being alone. If things go well in the South Atlantic she will have a House full of friends, followers who were with her right from the beginning. If it is a farce, or worse, the corridors will be abuzz with realists who knew from the start that this adventure was madness. But yesterday we were in that strange interlude between triumph and tragedy. Prudent men were hedging their bets.

Last Thursday she had been a Prime Minister whose fortunes were faintly, but perceptibly, turning for the better. At Hillhead, her candidate had been by no means humiliated. The opinion polls were beginning to move her way. She had had no trouble at the Dispatch Box that day. For an average Prime Minister's Question Time the House is well-attended, but not full. Yesterday it was full. The Peers' Gallery, a good guide to how much interest the Commons is arousing at any given moment, was crowded. Among their Lordships, the aged, the embittered, the patriots, the sympathetic, the worried, the simply curious or the half crazed all gazed down on the beleaguered commoner from Grantham.

She slipped into her place on the front bench while Social Service ministers meandered towards the end of their questions. There were some exchanges about the death grant. That is this month's cause among the compassionate classes. The grant is still too low apparently. Either that, or people should not have to die in order to qualify. Or it should also be paid on behalf of the living so as to make it a life grant. Who knows what the precise complaint is? Or cares. Mr John Silkin, the Shadow Secretary for Defence, lowered himself into his seat on the Opposition front bench opposite her, and began silently to ooze stratagems. Mr Eric Heffer squeezed in beside him. Into the small space remaining at the top of the bench, the Labour Chief Whip Mr Cocks, almost as ample a figure as the other two, determinedly forced himself. The frail form of Mr Michael Foot seemed to emerge from under Mr Silkin's armpit. The Prime

Minister rose.

In the second of silence before she embarked on her first answer, the Scots left-winger Mr Canavan shouted: 'Resign!' The cry was taken up by the Labour benches, pierced by the high cackle of another left-winger, Mr Winnick. When the noise subsided, Mrs Thatcher launched into an answer to two Tories about British Leyland. Labour remained silent. The second question on the order paper was about President Reagan's visit to Britain, and would afford greater opportunities.

The question about the visit came from Mr Cryer, an ally of Mr Benn's, a hater of Mrs Thatcher. She was trying to use the visit to 'cover up her failing position', he said. He added that 'even President Reagan' had called for a peaceful solution to this crisis. Someone else should receive Mr Reagan. She should resign. Mrs Thatcher welcomed Mr Reagan as: 'President of our senior Nato ally and the most powerful defender of liberty in the West and liberty in the world.' A Tory back-bencher showed his neighbour the London evening paper, with news of Mr Reagan's desire to mediate between his 'two allies'. We are being equated with Argentina, it seemed. Ominous.

Mr Foot made his first move. Were these reports true that we knew well in advance of Argentina's intentions? Mrs Thatcher in effect denied it. Several times Mr Foot persisted. Mrs Thatcher struggled through further denials, amid Labour glee. But her back-benchers looked on. They believed that we did indeed know, that she had not been told, and that the rules of politics forbade her saying so. The Opposition knew this too, particularly the cleverest or most cynical. Still, it was a good issue for them at this early stage. So there was an air of make-believe about those opening exchanges of the crisis, perhaps for the last time. Mrs Thatcher gathered up her papers quickly and left the Chamber on her own.

15 APRIL   Another emergency debate on the Falklands crisis: all the special effects of the previous two such occasions were still present. *** But much had changed: Mrs Thatcher, in particular. She was much more confident, less obviously under strain, than at any time since the crisis engulfed her a little under a fortnight ago. Her world had changed for the better. So too had the mood of her back-benchers. The despatch of a British fleet to the South Atlantic no longer seemed to be the preposterous, foredoomed adventure that the sophisticated originally assured us it was. The signs from the Argentines indicated that they did not see it as particularly hilarious.

Could it be, contrary to all advice we had been receiving for the last quarter of a century from the post-Suez generation of experts in these matters, that Britain could still prevail over an enemy?

It was too soon to be sure about anything as momentous as that yesterday. Between Mrs Thatcher and success lay General Galtieri, the United States, and the Labour Party, of whom, at the time of writing, the General appeared the least forbidding. On the Tory back benches, the United States was being given the benefit of the doubt at this stage. Mrs Thatcher's complimentary words about General Haig's strenuous efforts received polite murmurs of agreement, but no more than that. He was now reporting to Mr Reagan, apparently. And Mr Reagan's mind on the subject was clearly regarded as potentially hostile country which has not yet been penetrated.

Then there was this United Nations Ambassador, Mrs Kirkpatrick. The Liberal Mr Russell Johnston, who gave broad support to Government policy, showed admirable anger at some of Mrs Kirkpatrick's higher idiocies of the last few days. Only he called her 'Mrs Fitzgerald'. If only he spoke true. The drunken Zelda would have been a far more reliable ally at a time like this. ***

At the end, Members filed out of the Chamber amid the anxious buzz of a large number of people consulting one another as to how some perilous course of action would end. The beauty and drama of the situation is that none of them knows.

21 APRIL Still no sign of the eventual outcome in the South Atlantic: but there was some movement yesterday on the home front. It took the form of Mr Roy Jenkins.

The movement was initially confined to those rather distinguished jowls of his. They began to roll about the moment Mrs Thatcher arrived for Prime Minister's Question Time. While she answered other Members, the rest of Mr Jenkins began to move importantly in his seat below the gangway facing her. He consulted some notes. He advanced to the edge of his seat with some deliberation. It was clear that he was going to put a question. This was in itself an event of a certain significance. Nothing had so far been heard from him on this crisis. Since it arose, he had all but disappeared from the public gaze.

This absence was all the more marked because in the days immediately before the Argentine action he was the subject of all our attention. He had won Hillhead. He had taken his seat. He had put a notably incomprehensible, but no doubt distinguished, maiden question to the Prime Minister about micro-chips. All things seemed possible for him. But within days Dr David Owen had seized the SDP controls and was roaring away on the subject of submarines, frigates, and vertical take-off.

Dr Owen is at home with such matters. Mr Jenkins is not. Like Switzerland, he is prosperous, comfortable, civilized and almost entirely landlocked. His only previous contact with the high seas has been in various good fish restaurants. Instead of the vertical, he prefers the horizontal take-off: the unhurried rise to shake a few hands in a shopping precinct after an afternoon nap at a by-election. In addition to all these disqualifications for the times in which we at present live, one suspects that he is almost certainly a Carringtonian at heart: a man of the world who believes that the Falklands are a far away country of which we now know too much. So it is an appalling situation in which he finds himself so soon after his triumphant return. None the less, being officially registered as a statesman, he just had to put up a show sooner or later. So yesterday he rose.

There was a murmur of expectation on both sides of the House, much of it slightly ironic. They all knew that Mr Jenkins was not really the man for the hour. 'Will the right hon. lady, in view of the strong all-party support which the Government has rightly received during the past two-and-half weeks,' he began, 'bear in mind that she will be expected to take future, I hope and believe, unrushed decisions . . .' At this point, as well as the statesman's emphasis on the word 'unrushed', he made one of the two famous hand movements he deploys to illustrate anything. One is a turn of the wrist with half-closed palm as if he is unscrewing a light bulb. The other is a darting, fish-like movement of the whole hand. Yesterday we got the darting, fish-like movement. '. . . *unrushed* decisions in an equally non-party way. This demands more than merely asking the Paymaster General [Mr Cecil Parkinson], who is chairman of the Conservative Party, to a meeting of senior Ministers last night. Will she seriously consider the proposal made by the hon. Member for Cardigan?'

Whereupon, he sat down. And that was his grand design? Apparently so. But where did he stand on the blockade, the use of air and sea power, the UN, peace, war? And who was this Member for Cardigan? Furthermore, what was his proposal? Later research revealed that Mr Jenkins was referring to the Liberal, Mr Howells. He is the Member for Cardigan. And his proposal? All-party consultations, apparently. That, then, was the Jenkins strategy to deal with Galtieri: tea at Number 10. 'I must confess, I had expected a more fundamental point from the right hon. gentleman,' Mrs Thatcher told him.

But we still do not know Mrs Thatcher's intentions. In a few days, the Jenkins All-Party Tea Force may look the less risky plan. By then it may be too late.

23 APRIL 'Mr Speaker, I wish to make a statement about the future of the Schools Council for Curriculum and Examinations.' From the moment the Secretary for Education, Sir Keith Joseph, uttered those words yesterday, it was clear that the council did not stand a chance.

A few minutes later it was no more. In the absence of any hostilities so far in the South Atlantic, the Prime Minister, in order to satisfy the thirst for battle on the Tory back benches, had sent out Sir Keith to sink a quango. The operation, then, was closely bound up with domestic British politics. In a demagogic outburst, Sir Keith told the Government's followers: 'I have considered this matter in the light of Mrs Trenaman's report, which we published in October, and the comments on it. We are grateful to her for her review.' There was now no turning back. 'It has prompted us to give fresh thought to the two functions of the council and the best ways of performing them,' he said.

Strong words. But did the Government have the will to carry through such a threat? Sir Keith now began to indulge in the inevitable display of *machismo*. 'We have concluded that a single body, constituted as an elaborate network of committees on the lines of the Schools Council, is not well placed to carry out both functions,' he raved.

On the subject of examinations, he said bluntly: 'Radical changes are required.' Moreover, 'Ministers need independent authoritative advice on how these examinations might best serve national aims for education.' Such jingo talk sounded very easy from the safety of Whitehall. But how would such a policy be enforced in a world ruled by such powers as the National Union of Teachers?

None the less, Tory back-bench morale soared at this news of the destruction of the hated Schools Council for Curriculum and Examinations. Suddenly Sir Keith moved on to announce a sudden peace mission. He would 'discuss with the local authority associations the establishment of an Examination Council, appointed and funded by the Secretaries of State for Education and for Wales'.

So he had lain waste one quango in order to replace it with another. What kind of war was this? There was worse to come. He began talking about 'curriculum development'. It was a 'professional activity' which goes on continually throughout the education system', he said. 'This activity needs to be reinforced by a national body with the limited task of identifying gaps, helping to fill them and assisting with the curricular dissemination of curricular innovation,' he added ominously.

Identifying gaps and helping to fill them! What was wrong with continuing to rely on Britain's dentists for that job? But no, Sir Keith proposed instead 'a School Curriculum Development Council'. Another quango! That now made it two in place of the one he had blown to bits. 'Its constitution should promote the sensible ordering of priorities, and efficient operation,' he meandered on. By now there was a crisis of confidence on the Tory benches. Morale crashed.

'We shall discuss with local authority associations the establishment of such a body . . . envisage that it would be appointed by the Secretaries of State after consultation . . . financed jointly by local and central government . . . most members would be teachers.'

This last was a particularly deadening blow. But it was followed a few seconds later with the final admission of a British defeat: 'We hope that many of the expert staff of the council will be ready to join the new bodies.'

It was all over. Sir Keith sat down. 'How many additional ministerially-appointed quangaroos will be required to run the two quangos above those required to run one and what will be the additional cost to the public funds?' a dejected Conservative, Mr Phillip Holland, asked. He is a back-bencher who has for years demanded a war against Quangoland. Sir Keith claimed that both the numbers employed and the cost to public funds would be 'significantly less'. But this happy state would only be reached 'after the transition', he said. Mr Holland was by now such a beaten man that he could not raise even a feeble demand to know the length of the transition.

28 APRIL Yesterday's scene had been coming for days. The Opposition demand for 'negotiation' had all along been a code for no force. There is a clear Labour fear that, in using force, Mrs Thatcher might be responsible for a disaster. There is an even clearer Labour fear that, in using force, she might be responsible for a success.

One after the other yesterday they leaped up to urge Mrs Thatcher to rely on Senor Perez de Cuellar. Until a few days ago, the average Opposition back-bencher, like the rest of us, would have been hard pressed to tell the difference between Perez de Cuellar and Comodoro Rivadavia. There would have been much uncertainty as to which one was the Secretary General of the United Nations and

197

which one was the Argentine port. But by yesterday the entire Labour Party was united on the subject of the near miraculous negotiating powers of the Señor.

Mrs Thatcher had nothing against him personally, but manifestly suspected that Secretaries General of the United Nations were all right in principle, but were no good in a crisis. Understandably, she could not put it that way: she wrapped it up with many an assurance that she would be happy to talk to him if it would do any good.

Prime Minister's Question Time had begun with Mr Norman St John-Stevas urging Mrs Thatcher to seek 'the mediation services of the Holy See'. There was some mocking laughter at this on the Labour back benches, where they do not normally agree with Roman Catholics except Irish ones. *****

Labour bawled. Tories cheered. A Labour back-bencher cried 'Murderer!' There will be more scenes like this.

Labour regrouped to continue the struggle later in the week. What if Señor Perez de Cuellar mediates of his own accord, and without success? Labour will simply produce other admired mediators: Lord McCarthy; Lord Scarman; the Lord Warden of the Cinque Ports; the Dalai Lama; even the mocked Holy See—or Mr St John-Stevas himself.

29 APRIL Somehow, after nearly four weeks of it, the crisis still has a dream-like quality. Is it really happening?

Those of us who are essentially creatures of the world, as it has been post-Suez, had been assured all our adult lives that Britain was no longer capable of doing this sort of thing. All the best people said so. Yet we seem to be about to try and do it, though the precise nature of the 'it' remains unclear. Admittedly, the best people may have been right. There may be a débâcle. That does not bear thinking about, though think about it one must. But the best people have not been running this crisis. Grantham Woman has been in charge. As well as being much else, the crisis is thus a test between two ways of looking at the world. It is either her or them.

Yesterday at Westminster was a lull. Within a few days we would know what the outcome would be. But not yesterday. The situation seemed as unreal as ever. The rational part of our natures no doubt retained the hope that events would not turn bloody, that they would remain unreal. But what of the irrational part? That is the part whose existence politicians, like the rest of us, cannot acknowledge, except in others. That is the part that by now, after all this waiting and shuttling, wants there to be dramatic events on the islands so that the two great parties in the state can revert to their tribal passions. The Tories want to identify with the pomp and circumstance of glorious war. The Labour Party wants to accuse the Tories of wasting young lives. All of which is natural—natural in the strictest sense of the word, in keeping with nature. To deplore it is to deplore nature itself, rather pointless.

In yesterday's lull, Members moved about the place like ghosts. *****

But aloft in the gallery, one's mind kept drifting away into the South Atlantic. One does not really want anything horrible to happen, the inner voice of rationality kept on insisting. Was there any chance that, even at this late hour, the Falkland issue would revert to that harmless, Gilbert and Sullivan status it had always occupied until four weeks ago?

I began to invest high hopes in the effect on the enemy's morale of that dinner which our officers served those captured Argentine officers on board one of our ships after we took South Georgia. Word might now have spread among the Argentine forces that this is what they can expect unless they quit the islands immediately. They'll think twice about taking us on now that some of them have felt six inches of cold, British food inside them. They'll know that a nation which can serve up lethal stuff like an average British service dinner is not a nation to be trifled with, that is, if they ever dared eat one of our trifles. And there's plenty more where that dinner came from. Panic could even now be spreading among the Argentine brass hats that this is how the barbarous British treat captured officers. The choice is theirs. There is still time for them to avoid raising knife and fork against us.

6 MAY A decent restraint was observed by most of the Commons when, as he promised when breaking the news to the House late the night before, Mr Nott rose to make a fuller statement about the last hours of *HMS Sheffield*.

Decent restraint has not come easily to some Members these last four weeks. Some have had difficulty being decent. Others have had difficulty being restrained. Mr Ian Mikardo, the perennial Labour left-winger, for example, is one of those who have not been up to either. During Mr Nott's appearance the night before, some of us had sat in the gallery repelled as he had triumphantly asked the Secretary of State for Defence whether, after the loss of the *Sheffield*, the Prime Minister 'is still inviting us to rejoice, rejoice'. He was quoting from Mrs Thatcher's reaction to the *bloodless* retaking of South Georgia.

Stuff so vile and crude boded ill for yesterday's exchanges as Chamber and galleries began to fill. Mercifully we heard no more of it. No doubt it will be heard again in due course, but yesterday some vestigial decency counselled caution even among Mrs Thatcher's darkest enemies.

Mr Nott had little to add. He named the dead Harrier pilot. He put the number of missing at thirty. Next of kin were being informed. He said that the thoughts of the whole House were with them. Mrs Thatcher, seated next to him, was as pale as she had been when she sat in the same place, alongside the same Minister, at eleven o'clock the previous evening. Sometimes her gaze was lowered. Sometimes it scanned the Labour benches, looking with horror for some lurking Mikardo.

Twenty-four hours before this appearance in the Chamber yesterday, twenty-four hours almost to the minute, Mrs Thatcher had made a fateful remark to Mr Foot. He had contrived to suggest that the sinking of the *General Belgrano* had put British lives at risk, as if that risk were not already inherent in the very sending of the task force which he had supported. She had told him that she had to 'live hourly' with the worry that the Argentines 'might get through'. That was the way British lives would be put at risk. Her wording gave a suggestion that she believed it a danger, not something really likely. But now that hour had come, and here she was sitting on the front bench again, looking as if she was in a dream and perhaps wishing that she was.

Mr Healey, the Shadow Foreign Secretary, rose. He has been a party politician nearly all his adult life. He knows no other trade. He has continued to practise it over this last month. But he is also a man who can tell when an occasion is inappropriate to his professional skills. Associating the Labour Opposition with the tributes paid to the lost British servicemen, he said that they 'gave their lives in the defence of the principle which is regarded as of great importance by all members of the House'. There was a cheer at this, but rather more from the Tories than from Mr Healey's own party. Admittedly, the Shadow Foreign Secretary wandered off into a question to Mr Nott about the relative positions of the *Belgrano* and the British task force, a question designed to prove some point which Mr Healey had tried to score off Mr Nott the previous day. Mr Healey, being mortal, was not perfect, even on this day.

Mr Alan Clark, a Tory who represents the constituency of Plymouth, Sutton, asked Mr Nott to assure him that wherever possible next of kin would hear of these events before the news was released. And would it not be preferable for an officer to visit the relatives, to ensure that there was no immediate hardship, to explain entitlements? It was curiously right that so mundane a question— with its bleak reference to 'entitlements' and to the proprieties to be observed on these occasions—should have been the first from the back benches, heard while the House was still tense and silent.

Mr Pym, the Foreign Secretary, made a statement about the diplomatic aftermath. He was rather more interested in the United Nations than he had been a few days ago. By the time Mr Pym sat down, the impression was that the men of peace and negotiation were soon going to have their advice put to the test.

14 MAY   Mrs Thatcher, speaking during Prime Minister's Question Time, was implacable in the tone she adopted towards the Argentines. Mr Pym, opening the debate a few minutes later, was distinctly placable.

The Argentines may well feel that yesterday's proceedings demonstrated the difficulty they may have all along experienced in dealing with the sort of régime typified by the British junta. Who is really in charge? The leader tells her screaming back-bench followers, as she did yesterday, 'I have seen various reports in the press: we are working for a peaceful solution, not a peaceful sell-out,' only for her Foreign Secretary to get up just afterwards and suggest enthusiasm for all manner of peaceful compromises, diplomatic initiatives and interim administrations.

How can one do business with such people? Who has the power? That question was made even more difficult to answer by the sudden intervention yesterday, weeks after the crisis began, of Mr Edward Heath, who seemed to be some sort of deposed dictator-figure. He made a speech in which he said over and over again that he supported the Government. But which bit? As his speech wore on, it began to look as if he was on the side of Mr Pym and the fanatical Wet Ones (Los Humedos) as opposed to Mrs Thatcher and the Dry Ones (Los Aridos). For Mr Heath kept referring to the need to conciliate 'world opinion', a traditional anti-Thatcher slogan. ***

Mr Heath was subject to similar harassment. 'Foreign Office sell-out,' Mr Winterton shouted at him. But all were silent for Mr Enoch Powell.

The Government was prepared to accept what was six weeks ago unacceptable to it, he said. He mocked the idea that the task force should have set sail on behalf of a United Nations trusteeship. He seized on 'the internal difference of opinion in the Government', as good as invited Mr Pym to resign, but then said that it was Mrs Thatcher who had the 'prime duty' to maintain Government unity. She owed it to country, Armed Forces and Falkland Islanders. She looked across at him. With agreement? With renewed determination? With fear? We shall know soon enough.

19 MAY *** Finally, a last triumphant burst of peacetime slapstick: Mr Andrew Faulds rose on a point of order. It was to do with the media and with misquotation, he explained. Tory interruptions. Cry from Mr Faulds of: 'This is a serious matter, even for the Girl Guides opposite.' Cry from unidentified female Member of: 'There's nothing wrong with Girl Guides.' Boastful, chauvinist retort from Mr Faulds of: 'Perhaps I have known more Girl Guides than the hon. lady.' Reflection by myself: this man should be kept away from Girl Guides; he is a self-confessed Thespian.

Mr Faulds said he wanted to talk about 'my recent experience'. (What, with Girl Guides?) Further Tory interruptions. Speaker again asks him come to point. Mr Faulds uses phrase 'some of my colleagues . . .'. Tory voice finishes sentence by shouting: 'Laughed!' More of Speaker. Mr Faulds now getting closer to point. Refers to 'this new breed of political commentator and some of the termites that sit upstairs'. Further interruptions. Various termites collapse from the suspense of it all. Others from the boredom. Mr Faulds: 'In the particular column which I am discussing, which was in *The Times* . . .'

Progress, at last. But the Speaker would not allow him to go on. Not a point of order, apparently. Speaker not responsible for people being misquoted.

At least three rival termites last night claimed responsibility for the alleged misquotation. A quick check revealed that there had been only one reference to Mr Faulds in this column over the last two months, and that amounted to about half a line in which there was no quotation to misquote. A call to Mr Faulds' secretary reveals that none the less that was it. ***

25 MAY Seven weeks and three days ago, Mr John Nott, the Secretary of State for Defence, had stood at this same Dispatch Box, a sorry figure. The Falklands had been lost the previous day. So, it seemed, had his career.

War is not only about the serious matter of real lives, but also about the minor matter of political lives. Yet minor matters can still be the stuff of drama, and it was a dramatic reversal of personal fortune when Mr Nott entered the chamber yesterday to make the first Commons statement since British forces returned to the Falkland Islands. He was greeted with a cheer from the Tory back-benchers, not a prolonged or an ecstatic cheer, but a decent cheer none the less. Doubtless some of those cheering now were exactly the same ones cursing him seven weeks and three days before. But then, he had had about him the bedraggled air of fiasco; yesterday he was associated with success. Strictly speaking, he probably had little responsibility for either. It may eventually become apparent that his greatest contribution to success was to have supported the Prime Minister against the negotiation party within her Government and beyond. But the Chamber of the Commons is not a place for subtleties or layers of meaning. Yesterday Mr Nott was a winner, and that was good enough.

He began by saying that, seven weeks before, his right hon. friend the Prime Minister had stated that it was 'the Government's objective to see that the Islanders were freed from occupation'. He added: 'On the night of Thursday, 20 May, Her Majesty's forces reestablished a secure base on the Falkland Islands and the Union Flag is today flying over the settlement of San Carlos in East Falkland where it will remain.'

Mr Nott surely lived a lifetime of hope and anguish in those seven weeks. There was the original facing of the Commons on that Saturday, 2 April. There was the time of the loss of *HMS Sheffield*, when the anti-war faction on the Labour benches flocked into the Chamber during some Scottish local government debate to bay for a Government statement, and Mr Nott had to hurry to the House to confirm the bitter news.

There were the last few days, when the forces for which he was responsible eight thousand miles from home and exposed to onslaught from the air, began the operation in Falkland Sound, with Opposition politicians able to quote from their small print if it all ended in tragedy.

Through these weeks Mr Nott has gone about these occasions with dignity, avoiding both the bellicose and the feeble. Yesterday he was manifestly relieved to be announcing a success but he also had a warning. Our forces still faced 'formidable problems in difficult terrain with a hostile climate'. As he read on, it was clear that victory was being won at a steady cost in lives, as all victories so often are. He confirmed the toll on *HMS Ardent*: twenty-two dead, seventeen injured. And *HMS Antelope*: one dead, seven hurt. But one thing was certain, he concluded: 'It will not be long' before victory. Several

Labour back-benchers seized on the losses to urge a ceasefire and negotiation. They were figures such as the left-winger, Mr Frank Allaun, for whom this was a consistent attitude since they had opposed the use of the force from the start. Such a recommendation would have sounded especially shameless coming from the Opposition front bench, which was why we did not hear it. Perhaps, if the capture of Port Stanley costs many lives and proves protracted, we will hear it soon enough. *****

26 MAY Faced with the (to him) appalling prospect of the Argentines being removed from the Falkland Islands without the assistance of the United Nations or the President of Peru, Mr Michael Foot flew a historic last mission against Mrs Thatcher at Prime Minister's Question Time yesterday. 'Can she clarify the attitude of the Government on the state of, or possibilities of, negotiations now,' he asked, braving a Tory back-bench surface-to-air missile: a cry from the direction of Sir William Clark of: 'Come off it, Foot.'

It was sheer suicide. How long can Mr Foot go on flying these missions? That was the question defence analysts were asking themselves last night. Mr Foot has kept it up now for seven weeks. First, he bombarded the Prime Minister with demands that Mrs Thatcher put her faith in the negotiating skills of the United Nations Secretary General. He is a Peruvian. When Mrs Thatcher withstood that onslaught, Mr Foot roared down on her with a new negotiator, the President of Peru. He, too, one assumed was Peruvian. What was this mystical bond, we asked ourselves, between Mr Foot and Peru? One assumed it must have been because Ebbw Vale was a traditionally pro-Peruvian part of South Wales.

Yesterday, Mr Foot did not name his new negotiator. But it was clear that the Leader of the Opposition was prepared to negotiate to the last Peruvian. With the UN Secretary General and the Peruvian President seen off by Mrs Thatcher, the only other powerful Peruvian is Paddington Bear. (Readers with young children—or readers who *are* young children—will recall that Paddington was born in Peru.) He was presumably the mediator whom Mr Foot had in mind when he yesterday told Mrs Thatcher: 'Does she not agree that it is essential, in the interest of saving lives, British or others, that the possibilities of negotiation should be kept open along with the military action.'

The precise opposite was of course the case. The possibilities of negotiation would *prolong* the military action. But Mr Foot is the Leader of the Labour Party while a Tory Government is engaged on an apparently victorious military operation. He is not expected to make sense. Mrs Thatcher declined Mr Foot's implied suggestion that we call in Señor Paddington. She pointed out that United Nations Resolution 502, the one which called on the Argentines to withdraw seven weeks ago, had not yet been implemented. 'If it were and Argentine troops withdrew, peace would follow,' she told Mr Foot.

Mr Foot had resumed his seat to refuel. Bravely, within seconds, he set out again. He told her: 'That is not the question.' Of course it wasn't. It was the answer: He was the one supposed to be asking the questions. The war has rather confused Mr Foot.

None the less, to humour Mr Foot, we were all prepared to agree that that was not the question. It turned out to be: did Mrs Thatcher fully agree 'with what was said by the Foreign Secretary at the end of the debate on Thursday when he said we remain ready to negotiate'.

Of course Mrs Thatcher does not 'fully agree' with her Foreign Secretary. Otherwise it is extremely unlikely that we would be pressing ahead with the war. Everyone knew that, including Mr Foot. But Mrs Thatcher could hardly be expected to phrase it that way. So she avoided the question, and repeated what she had said about resolution 502.

Gamely, Mr Foot struggled to his feet yet again, displaying magnificent fighting spirit—that is to say, from his point of view, negotiating spirit. 'She cannot leave the matter there,' he protested. Did she agree with the Foreign Secretary, he repeated. She replied that she did not think the Foreign Secretary disagreed with her 'for one moment', a remark which caused widespread hilarity.

Mr Foot called off his attacks for the day. But where was Mr Healey? Why did not Mr Silkin put to sea? The Labour back-bench masses will undoubtedly turn on their leaders when this war is over. In turn, the junta will accuse each other of cowardice. The régime could totter. Mr Benn is waiting and watching. There could be terrible times ahead, we must hope.

9 JUNE Mr Reagan's address yesterday was the sort of thing that, before the presidency restrained him, he presumably gave for years to small town rotary clubs: naïve, simplistic, determined to depict the Soviet Union as the supreme evil, insensitive to the multipolar nature of the modern world. For all those reasons, I liked it.

The speech was a sophisticate's nightmare. But, then, so is everything about Mr Reagan. This is his great virtue. He knows that there is something fundamentally wrong about the Soviet Union and something fundamentally right about his own country and ours. Most people start out on their adult lives with this understanding, and most people retain it. But a number of people have it bludgeoned out of them by years of watching and making rotten television documentaries, or reading and writing rotten journalism.

One had feared that, because he was among Europeans, Mr Reagan might have felt that he had to make his tone more acceptable to polite society. He had been as much mocked in our enlightened prints as in those of his own country for his reliance over the years on such sources as the *Reader's Digest* for his information.

Now, no dispassionate soul, presented with the relevant material, would deny that *Reader's Digest* has been a more reliable source of understanding about the world than, say, *Le Monde*. But it just does not have the same social cachet.

At one stage in his speech yesterday, Mr Reagan launched into a passage about Soviet agriculture. 'A country which employs one fifth of its population on agriculture is unable to feed its own people. Were it not for the tiny private sector tolerated in Soviet agriculture, the country might be on the brink of famine. These private plots occupy a bare three per cent of the arable land but account for nearly one quarter of Soviet farm output and nearly one third of meat products and vegetables.' There was a *Reader's Digest* ring to that passage, but there was also a ring of truth. More sophisticated speakers or journals would blame that Soviet agriculture problem on the dislocation caused by the Second World War or by the Tsars. But Mr Reagan, and the rest of the unfashionable classes, suspect that it is because there is a bit of a flaw in Marx's ideas about agriculture.

Mr Reagan was equally interesting on the subject of El Salvador. 'For months and months the world news media covered the fighting in El Salvador. Day after day we were treated to stories and films slanted towards the brave freedom fighters battling oppressive government forces on behalf of the silent, suffering people of that tortured country . . . Then one day those silent, suffering people were offered a chance to vote to choose the kind of government they wanted . . . an unprecedented 1.4 million of them braved ambush and gunfire, trudging miles to vote . . . The real freedom fighters of El Salvador turned out to be the people of that country . . .' Now, no doubt that account of Mr Reagan's was a partial account of recent history in El Salvador. No doubt, proportionately, the poll was indeed low—though not much lower than the ones that elected Mr Kenneth Livingstone. But Mr Reagan's version of El Salvador was at least as well-documented as the one on *News at Ten*, and I suspect more informative.

Mr Reagan had a respectful audience. This was largely because of the absence of many Labour MPs. But Mr Foot wandered in. Because of the heat, he was without the donkey jacket he wears on grand occasions. He wore a rather smart suit, giving himself another black mark with the Bennites.

Mr Reagan entered, preceded by a blast of trumpets, some Yeoman wardens, more men with moustaches, the Lord Chancellor, and a Britisher who would not go down well in Middle America on account of the fact that, though wearing black tights, he was a man. He was the Speaker. The President turned out to be a genial man, a walking tribute to the avoidance of jogging, health foods, and psycho-analysis. It was a privilege to have him among us.

10 JUNE With British forces poised to retake Port Stanley, the Labour front bench was by yesterday completely cut off from the outside world.

It was Foreign Affairs Question Time. Now, there are only a very few foreign affairs questions in which the electorate is at all interested just now. When will the assault on Port Stanley begin? Is it already under way? Dare we hope that our casualties will be small? But the Labour front-benchers pride themselves on not pandering to the illiberal, patriotic prejudices of the easily whipped-up masses.

That is because the Labour front-benchers have to pander to the liberal, anti-patriotic prejudices of the easily whipped-up Labour back-benchers. So from the Labour front bench yesterday came a series of questions of no interest to the electorate as a whole, or relevance to the situation, but entirely intended for domestic Labour consumption.

What about the United Nations? Where had all the negotiations gone? Why did Britain veto that UN resolution at the weekend? What about Mr Alexander Haig's failure to support his own support for our veto, as the case may be? It was further evidence that the beleaguered Labour front bench was almost entirely lacking in reality. Supplies of reality have not been getting through to it for weeks. None the less, Mr Denis Healey, the Shadow Foreign Secretary, got up three times yesterday to ask Mr Francis Pym more or less the same question. The question, pared of its sophisticated apparatus about resolutions and vetoes, amounted to this: why did not the Government rely on the United Nations to liberate the Falklands rather than the paratroopers, the Gurkhas, the Harriers and the Royal Navy? Put that way, the question sounds ridiculous, which is why I put it that way. I thought it would bring out its essential dottiness.

Mr Healey was no doubt being forced to go out on these patrols because of his notorious garrison commander, the fanatical, negotiation-crazed General Footez. He was safely absent from the front bench yesterday. No doubt, he intends to save his own skin. That is always the way with such tyrants. Instead, he left the fighting to Mr Healey, a man clearly demoralized by the stunning successes of the British forces so far, a man sixty-four years of age, dripping wet, wanting only to return to his farm in Sussex. * * *

So Mr Healey went for a simple, straightforward, brave, last-ditch request that no doors be closed to further negotiation. Mr Pym used a complex metaphor about no doors being closed and indeed doors being left open even when they were being closed. Mr Healey, being a worldly soul, was doubtless well aware that his questions were ridiculous at this late stage. His excuse, at this difficult time, is that he *is* Shadow Foreign Secretary. He achieved the difficult feat of making Mr Pym sound a hawk. So much so that Mr Tam Dalyell, the Labour back-bencher, asked in exasperation: 'Who is running British foreign policy, the Foreign Office or No 10 Downing Street?' The honest answer (*'She* is, you fool') was avoided by Mr Pym.

25 JUNE Suddenly made real in the Chamber for Mrs Margaret Thatcher yesterday were her own dreams of these last eleven weeks, and the nightmares of those on both sides of the House, and in the world of the high-minded beyond, who loathe her.

For as she slipped on to the front bench for Prime Minister's Question Time while a junior social services minister meandered through some statistics, her triumph was total: the most complete a British Prime Minister had achieved in a generation. Overnight the news had got better and better. Not only had the Argentines accepted a ceasefire, that much she had told the House the night before. Now they had surrendered—moreover, thousands more of them than we even thought were there. Amid the derision and disbelief of Britain's sophisticated classes, she had vowed to the world all those weeks ago that she would free those islands. And now she had. As she sat there, much of the House must have pondered in relief, exultation or dismay: the old girl had actually done it. Meanwhile, she leafed through her notes, perhaps trying to give the impression that she regarded this as just another working day, from time to time smiling sweetly about her. But she knew that, life and politics being what they are, she will never again have a day such as this.

Naturally, she rose to the great Tory cheer. If things go well in the South Atlantic, I remember writing in this space shortly after the fleet set sail, 'she will have a House full of friends who were with her right from the start.' If it ended in farce or worse, 'the corridors will be abuzz with realists who knew that this adventure was madness.' I thought I would keep the cutting to hand, whatever the outcome. Yesterday they were with her from the start.

Her first questioner was a Tory back-bencher, who asked her to give thanks for the task force and to agree with him that it was a fine moment for the country. 'I entirely agree,' she said, and went on to say she hoped we had let every nation know that we would defend our sovereignty. Mr Foot remained seated. A pro-Arab Tory asked her about the Lebanon. One or two Labour Members put questions about the sort of economics to which our politics must soon return. One of them mentioned the Welsh miners striking in support of the health service workers.

When Mr Foot eventually did rise it was to ask about some United Nations 'special session' on disarmament which she was apparently to address in New York this week, though what was special about it was unclear. She replied by denouncing unilateralism. Labour bayed. The Tory Mr George Gardiner asked her to designate a Sunday soon as 'a national day of prayer and thanksgiving'.

Mr Gardiner is not noted for especial religious fervour or piety, except towards Mrs Thatcher. So the left-winger Mr Bob Cryer shouted 'give over' and his friend sitting next to him, Mr Dennis Skinner, shouted 'Uriah Heep', or perhaps it was the other way about, though both shouts were well-deserved by Mr Gardiner.

When the business moved on to the Prime Minister's statement on the latest from the Falklands, Mr Foot had to reply. On and on he went, like a barrel organ much-loved but capable of only one tune. When he eventually sat down, she rejected everything he had said.

And Mr Tony Benn? In the early days, he had told her to her face across the chamber that she could not win, that Mr Reagan would stop her exactly as Eisenhower stopped Eden in 1956. I remember her staring at him palely as he said it—perhaps half fearing that it might come true. Yesterday he found some words to prove that she had not 'provided an answer to the problems of the Falklands'. Tremendously, she replied that he enjoyed free speech because of the sort of sacrifices which our forces had made. The Tories roared.

Post-war

The need to protect a British dependency on the other side of the world had understandably engendered a mood of drama and heroics. And–victory achieved– life in the Commons did not immediately revert to its former even tenor.

With Galtieri fallen, and Weighell and Buckton locked in inter-service rivalry over who should rule British Rail after the NUR's humiliation, the world strategic situation, though complex, was favourable to Mrs Thatcher yesterday.

The time during which she has been a successful Prime Minister was now approaching a matter of weeks, which was considerably longer than most of her living predecessors in the office had achieved. Finally, Mr Edward Heath could stand it no longer. He staged an elaborate attack on her during Prime Minister's Question Time. He lay in wait below the gangway as Mrs Thatcher answered questions from Mr Foot, among others, on the threatened Aslef strike.

Rejecting calls for a further independent inquiry into the dispute, she said that the dispute had already been examined by everyone. That did not satisfy Mr Foot, presumably because the case had not gone before Señor Perez de Cuellar. Mr Foot rose and discerned 'a glimmer of light' if only the Government would initiate 'fresh discussions'.

Contentedly, Mr Foot and Mrs Thatcher clashed with one another over whether the light was still on. Meanwhile, the rest of us discerned a glimmer of dark: Mr Heath, below the gangway, getting ready to intervene. But still he was content to wait. The Tory back-bench ideologist of the Falklands campaign, Mr Alan Clark, asked about a report in *The Times* that there was 'no question' of a parade by returning units of the task force prior to the thanksgiving service in St Paul's Cathedral 'and also that the form of the service is to contain passages in Spanish as a gesture to the people of Argentina?' It is safe to assume that Mr Clark is not, in principle, against gestures to the people of Argentina provided they are sufficiently rude.

He went on to ask her to congratulate the Lord Mayor of Plymouth, in which city Mr Clark's constituency is to be found, on having a proper victory parade'. ***** Mrs Thatcher confirmed that there would be a Falklands thanksgiving service. She congratulated the Mayor of Plymouth. She added that a final victory parade would be decided later. She manifestly knew nothing about whichever uncontrollable ecumenicist in the C. of E. had thought up the idea of the Spanish prayer. One could see her eyes glaze over at this further confirmation that the Wets are everywhere.

With all this talk of victory and victory parades, Mr Heath's nerve finally snapped. He has not yet got over her last victory, which was in 1975 and happened to have been over himself. So he rose. He began to ramble about the proposed inquiry into the Falklands episode. If it was true that it would pre-date recent incidents, 'then there are five former Prime Ministers alive who have an equal right to take part in the decision about the inquiry—in fact, just as equal a right as the leaders of the Opposition parties in this House'.

Labour Members oooed and aaahed with delight. Mrs Thatcher started taking notes. Mr Biffen, the Leader of the House, an early anti-Heathite when it was still unsafe (i.e. when he was still at large as Prime Minister) laughed. On and on went Mr Heath. '. . . by what constitutional right? . . . What consultations . . . As far as I am concerned, none . . . I have no objection to the record of my administration being examined . . .' In that case, sit down, one mused. 'But I have not been asked to give authority . . .' Ah, so that was it. It was all to do with his authority.

Mrs Thatcher replied that she was advised that she did not necessarily have to ask permission to consult the papers, but would do so 'as a matter of courtesy'. Mr Heath subsided. Mr Biffen laughed again, perhaps at the sheer pride and simple malice behind it all. But Mr Heath can be excused of having a political motive. It was purely personal.

Members on both sides of the House laughed at Mr Roy Jenkins yesterday. All he had done was intervene in Scottish Question Time. That was why they laughed.

We none of us can get over the fact that Mr Jenkins now represents a Scottish constituency. He is somehow so *un*-Rob Roy. Yet here he is condemned to a stretch in Scottish Question Time, which is Parliament's equivalent of Barlinnie. It is the place which contains the MPs whom society would prefer to forget. These are the men who represent Scottish seats. (There are few women.) Some of these men, such as Mr Dennis Canavan, a lifer who sits for the safe Labour seat of Stirlingshire West, will probably never be integrated into society again. There is this constant air of tension and latent violence in the place.

The visitor feels that at any moment something could spark off a flare-up—some unemployment statistics being announced by a Scottish Officer, the housing figures, the refusal of a subsidy. It is no place for a man like Mr Jenkins; yet there he must be. Ideally, he would like to have been elected at Warrington or Crosby—more ideally still Belgravia, where he at least speaks the language. But fate had it that Hillhead elected him, condemning him to the living death that is Scottish Question Time. There he wastes away, on the bench below the gangway on the Opposition side of the House. Mr Canavan is only a few feet away. So is Mr Dennis Skinner. The latter sits for a Derbyshire seat, but is considered sufficiently aggressive to be an honorary Scotsman. The bench, then, is Scottish Question Time's maximum security wing.

But in fairness it must be admitted that, to anyone looking down from the public gallery and having no knowledge of the reality of the situation, Mr Jenkins has no connection with these people. He is suffused with respectability. He occasionally inspects his fingernails. When Mr Canavan or Mr Skinner become agitated, he draws his jacket more tightly across his lap and moves a few inches away from them. The uninitiated would assume that he is the prison visitor or the padre—perhaps even the psychiatrist, the man who comes every few months and asks Mr Canavan to make ink blots on the order paper, which blots will tell whether Mr Canavan is still a danger to the public.

But those of us with some knowledge of Mr Jenkins's case know that he is very much an inmate, just like the others. It is no good his being snobbish about them. He is now one of them. True, unlike most of them, it was a white-collar ploy that brought him to his present sad pass. He was elected for a middle-class constituency. But Scottish it nonetheless is. So every now and then he has no alternative but to put a question about Scotland. As the laughter died away yesterday, he asked whether there was 'any realistic hope of a reduction in the appalling level of unemployment in the life-time of this parliament'.

Replying, Mr Fletcher, a junior minister, conceded that the level was likely to increase in the short term, but seemed confident that it would improve in the longer term. He added that the Government's policies were 'rather close' to those pursued by Mr Jenkins when he was Chancellor of the Exchequer, especially with regard to public expenditure.

This observation delighted the Labour brutes. Mr Fletcher may be one of the screws. But they regard violence against Mr Jenkins as justifiable. Appropriately, Mr David Alton later sought leave to introduce a Bill about compensating victims of violence. Mr Alton is a Liberal, so his policy involved, not more punishment for the criminals, but more aid for the victims.

He seemed to be arguing that the best bulwark against crime was the old-fashioned social worker on the beat. As for prisons, all he had to say about them was they were too full of 'vagrants, alcoholics and prostitutes. These are people who should be receiving help.' What if they did not want help? What if they wanted to get on with boozing, being vagrant, and whoring—without being pestered by Mr Alton's crack squad of social workers? But there Mr Alton's compassion for them stopped.

*

Mr George Gardiner, MP, fanatical leader of thousands of commuters trapped in his constituency of Reigate, vowed a fight to the death as Aslef forces closed. He moved a motion grimly entitled: 'Travelling Public and British Rail.' The wording urged his followers to still greater sacrifice and effort in this dark hour for the commuter movement. 'That this House saluted British Rail travellers for their determination to overcome the effects of industrial action; condemns those union leaders who refuse to accept modern working conditions; and believes that until these are adopted there can be no hope of achieving an efficient railway system that . . .'

On and on the emotional rhetoric swirled. For Mr Gardiner is a brilliant demogogue who knows how to play on the passions of the dispossessed suburbanites, victims of the second rail war in a week. Then, in Mr Gardiner's speech commending the motion, came the talk of death. 'I was interested to read of Mr Buckton saying this was a fight to the death,' he said, beginning the passage in a deceptively low key.

Then, voice rising as he sensed the hysteria his words were creating among the home county Conservative MPs who had come to hear him, he went on: 'The death of thousands of jobs on the railways for his own members and of members of other unions. The deaths of other jobs like those in holiday resorts which depend on the railways bringing their customers or the death of the railway system?' Then, after this macabre imagery, came the final flourish of the born orator: 'Or would the fight to the death be the death of Aslef? What a welcome event that would be.' (Some Conservative cheers; some Labour cries of outrage; women fainting, etc.)

Day One of the Anglo-Aslef war found the House in tense mood, then. *** The situation was confused. Both sides were claiming early victories. Members of the Labour front bench opted for the role of the pathetic civilian caught in the crossfire. One old man had fled from the front bench entirely. He wore a donkey jacket and hobbled on a walking stick. He had not asked for this war. Now he was one of its countless Labour victims. No doubt he hated Aslef as much as anyone. But how was this Mr Foot to get rid of them?

Meanwhile, in the incredibly complex politics of the back benches behind him, NUR and Aslef, though still hating one another, united in the face of both the Government and Mr Gardiner. Who is this man Gardiner? His enemies say he is only interested in power for himself and is using the suburban cause to get it.

But he seems to be sincere. Nonetheless, his claims yesterday had to be treated with caution. He insisted that thousands of his followers had broken out of Reigate and managed to fight their way through to the City of London that morning. In an Aslef broadcast Mr Huckfield denied it. The situation could become clearer today, though not if Mr Gardiner or Mr Huckfield can help it.

*

Members learned yesterday that the soccer hooligans whom Britain had entered for the World Cup were still leading the world.

Mr Dennis Canavan, the Labour Member for Stirlingshire West, raised at question time the fighting which had taken place between English and Scottish fans in two disco-pubs in Lloret de Mar the previous evening. So cowed were other nationalities, it seemed, that the English and Scottish hooligans, in order to find any worthy opposition at all, were reduced to playing each other. Soccer hooliganism is the game that Britain taught the world. For a while, people like the Brazilians played some brilliant riots. But in the end sheer experience has told. It was glory night for Britain. But Mr Canavan took a rather censorious attitude—even though, all his life, he has been a practising Scot.

Questioning Mr Neil McFarlane, the Minister for Sport, he demanded: 'Has the Minister yet been able to inquire into the exact circumstances of the violent confrontation between Scottish and English football fans? Would it not be appropriate for the Scottish Office Minister, who was reported to have been at the match, to conduct an on-the-spot investigation into this tragic and deplorable incident which should not have been allowed to mar one of the greatest sporting occasions in the world?'

Mr MacFarlane said that so far he had not had detailed reports of this incident. 'I and other Ministers have attended some of the matches,' he added. And these Ministers, we were left to deduce, had never once joined in a riot. 'The behaviour of our fans has been exemplary,' he said; a remark which might well be regarded by our lads in Spain as a challenge. 'There have been one or two bad examples outside of grounds. I will look into this matter and report back.'

Whereupon, the Conservative back-bencher Mr David Crouch, a silver-haired gentleman of ostentatious respectability who is not normally given to provocative behaviour, ran on the pitch to ask whether the Minister was aware that the most important thing about the World Cup was the matches involving the English team. He proclaimed his confidence in their outcome. Mr Canavan snarled at him: 'That's cos ye got an easy draw,' or, as he put it, 'eeezie drarrr'. The Speaker moved quickly to separate the two fans before there was further trouble.

The problem for society is that, since the end of the Falklands War, we have lacked a means by which the natural aggression of healthy MPs can express itself. This is one of the greatest challenges facing Britain today. * * *

*

Labour members, front and back, may not have shown much enthusiasm for the Falklands War while it was being fought, but they are determined to win the inquiry into it.

Yesterday Mrs Thatcher told the House that the inquiry, under Lord Franks, would be carried out by a committee of Privy Counsellors. They would include representatives of the two main political parties 'chosen in consultation with the right hon. gentleman the Leader of the Opposition'.

The terms of reference were also announced. They include the reviewing of 'the way in which the responsibilities of Government in relation to the Falkland Islands and their dependencies were discharged'. They ended with the stirring phrase '. . . taking account of all such factors in previous years as are relevant'. Here was the sort of sea and terrain on which the Labour Party is superbly equipped to fight. Terms of reference! Consultation with the right hon. gentleman! The mighty roar of discharging responsibilities! The pomp and circumstance of such factors as are relevant!

When Mrs Thatcher mentioned the inquiry during Prime Minister's Question Time, and when the Leader of the House later rose to announce that there would be a debate on the terms of reference later this week, Labour's crack proceduralists and trained windbags went into action. Question after question were trained on Mrs Thatcher and Mr Biffen. The air was filled with the acrid smoke of Labour's deadly points of order. No troops in the world could wage an inquiry with such skill and sheer nerve.

Suddenly, Mr Roy Jenkins joined the hostilities, apparently on Labour's side. Mr Jenkins and the Labour Party have historically hated one another. This was especially true when he was the party's Deputy Leader. But, on the inquiry issue, their hemispheric interests are the same. During the actual fighting in the South Atlantic he was of course almost entirely silent in the House. But he too is a man whose blood stirs at the sight of a committee of Privy Counsellors under Lord Franks setting sail with a full complement of relevant factors. So he rose. It was his first intervention in the House since he officially became the leader of Britain's seething, raging mass of moderates. So there were jeers. He smiled and remained calm.

Then, within seconds, he showed his mastery of modern committee warfare. 'Can the Prime Minister confirm that the terms of reference will not now involve any leisurely ramblings over the history of the last two decades, but will concentrate on immediate events?' This was thought to be the first leisurely ramble ever opposed by Mr Jenkins, perhaps because the rambling was not being done after a good lunch at a stately home. 'Bring back Owen', cried an irreverent Tory. Mrs Thatcher assured Mr Jenkins that there was nothing wrong with the terms of reference.

Later Mr Biffen, after announcing that there would be a debate tomorrow on the inquiry, came under tremendous fire. Mr Christopher Price and Mr George Foulkes were anxious that not enough consulting was going to be done. Mr George Cunningham, a Social Democrat and a bloodthirsty proceduralist, demanded that the House be allowed to inquire into Mrs Thatcher's claim that the original inquiry be allowed to examine previous governments' papers (Mr Cunningham believes that you cannot have too much inquiring). Mr Dick Douglas demanded that the names of the other committee members not become known before the debate.

Mr Michael English, Labour's most lethal pedant, spotted that Mr Biffen had referred only to the Falklands and wanted to know whether that included South Georgia. Mr Biffen (wearily): 'Yes'. The exchanges ended with morale high on the Opposition benches. Our boys down there just wanted to get on to the next point of order later this week.

*

Yesterday dawned: the day of the Commons debate agreeing to a committee of inquiry into the Argentine seizure of the Falklands and the events leading thereto.

This was the day Britain's politicians had been waiting for. Their years of training had led up to this day. If there is one thing they look forward to, it is a debate on an inquiry—apart, that is, from an inquiry itself. It was perfect inquiring weather. A low cloud hung over the Chamber. This was the speech of Mr Roy Jenkins, the new Leader of the Social Democrats. He was sitting in the first seat on the front bench below the gangway. Mr Edward Heath occupies the corresponding seat on the opposite side of the House.

Ever since being re-elected to the Commons, Mr Jenkins has longed to sit in the seat he occupied yesterday. But various members of the lower orders had been determined to deny it to him. For weeks one of their number has defiantly sat there. In order to be sure of the seat, a Member must seize it as soon as business starts, with prayers, at 2.30 p.m.

Mr Jenkins has never quite reached it by that unearthly hour. It is assumed that, at that time, he is just finishing breakfast. But yesterday—inquiry day—it was essential that Mr Jenkins's stupendously statesmanlike contribution be delivered from that seat. So Mr Christopher Brocklebank-Fowler, who seemed to be some sort of valet or gentleman's gentleman to the old statesman, was found sitting there during Question Time, so as to make way for Mr Jenkins later. This occasioned a point of order from Mr Christopher Price, a Labour Member who, though of gentle birth, consorts with his party's brutes, a mild case of Benn's Syndrome. Was it in order for one Member to reserve a seat with one of the cards designed for that purpose, only 'to hand it over to another right hon. Member who seems unable to rise early enough'. The Speaker prudently avoided giving a ruling. Mr Price resumed his seat directly next to Mr Jenkins, who looked the other way. All the seats below the gangway are now disputed between the SDP and the Labour Left. It would appear to be a suitable subject for the next inquiry.

On to the debate. The committee doing the inquiring has turned out to be of such paralysing respectability that Mr Michael Foot felt he had no alternative but to endorse it, especially since one of his front-benchers, Mr Rees, had ended up a member.

Mr Jenkins had nothing to say. But with what style he said it! He approved the inquiry's membership, for that gave him the chance to say things like: 'I think it is a good choice of chairman . . . Sir Patrick Nairn too, outstanding civil servant . . . integrity . . . distinguished . . .' Mr Jo Grimond asked whether or not, as an historian, he agreed with something or other. 'I hesitate to speak with absolute authority,' said Mr Jenkins. Nonsense, Mr Jenkins does little else. He went on to speak with absolute authority about the inquiries into the Crimean War, the Jameson Raid, the Marconi scandal, Mesopotamia and the Dardanelles.

For the rest, Mr Callaghan was angry with Mrs Thatcher for not being sufficiently impressed by his own naval triumphs in the Falklands, and Mr Heath's speech passed off peacefully.

*

Mr William Whitelaw, the Home Secretary, rose to make a statement about the man who intruded into the Queen's bedroom and demanded a cigarette.

All eyes turned towards the leading critic of the monarchy, Mr William Hamilton, who was in his usual seat above the gangway. It turned out that he could not have been the intruder. He does not smoke. But he took a close interest in the exchanges yesterday.

He did not intervene. But as Mr Whitelaw confirmed the astounding tale, Mr Hamilton allowed a smile occasionally to disturb the expression of genial outrage at life that is his normal look. Others on the Labour benches scoffed with equal satisfaction. And who could blame them?

The Conservative Party—the party of the Crown, of law and order, of more policemen, of richer policemen, of Mr Eldon Griffiths—this, of all parties, had failed to secure the Royal bedchamber itself.

Mr Roy Hattersley, the Opposition spokesman on Home Affairs, who is a contented soul in any case, was in a particularly good mood as a result of this turn of events. He rose three times. First, he said that it was 'to say the least, a wholly extraordinary state of affairs'. The second time round, he devastatingly observed: 'The Home Secretary has said that security had recently been improved. Since that resulted in a man getting into the Queen's bedroom, how bad was it before the improvement?' The third time, he found himself saying: 'None of us want this to become a matter of controversy across the House. But I must press the Home Secretary on one point . . .'

Mr Hattersley was colossally concerned, pulverizingly pompous. His aim was to depict the Home Secretary as a man dangling perilously from the end of his tether. In this, Mr Hattersley was entirely successful. 'I have to report to the House that a man was arrested in Buckingham Palace on Friday morning after entering the bedchamber of Her Majesty the Queen,' began the statement of the wretched Mr Whitelaw.

This was one of the sentences least likely to be heard in the House of Commons, the sort of thing which forms the first sentence of one of Mr Jeffrey Archer's vastly successful novels. Mr Whitelaw seemed to be determined to discover who was responsible for this incomparable blunder. As a matter of fact, *he* was. But happily Mr Whitelaw is no great student of the constitution. Apparently, he will not be resigning. Instead, he roared through a statement which contained such phrases as: 'I am determined, as is the Commissioner, that the arrangements for safeguarding the security of the Queen should be as comprehensive and effective as possible . . . rapid implementation . . . utmost urgency . . . further statement as soon as I can.'

During the statement, it emerged that the incident was related to another last month. Mr Hattersley moved in. What steps were taken to improve security after the first incident? 'Or was it necessary for the *Daily Express* to enjoy their extraordinary scoop before these matters were taken with the seriousness that the situation warrants?'

Mr Hattersley had found his line and length. He was away, welcoming the urgent and immediate inquiry, looking forward to the future statement, leaning importantly on the Dispatch Box. Faced with such gravitas, Mr Whitelaw was a sorry figure. It takes a Hattersley, with his breeding, to protect the person of a British sovereign, it seemed—not this floundering Tory. For Labour, the situation almost made up for the British triumph in the Falklands war.

As questions were directed at him, not least from the outraged Conservative back benches, Mr Whitelaw adopted a policy of complete bewilderment. Over a furious weekend he had obviously drawn on all his experience to come up with an explanation as to how that man ended up in that bedroom. People would do anything to try and get a peerage, he no doubt mused to himself at one stage, as he toyed with the possibilities. But, as he confessed to Mr David Ennals, a Labour questioner: 'No one is likely to have been more shocked or staggered than I was.'

Sir Geoffrey Howe* rose to make his important *economic* statement yesterday wearing a dark jacket and a pair of hush-puppies. In between, contrary to newspaper reports last week, was a pair of trousers.

As he rose, his trousers were on all our minds. This on the face of it was an unusual place for them to be, but in reality no odder than on the railway line between London and the North, which was the last reported sighting of the trousers in question. Happily, they have now been restored to the nation.

Moreover, Sir Geoffrey's loss of his trousers was in a great British tradition. Most British humour is about people losing their trousers. Sir Geoffrey has been Chancellor of the Exchequer since May, 1979. But it is only now, with this traditional loss of his trousers, that he has entered the folklore of the nation.

Ideally, he should not have had a spare pair of trousers available on the train on which the original pair were apparently stolen. The British would have liked the idea of their Chancellor on a train in early winter, trouserless, civil servants panicking, station masters being summoned at Crewe, searches of the line being ordered, Sir Peter Parker being hauled out of a board meeting or bed or dinner party to supervise the operation.

Alas, our Chancellor, it seems, is a prudent man as befits a monetarist and a careful husbander of the nation's resources. For the fact that a reserve pair was available suggests that Sir Geoffrey always travels with a spare pair of bags. He is an inspiration to us all.

That fact will not deter the British people from devising their own mythology of the event. Sir Geoffrey has entered history as the Chancellor who lost his trousers.

Pretty soon, people will believe that he lost them in the presence of Mrs Thatcher, or at a cocktail party for visiting heads of central banks, or in the chamber of the Commons itself.

Eventually, it will be said that he does it all the time—enlivening Cabinet meetings thereby. He will become the Brian Rix of monetarism. In the esteem of the British people, his future is assured.

* Who, a few days before this Commons appearance, was reported to have had a pair of trousers stolen from his baggage while returning by train from a speaking engagement.

And so, relishing Labour cries of 'keep your trousers on this time' and similar ribaldries, Sir Geoffrey launched into his statement about public expenditure, and related matters, for the year ahead. He announced some changes to mitigate the worst effects of recession.

Replying, Mr Peter Shore, the Shadow Chancellor, said these were just cosmetic. We should all hope that Mr Shore was right. If they are anything more than 'cosmetic', they would undermine the Thatcher-Howe policy of curbing, at this stage, inflation rather than recession.

Sir Geoffrey would then achieve inflation *and* recession next year. There would thus be nothing to show for all the pain, real and imagined, that they have felt it necessary to inflict in the cause of defeating inflation.

Perhaps we will have both recession and worse inflation next year come what may.

Mr Roy Jenkins, for the Social Democrats, challenged Sir Geoffrey to say whether the London Business School was correct in forecasting that inflation, after falling in the second quarter, will begin to rise again after that.

Sir Geoffrey replied that he did not 'accept' the school's forecast for the end of that year. Inflation may still be at five per cent at the end of 1983, he added. He went on to imply that it all depended on pay settlements. So he did not sound sure.

The dread spectre of inflation rising again after all this anti-inflationary misery, and with a general election approaching, hovered momentarily over the Tory benches. However, this was Sir Geoffrey's only worried moment yesterday. After these years of being abused, Sir Geoffrey, with the recent improvement in the inflation figures, has achieved a sort of dogged serenity.

In the face of the foulest denunciations from Labour members on the subject of old age pensioners or whatever, Sir Geoffrey simply remains good-natured and makes a polite reply about the honourable member not being entirely fair.

After all these years, he probably feels he can endure anything with complete equanimity. The stoicism with which he accepted the loss of those trousers was almost symbolic, coming as it did after all the other indignities heaped on him by his critics.

Sir Ian Gilmour, the Conservative opponent of the present regime, speaking from his place of exile on the back benches on Monday, asked for 'major reflation.'

Yesterday, the last day of the week-long Queen's Speech debate, Major Reflation himself put in an appearance: Mr Edward Heath. We knew he would turn up sooner or later. There is a theory that, if you put your head around the door of any pub in the Home Counties, and shout out, 'is the Major here yet?' you would always get an answer.

Either the reply would be 'yes' or the landlord would explain that the Major had just left, or was on his way, or had sent word that he would not be in today, or was at a regimental funeral, or whatever.

The crucial point is that, for every pub of this sort, there is a Major. So it is with the House of Commons. Major Reflation is always a popular figure. Several members covet the title.

Some of them, as is the way with certain majors, are impostors, the sort who diddle genteel old ladies out of their savings. Other members, such as Sir Ian, just go around calling for the Major, and are thus the equivalent of people who put their heads around those pub doors. But at present the most famous Major named Reflation is Mr Heath.

True, many people regard Mr Heath, not as Major Reflation, but as Field-Marshal Inflation. Others remember him as General Chaos. But, in the eyes of the Labour Party, the Liberal-Social Democratic Alliance, and the indeterminate number of Tory wets, this Mr Heath is the rightful holder of the rank of Major.

Yesterday he was in cracking form, rambling on for half an hour explaining what needed doing, not just about Britain, but about the rest of the world. For like so many retired military gentlemen, he tends to go on a bit. And, again like most of his profession, he was very hot on 'leadership'. He called for bags of it all round.

'Leadership' was the thing—particularly, we were led to deduce, if he was the one doing the leading. 'This is a place where the British can give leadership', he said, of something to do with international economic relations.

Later, he decided that leadership was something which was required by the entire world. Towards the end of his speech, he announced: 'It's got to be brought about by world leadership'. By this time it was not entirely clear to all of us what the 'it' was that needed to be brought about by all this leading. But no matter.

We marvelled at his ability to sum up whole countries on the basis of his random wanderings: 'The American people . . . Australia . . . what I want to point out is that the situation is deteriorating in Germany . . . Brazil . . . Nigeria has already had to clamp down very much on imports twice.' Suddenly, he started talking about old-age pensioners: presumably ours rather than Nigeria's.

'At last, we've got to the latest anti-Thatcher bit', pro-Thatcher Tories no doubt mused at this point.

Mr Heath conceded that the decision to make the pension increase less next year was 'arithmetically correct.'

But he added: 'You can never convince old-age pensioners of the correctness of arithmetic.' For someone perhaps anxious to appear as the champion of the old folk, this sounded a little patronizing ('Heath says OAPs innumerate'). But it got him lots of Labour cheers.

Mr Roy Jenkins, for the Social Democrats, was not as much of a tourist as the Major. But he too sought to impress us with his knowledge of abroad. He noticed that, in her discussion of unemployment, Mrs Thatcher had not mentioned Austria. But Austria had low unemployment and social democratic government, he triumphantly claimed. Johann Strauss was a moderate, he no doubt would have argued, had he thought it served his purpose.

Nonetheless, Mr Jenkins said he was just as opposed as Mrs Thatcher to general financial indiscipline. General Financial Indiscipline, with his double-barrel name, is a less popular figure than the Major with the Labour Party, the Social Democrats and the Tory wets, but amounts to the same thing.

Mrs Shirley Williams, the SDP member for Crosby, made a speech on unemployment in the House last night.

This was seen as the relaunch of Party 4 after audience ratings which have been disastrous. Over the last few opinion polls, audiences for the party have regularly fallen towards a 'zero rating,' one so low it cannot be measured. Mr David Steel, head of the main organization backing Party 4, has been reported to be worried about the performance of certain anchormen. This was believed to be a reference to Mr Roy Jenkins. Mr Steel is also said to be concerned about stodgy programme content—too much emphasis on people just giving their own opinions. This is also said to be a reference to Mr Roy Jenkins.

Some of the anchormen have moved across from other parties. It is thought that it would be very difficult to make changes in their methods of presenting the news. This is also understood to be a reference to Mr Roy Jenkins.

Despite these problems, it was considered essential to come up with a bright new face by last night's unemployment debate. So they put on Mrs Williams.

She is in fact a bright old face. But the party's controllers were in no position to argue. Mrs Williams is now one of the few big names still ready to appear in the party's programmes.

This is principally because, long before she knew about these ratings, she joined it. So she has no choice. Gamely, she rose and chattered for half an hour about unemployment.

Mrs Williams touched on such subjects as the loan guarantee scheme, regional support, the way they do things better in West Germany and Japan, and the need for more 'high-tech'. Actually, this 'high-tech', whatever it may be, sounded the sort of thing which would make *more* people unemployed—at least initially. But no one noticed that flaw in her argument because Mrs Williams was speaking so knowledgeably—or at least so quickly.

What was the audience reaction? After she sat down, some viewers—particularly Conservative and Labour MPs—seemed to feel that she had done her best, but that her programme was 'too complicated' or 'did not have enough humour' or that 'she just seemed to be saying the first thing that came into her head'.

But, as is usual with programmes of this sort, most viewers could not remember what the subject was. They remembered the superficial details, such as her woolly sweater, rather than the important points, such as her woolly opinions.

There was one technical hitch when Mrs Williams, in quoting a particular MP, could not remember whether he was the member for Truro. Turning to him, she inquired: 'Truro, is it?' 'Yes, Truro', said David Penhaligon, a member of the same Alliance as her. 'Geography is not her strong point', muttered Mr Ronald Leighton, a Labour whip.

She sat down after making the serious charge: 'The Government seems unaware of the scale of the despair that is now arising.'

This seemed rather an exaggerated way for her to describe the situation in the SDP. There is still a chance that the ratings will improve.

The problem, it seems to me, is that the party is not a suitable medium for current affairs. There will have to be a greater emphasis on entertainment. A man from whom they would be well advised to seek advice is Mr Gerald Kaufman, the Labour spokesman on the environment. Yesterday was his first big show since the arrival of the new Secretary for the Environment, Mr Tom King. Mr King had to make a statement about the water dispute.

Mr Kaufman got up and unhesitatingly blamed the entire dispute on Mr King personally. The amiable Mr King laughed away just like the rest of the audience. It is performances like this that have taken Mr Kaufman to the top of the poll, in which the Parliamentary Labour Party chooses the Shadow Cabinet: the sophisticated, audience-sensitive PLP ratings.

Mr Kaufman is neither right wing nor left wing. But, unlike Mrs Williams, he always sounds as if he knows what he is talking about, even when he has obviously made it all up.

Yesterday, he demanded to know what Mr King made of 'paragraph eight of the mediator's recommendation'. Mr Kaufman is a man who believes in giving his viewers what they want.

Gazing across at the public gallery during a repetitive passage in Prime Minister's question time yesterday, the eye was caught by a visitor who seemed to be vaguely familiar. A colleague with a wide knowledge of the arts informed me that it was Miss Diana Dors.

It is not unusual for personalities from the world of entertainment to visit our proceedings from time to time. One of them, Sir Harold Wilson, stayed to become Prime Minister. Unfortunately another one, the Labour back-bencher Mr Andrew Faulds, just stayed.

But a visit from Miss Dors was something special. Here was a figure out of Britain's past greatness; a rose-red woman half as old as Miss Joan Collins. Now a matron of intimidating respectability, Miss Dors was once the very embodiment of how an actress should behave before actresses took up muesli, disarmament, workshops and being generally boring. She was blonde, outrageous, publicity-seeking. She was the Michael Heseltine of her day.

Miss Dors, accompanied by a fortunate man who was identified to me as her husband, was ushered into the gallery by the member for Bassetlaw, Mr Joe Ashton, who is the Labour cultural attaché. This was rather surprising. One had always assumed her to be a Conservative.

As she sailed majestically into her seat, it was clear that she was in magnificent condition—like a warship with a turbulent history of battle, now rendered obsolete by faster craft, but still doing sterling service as a training vessel. Intently, she followed the proceedings in the chamber. What did she make, one wondered, of the woman at the Government dispatch box who had succeeded her in the newspapers as Britain's wildest blonde?

Well, Mrs Thatcher was a different sort of star from Miss Dors's day. Instead of falling into successive swimming pools and marriages, Mrs Thatcher goes around giving her opinions on politics—something which the studio bosses made sure was strictly out when Miss Dors was at the top of this business.

But Mrs Thatcher showed yesterday she knew how to handle men.

227

Miss Dors would have approved of that. Mr Michael Foot got up and tried to make trouble over the zero option. This was a reference, not to his recent standing in the public opinion polls, but to something connected with nuclear missiles. Mr Foot seemed to think that the zero option, an American policy, was evidence of obduracy towards the Soviet Union.

For the same reason, Mrs Thatcher was in favour of it. She bullied Mr Foot for some time on the subject. He lapsed into moody silence. Nothing was so far new to Miss Dors. All show business relationships are said to be like this.

Mr Foot remained silent for some time. After a while, the subject turned to that of the loans being made by British banks to Argentina as part of an attempt by the banks of several countries to stop the Argentine economy from collapsing.

A Labour left-winger, Mr Stan Newens, demanded to know if Mrs Thatcher approved of this. She said she shared Mr Newens's concern, but that it was in our interests to prevent the Argentine economy from collapsing because of the effect on other economies. Labour members, sensing the Prime Minister's undoubted vulnerability on the matter, started to rage. Whereupon, Mr Foot perked up and started to rage as well. By the end, Mrs Thatcher was quite forced on to the defensive.

Some relief was provided by the Labour member, Mr Giles Radice, becoming slightly petulant over what he called Mr Norman Tebbit's attacks on 'my union, the General and Municipal Workers'. Mr Radice is an extremely middle class Wykehamist, which must make him a very general rather than municipal kind of worker.

Mr Ashton, the impresario who brought us Miss Diana Dors, kept trying to get in a question, obviously in order to impress his distinguished guest. He failed. Rightly. He had had enough glory for one day.

The piece about Miss Dors was followed by a postscript a few days later.

. . . I have had the honour of an appreciative letter from Miss Diana Dors (see this space, last Friday). It contained no address. At the top, in gold lettering, were the words: Diana Dors Lake. This I took to be her married name rather than her address.

Readers may recall that I expressed surprise that she was escorted into the public gallery by the Labour member Mr Joe Ashton, since I had assumed her to be a Conservative. She writes: 'The only point on which I would like to correct you is your assumption that as I was a guest of Joe Ashton, Labour MP I must also embrace his politics. This I hasten to add is not so! Indeed, like my father before me, I am a staunch Tory. Therefore, you were right to state that it came as a bit of a surprise to think I might be anything else. I would like this put straight if it is at all possible?'

I am delighted to do so, madam. Somehow I never really doubted the Conservatism of this great woman who was so important an influence on my generation of schoolboy art collectors.

Mrs Thatcher has been accused of seeking, for electoral purposes, to identify the Conservative Party with the Harrier pilots and other heroes of the Falklands conflict. But yesterday all parties sought to identify themselves with the British milkman.

The European Court had ruled that Britain must remove all impedimenta to the import of a continental secretion known as UHT (ultra heat treated) long life milk. According to some reports, this substance, being cheaper than British milk, would be bought in our shops in such quantities that the national milk would become uneconomic. Home deliveries would therefore cease.

The milkman would be dislodged from his central position in British culture. The danger sounded so implausible that all parties spent an enormous amount of time in the House yesterday promising voters that, if elected, they alone could be trusted to avoid it.

'Britain's unique doorstep delivery service not only provides milk of quality to housewives, but is an important social service, especially to old people,' proclaimed Mr Peter Walker, the Minister of Agriculture, Fisheries and Food.

Members of other parties nonetheless proceeded to prove, to their own satisfaction, that the Conservatives could not be trusted to protect the milkmen of Britain. Labour, or the Liberals, or the SDP were the Milkmen Party. So, at strategic intervals during the questioning, Mr Walker repeatedly identified Conservatism with home deliveries.

After a while some of us became rather shocked at the way in which the politicians were trying to make political capital out of the sacrifices made by our country's milkmen. Morning after morning, they roar off in their electrically operated carts to face ceaseless, sometimes suicidal attacks, from overwhelmingly more numerous, sexually ravenous housewives.

Or so all Britons are brought up to believe by the seaside postcards, and Mr Benny Hill. In threatening our home deliveries, the continentals were threatening the very basis of the British joke.

Housewife: 'Milkman, I'd bet you'd like to sell me enough milk to bath in?'

Milkman: 'Pasteurized?'

Housewife: 'Not quite. Up to m'chest will do.'

That is the heritage which members from all parties were yesterday competing to preserve. So, despite the element of political exploitation, they were indeed acting in the national interest. Members could not wait for the statement to be made yesterday by Mr Walker on the recent meeting of EEC ministers of agriculture during which the European Court's judgment became known.

The first mention of the issue came earlier during questions to Foreign Office ministers. Mr Roy Hughes, the Labour member for Newport, confronted Mr Douglas Hurd, the Minister of State.

'The Minister should be delivering a clear repudiation of the dictat from the Common Market, trying to force down the throats of the British people imported so-called milk, in substitution for our most excellent product which has been so superbly delivered in all weathers,' said Mr Hughes.

Mr Hurd took care immediately to establish his patriotism. What he disdainfully called 'this product' was only 1 per cent milk, he said, and nobody was forcing Mr Hughes 'or anyone else, to drink the nasty stuff.'

Shortly afterwards Mr Eric Heffer, the chief Opposition spokesman on European and Community affairs, sought an assurance from the Foreign Secretary, Mr Pym, that 'doorstep deliveries of milk will in no way be affected'.

Mr Pym swiftly gave it, and added that the stuff would not be 'forced down the throats of the British people'. Then Mr Walker arrived. The more other parties praised our boys who fly the carts, the more Mr Walker identified the Tories with those who go out at dawn from the Co-op and United Dairy bases throughout Britain, the location of which, for security reasons, he was careful not to divulge.

He clinched the Union Jack vote with a final remark: 'Although my dog loves Lymeswold cheese, he wouldn't touch UHT milk', being careful, like a true Briton, to establish that he was also a dog lover. So at the election the Tories will have on their side the Doorstep Delivery Factor.

'Pasteurized, lady?'

'What are you trying to do, drown me?'

Epilogue

Experience has taught me that one interesting thing has happened to everybody, but *only* one. Politicians, most columnists and nearly everyone who goes on television are under the impression that *everything* that has happened to them is interesting. Such people are no exceptions to this remorseless law. Only one thing is likely to have happened to them too, if as many as that.

All of which is by way of being an overture to the announcement that the interesting thing that happened to me took place amid the fog of pre-Clean Air Act London 25 years ago this very night* when I appeared with Maria Callas in the first two performances at Covent Garden of Bellini's *Norma*.

The secondary school in Shoreditch of which I was an inmate happened to supply the human material for the children's parts at the Royal Opera House. The qualification for getting into this academy was stiff: one had to fail the 11-Plus. In my day one had to be almost feral to fail the 11-Plus. I shall always be grateful to my early teachers that I managed the feat.

Having won a place in the school, the privileged pupils discovered that, because the rehearsals took place during the day, if you volunteered for the opera, you got out of maths. On the strength of a few mid-1950s television productions, I disliked opera. On the strength of a few lessons, I feared maths. I volunteered for the opera.

My Covent Garden debut was in 1955 as one of the Nibelheim dwarfs in *Das Rheingold*. We were required to scream when the late Otakar Kraus, the greatest of Covent Garden Alberichs, cursed the ring. Over the next three years we were the urchins in Act One of *Carmen*, the urchins in Act Two of *Bohème*, the urchins in Act One

*This piece first appeared in THE TIMES of 2 February, 1982.

of Janacek's *Jenufa*, the urchins in Acts One and Two of *Otello*, and both Trojan and Carthaginian urchins at various stages of Berlioz's immense *The Trojans*, wearing, in both Troy and Carthage, I seem to recall, the same costume.

We were also the aristocratic officer cadets marching around the garden in St Petersburg in which is set Act One of Tchaikovsky's *Queen of Spades*. In this latter role we were less convincing, the Shoreditch school being long on urchins and screaming dwarfs, but short on aristocrats.

It was extraordinarily casual. In some of these works we were required to sing. *Carmen*, after all, contains an urchins' chorus of some complexity. But of the vocal arts we were entirely deficient. We simply shouted with the utmost vigour, usually in English, such was Covent Garden's linguistic policy at that time, but in *Otello* in phonetic, cockney Italian. Happily, this dark era in Covent Garden's history has ended, and the school which provides the lads today achieves higher standards.

Early in 1957, we learned that there was an opera coming up which would require only two of us: *Norma*. Apparently the heroine of that name had two children whom she decides to stab to death, changing her mind at the last minute and opting instead for a duet with a mezzo soprano. I and a boy called Arthur were chosen. The choice was dictated by our height rather than innate musicality, which was just as well since no singing was required. Furthermore Arthur and I had no history of artistic collaboration. Being even smaller than me, he was the one by whom I was always courageously refusing to be bullied.

I embarked on this memoir resolved to be honest, to tell only that which I could remember. So now the sad truth must be faced: of this, the one moment of my life which makes me immortal, I can recall very little. Just a few images in my memory. For it was 25 years ago, and I was just turned 14. So today I never trust the childhood reminiscences of autobiographers.

I remember that there seemed to be something exciting and tense about the atmosphere in the weeks before the performance. Arthur and I were constantly enjoined to be on our best behaviour, especially at the first rehearsal. At some point we must have learned that someone exceptional was involved, which meant someone with a foreign name. Hitherto, under the Covent Garden régime, the singers tended to have such names as Elsie Morrison and James Johnston, the latter a ringing Irish tenor who used to tell Carmen: 'Carmen, oil never leaf your soid.' But we had been the choirboys whom Mr Tito Gobbi had terrified in Act One of *Tosca* and he had seemed jolly enough, for he had fed us Italian gob-stoppers during a rehearsal and asked us about football.

Then, probably in the *Daily Mirror*, Arthur and I learned with some consternation that a woman was coming to Covent Garden who was known as 'Opera's Tigress'. Furthermore, she had been in a 'storm' in New York. She had got the sack for a baritone who had held a final note longer than she had in a duet.

The latter was untrue, as the books now make clear, but that was no good to Arthur and me at the time.

This tigress sounded like trouble for us. I suppose that this stage in her career, 1957, was the one in which Callas emerged into the consciousness of the masses. She still included 'Meneghini' in her name, after the doddery industrialist of some antiquity whom she had married. But the liaison with Onassis lay only a matter of months away, as did Elsa Maxwell's ruinous seducing of her into international café society. By 1957 she had slimmed, but the voice, I now know from her recordings of the time, was still full. At 33, she was at her apogée.

As a result of the *Mirror*, household and neighbours were alerted. There was some doubt as to whether Norma was the name of the opera or the name of the great singer. 'My boy's appearing with that Norma,' my father would sometimes explain. By word of mouth down the street, this was occasionally transmuted into the Johnson boy appearing with Yana, a popular television artiste of the period.

Came the rehearsal. The late Christopher West, the producer, seemed nervous. An efficient-looking woman came in wearing sculpted horn-rimmed glasses, a tight black sweater, a green two-piece suit and stockings with black seams down the back to which were affixed stiletto heels in accordance with the fashion of the day. (Pubescent boys take note of such details.)

'That's her,' Arthur said. 'Don't be bloody daft,' I distinctly remember telling him. 'That's West's secretary.' But Arthur was right.

'These are the children,' West said to the great soprano of the age. 'They're a little big,' she replied, speaking I recall with a sort of American accent. At this, West, a somewhat epicene figure, began to flap his wrists with some consternation. He gabbled something about younger ones not being allowed on stage under British law. Callas stared at us. Arthur and I cowered. If this bitch gets the boot for baritones, what would she do to us, we no doubt pondered, I regret, in our rough way.

'I understand,' Callas told West, who breathed again. But there was still trouble. It came, however, not from Callas but from the mezzo soprano, the late Ebe Stignani.

She was singing Norma's rival in love, the 'young temple virgin Adalgisa'. Stignani was 53 at the time. I now know that she was a singer of much distinction. 'Her acting was all in the voice,' says my edition of the *Oxford Dictionary of Opera*, which was just as well because she was a short, round woman with a terrifying face. 'Not understand to him, not understand to him, Maria,' she told Callas. 'They're too bigga.' Though I cannot claw the precise words back from memory, Callas replied with something about even the great Stignani having to abide by the law. West giggled.

I forget the actual rehearsal. Indeed, the policy of honesty compels the admission that I remember little of the two performances themselves. But I do recall that when we emerged from Covent Garden underground station, people were already at the barriers offering clusters of £5 notes for return tickets.

And I could not forget that when Callas bore down on us with the knife, her nostrils flared; that when, dropping the knife, she repentantly clasped us to her bosom, her perfume smelt like that of an aunt who was always kissing me; and that at the first performance on 2 February there penetrated, into my left eye, the tip of the diva's right breast, which partnership remained throughout the subsequent duet with Stignani.

In that eye I felt the most distinct pain as that voice of myth and legend rose and fell. In the other eye, all I could see was the exit sign at the far corner of the gallery. At the second performance, I ducked and secured a safer refuge in a more central portion of the diva's bosom.

Furthermore, listening to the loudspeakers which carry the performance to the dressing rooms, I remember coming to the conclusion that the bloodthirsty chorus in Act One, *Dell'aura tua profetica, Terribil Dio, l'informa* ('Inspire her, O terrible God, with your prophetic spirit') was the same tune as *Over the Mountains, Over the Sea, That's Where My Heart Is Longing To Be*, to be incessantly heard at the time from Miss Anne Shelton.

And that is all. Still, there are few men who can truthfully say that their eye made contact with the right nipple of Maria Callas. So it is not necessarily true that someone who has passed much of his adult life in the press gallery of the House of Commons has never glimpsed greatness.

ROYAL OPERA HOUSE*

COVENT GARDEN
CHARACTERS IN ORDER OF APPEARANCE

NORMA, High Priestess of the Druids MARIA MENEGHINI CALLAS

ADALGISA, a virgin of the Temple   ...   EBE STIGNANI

CLOTILDE, Norma's Confidante ...   ...   MARIE COLLIER

The two children of Pollione and Norma   ARTHUR MACKENZIE
                                          FRANK JOHNSON

Druids, Bards, Priestesses, Warriors and Gallic Soldiers.

* From the Covent Garden Programme for 2 February 1957.

Index

241

Rubens, Peter Paul, 155

Salvador, El, 143–4, 174, 175, 206
Sandelson, Neville (Lab., Hayes and Harlington), 144
Sands, Robert, 77, 95
St Paul, 41
Scarman, Lord, 198
Schools Council for Curriculum and Examinations, 196–7
Scott, John, 105
Scott, Norman, 97
Scottish Questions, 212–13
S.D.P., *see* Social Democratic Party
Semiramide Overture, 79
Semprini, 83
sex shops, 169, 170
Shankly, Bill, 101
Sheffield, HMS, 199, 203
Shelton, Anne, 224
Sherman, Alfred, 130–1
Shore, Rt. Hon. Peter (Lab., Stepney and Poplar), 46–7, 152–3, 156, 226
Short, Mrs Renee (Lab., Wolverhampton, N.E.), 52, 155, 159, 183, 184
Short, Rt. Hon. Edward (Lab., Newcastle Central; later Lord Glenmara of Glenridding), 20, 61, 68
Sieff, Lord, 67
Silkin, Rt. Hon. John (Lab., Deptford), 191, 192, 205
Silvester, Brian, 115
Sinn Fein, 75
Skelton, Mick, 82
Skinner, Dennis (Lab., Bolsover), 17, 38, 46, 48, 49, 59, 127, 143, 144, 145, 163, 165, 168, 177–8, 187, 209, 213
Smith, Adam, 153
Smith, Cyril (Lib., Rochdale), 128, 160
Smith, Ian, 22, 23
Smith, Rt. Hon. John (Lab., Lanarkshire, N.), 39
Social Contract, the, 18
Social Democratic Party, 63, 64, 65, 88, 89, 90, 91, 92, 129, 130–1, 135, 152, 163, 171, 195; Conference (1981), 106–13
Somerset, Guy, 111

South Africa cricket tour, 179–82
South Atlantic, battle in, *see* Falklands crisis
South Sea Bubble, the, 30
Speaker, The, *see* Thomas, Rt. Hon. George
Spender, Stephen, 121
Squire, Robin (C., Hornchurch), 174–5
Stalin, Josef, 147, 163
Stallard, Jock (Lab., St Pancras, N.), 159
State Opening of Parliament, 148–9
Steel, Rt. Hon. David (Lib., Roxburgh, Selkirk and Peebles), 26, 34, 100, 128, 136, 149, 229
Stevas, Rt. Hon. Norman St John (C., Chelmsford), 36–7, 44, 113, 118, 119, 154, 198
Stewart, Donald (Scot. Nat., Western Isles), 26, 48, 53
Stignani, Ebe, 224
Stockhausen, Karlheinz, 77
Stokes, John (C., Halesowen and Stourbridge), 35, 54, 167
Stoppard, Tom, 137
Strauss, Johann, 228
Strauss, Richard, 29
Stravinsky, Igor, 29
Straw, Jack (Lab., Blackburn), 182
strikes, *see* industrial relations
Strindberg, August, 150
Suez crisis, 189, 194, 198
Sun, 8, 9
Sunday Express, 155
Sunday Telegraph, 18
Swain, Tom (Lab., Derbyshire, N.E.), 23–4
Synge, J. M., 95

Take It From Here, 78
Tatchell, Peter, 157–8
Taylor, Teddy (C., Southend, E.), 175, 176
Tchaikovsky, Piotr, 222
Tebbit, Rt. Hon. Norman (C., Chingford), 24, 28, 29, 132, 163–5, 171, 232
television: future of, 39–40; licence fees, 73, 74, 136
Thatcher, Denis, 58, 67, 68

THE EMPEROR OF THE UNITED STATES OF AMERICA AND OTHER MAGNIFICENT BRITISH ECCENTRICS

BY CATHERINE CAULFIELD

Wildly funny stories of over 1,000 delightfully dotty individuals who actually lived: glorious eccentrics given to dining their pets at table, conducting elaborate practical jokes, wearing odd clothes, indulging in strange phobias and leaving outrageous wills, including:

WILLIAM BUCKLAND (1784–1856) who, until he ate a bluebottle, maintained that the taste of a mole was the most repulsive he knew...

OSBORNE DE VERE BEAUCLERK (1875–1964), 12th Duke of St Albans, who proposed attending the 1953 Coronation with a live falcon on his wrist...

SIMEON ELLERTON (1694–1799) who preferred walking with a large stone on his head...

JOHN ALLINGTON (1795–1863) who enjoyed being carried around in an open coffin. 'You see,' he would explain, 'I'm getting ready...'

'Weird, wonderful and so eccentric'
Peter Grosvenor, Daily Express

'When life seems weary, stale, and exactly the same as last Monday, this is a cheering book'
Irish Times

0 552 99007 8   £1.75

CLASS

<small>BY</small> J<small>ILLY</small> C<small>OOPER</small>

CLASS IS DEAD! Or so everyone claims. Who better to refute this than Jilly Cooper!

Describing herself as 'upper middle class', Jilly claims that snobbery is very much alive and thriving! Meet her hilarious characters! People like Harry Stow-Crat, Mr and Mrs Nouveau-Richards, Samantha and Gideon Upward, and Jen Teale and her husband Brian. Roar with laughter at her horribly unfair observations on their everyday pretensions – their sexual courtships, choice of furnishings, clothes, education, food, careers and ambitions. . .

For they will all remind you of people that you know!

'Highly entertaining, acerbic and wickedly observant . . . certain to become as much part of the verbal shorthand as was Nancy Mitford's *U and Non-U* a generation ago'
The Economist

'Enormously readable and very funny'
Cosmopolitan

0 552 11525 8   £1.95

SUPER JILLY

BY JILLY COOPER

Here's our famously zany social commentator on top form once again! This collection of Jilly Cooper's witty anecdotes includes 'Paws', the tale of her dreadful dog, a hazardous visit to Harrods' sales and an hilarious account of judging a well-dressed turkey competition!

Whether interviewing Mrs Thatcher, lunching with the mums of today's Debs, or defining the magic of 'machismo', Jilly's acerbic wit and shrewd observations make SUPER JILLY an entertaining and provocative read.

0 552 11802 8   £1.25

THE CULT OF THE EXPERT

BY BRIAN J. FORD

'Splendidly irreverent, mischievous and sardonic'
Sunday Express

The Cult of the Expert is a highly entertaining and ingenious attack on the Experts who blind us with science, confuse us with jargon, frustrate us with bureaucracy, intimidate us with superiority – and yet – precisely because they are so successful at this – have the power to appropriate huge shares of public funds and to make decisions which fundamentally affect our daily lives.

Stephen Potter delighted us with *One-Upmanship*, Parkinson coined his famous *Law*, Nancy Mitford brought us *U and Non-U*. Now Brian J. Ford has added to the English language *Fashionism* and *Nonscience*.

The Cult of the Expert is a timely and important book, for its message is that our blind subservience to the Experts is leading to the decay and destruction of our society.

O 552 12249 1   £1.50

A DIRECTORY OF DISCARDED IDEAS

BY JOHN GRANT

AN ABSORBING AND HILARIOUS A–Z OF LUNACIES AND CURIOS.

Throughout history, people have got their ideas and theories wrong just as often as right. And the wrong answers are frequently more interesting...

In the US during 1943 there was high absenteeism among women working on the filling of fire-extinguishers. It was discovered this was due to a rumour that carbon tetrachloride could make you pregnant...

Dr Edward Clarke warned in 1873 that education could cause a woman's uterus to shrivel...

A palmist, Patrick Cullen, devised a technique to take prints of female breasts to predict their owner's future. Subsequently he tested virginity by examining women's silhouettes as they stood, illuminated, behind sheets...

The flat earth – the hollow sun – the World Ice Theory – leeching, perpetual motion, the music of the spheres – an exhaustive search through the litterbins of the past has resulted in a rich harvest of amazing and entertaining notions.

0 552 99013 2   £1.95

WEASEL WORDS

by Philip Howard

THE WORD ACCORDING TO HOWARD

Is the English language being strangled by a sort of Double Dutch Elm disease of jargon, slang and obfuscation? Why do we say 'cheers' when we mean 'sorry' and 'lovely' when we mean 'thank you'? How Platonic is platonic love these days? What would you do with a module? Not to worry, the answer is here, and so is the gen on 'not to worry'. What is a personality? Is there a person inside trying to get out? How big is a quantum jump, and is data not what they used to be at this moment in time?

Philip Howard, Literary Editor of *The Times*, conducts a lively examination of over forty specific examples of words and phrases that have recently changed their meaning. Basically, the result is an on-going entertainment situation!

'Philip Howard once more applies an entertaining erudition to a well-manured field of gobbledygook, vogue words and solecisms'
Daily Telegraph

'It is a pleasure to be told so politely how ignorant we were about to seem'
The Times

'Mr Howard is witty. His book is one that no logophile should miss'
Birmingham Post

0 552 99025 6   £1.95

THE BOOK OF WORLD SEXUAL RECORDS

BY G. L. SIMONS

The biggest...the smallest...the longest...the shortest...the oldest...the youngest...the cheapest...the oddest...

G. L. Simons presents a compendium of extremes, firsts, excesses and the like – all that is great and small, beautiful and not so beautiful in the recorded history of sex.

Whether your curiosity is aroused by the world's heaviest breasts (fifty-two pounds) or the longest session of love-making (15 hours – recorded by Mae West!), this book brings accurate and up-to-date information to those with a genuine interest in sex, a book to entertain, inform, titillate or simply amuse.

0 552 12258 0   £1.95

HUMOUR TITLES AVAILABLE FROM CORGI BOOKS